NEPAL

Second Revised Edition
1995

TABLE OF CONTENTS

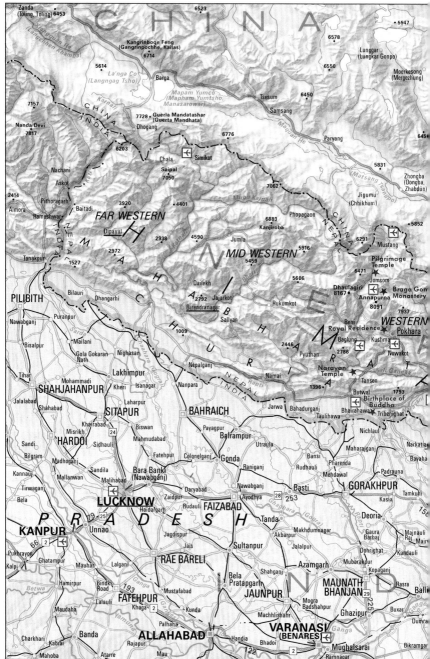

LIST OF MAPS

Please note: in some cases the spelling of the place names on the maps is not the same as in the text, because the spelling on the maps is according to UN guidelines, whereas the usual English spelling is used in the text.

Nelles Guides

... get you going.

TITLES IN PRINT

Australia
Bali / Lombok
Berlin and Potsdam
Brittany
California
  Las Vegas, Reno, Baja California
Cambodia / Laos
Canada
  Ontario, Québec,
  Atlantic Provinces
Caribbean:
  The Greater Antilles
  Bermuda, Bahamas
Caribbean:
  The Lesser Antilles
China
Crete
Cyprus
Egypt
Florida
Greece - *The Mainland*
Hawaii
Hungary
India
  Northern, Northeastern
  and Central India
India
  Southern India
Indonesia
  Sumatra, Java, Bali,
  Lombok, Sulawesi
Ireland

Kenya
London, England and Wales
Malaysia
Mexico
Morocco
Moscow / St Petersburg
Munich *and Excursions to*
              Castles, Lakes & Mountains
Nepal
New York *and New York State*
New Zealand
Paris
Philippines
Prague - Czech Republic
Provence
Rome
Spain, *North*
Spain, *South*
Thailand
Turkey
Tuscany

IN PREPARATION (for 1995)

Israel
South Africa
U.S.A.
  The West, Rockies and Texas
U.S.A
  The East, Midwest and South
Vietnam

NEPAL
© Nelles Verlag GmbH, 80935 München
  All rights reserved

Second Revised Edition 1995
ISBN 3-88618-046-8
Printed in Slovenia

Publisher:	Günter Nelles	**Translation**:	R. Rosko, E. Szasz
Project Editor:	Dr. Susanne von der Heide	**Cartography**:	Nelles Verlag GmbH
Editor:	Berthold Schwarz, J. Martina Schneider	**Color Separation**:	Priegnitz, München
		Printed by:	Gorenjski Tisk

                                                                          - 04 -

GEOGRAPHY

In Nepal the traveller enters an area which is unique in its orographic, botanical and zoological diversity. The geo-historical origins of the imposing Himalayan range, which comprises a considerable portion of Nepal, makes fascinating reading. The Indian continental plate separated from the old southern continent of Gondwanaland and moved north, where it slid under the old Eurasian plate. In the process, the southerly Sea of Tethys narrowed, and when at the meeting point of the two plates the Himalaya emerged, the sediments of this sea were pushed up in the process. The proof are fossiles of sea animals at a hight of over 4,000 m.

As the Himalayas arched ever higher, rivers, whose sources are found on the Tibetan plateau, carved deep into the young mountains. This created the impressive traverse valleys which to this day serve to make the range penetrable to traffic and trade at a few points. With the incessant pressure of the Indian continental plate on the Eurasian, the growth in height of the Himalayas continues at a rate of one millimeter per year. A permanent levelling in the form of natural erosion counteracts this process.

The Kingdom of Nepal comprises an area of about 147,000 square kilometers. It stretches over 800 kilometers from the northwest to the southeast, and is an aver-

Preceding pages: A Newar wearing his traditional headdress, the topi. The clad statue of the monkey god Hanuman. A pilgrim crosses the Kali Gandaki.The all-seeing eyes of the Buddha of Svayambhunath. The sleeping Vishnu in Budhanilakantha. Left: The landscape in the upper Kali Gandaki Valley.

age of 200 kilometers wide. From the Ganges plain to the main range of the Himalayas, Nepal ranges in altitude from 60 meters above sea-level in south-eastern Terai up to 8,846 meters at the summit of Sagarmatha (Mt. Everest). More than a quarter of country is higher than 3,000 meters, and it is boxed in by mountain ridges, plains, valleys and basins so that roads are difficult to build.

It is impressive to find, within the confines of one single country, almost every form of vegetation and landscape, from jungle to glaciers, on a horizontal width of only 200 kilometers. Its geographical position between 30 degrees and 26 degrees 15" north, puts Nepal on the same level as Libya, but the summer monsoon brings the Himalaya region record precipitations. Because the country "leans" from northwest to southeast, its southeastern tip is 450 kilometers further south than its northwestern extremity.

The Terai and the Siwaliks

The geography of the country has led to the development of very clearly distinguished landscapes and natural regions. Drawn along the Indian border, the Terai is a lowland with an altitude of between 60 and 280 meters above sea level. It is covered with a thick, dry jungle, and was long called Nepal's "fever hell" because of the malaria which was endemic there. Since this danger has been brought under control, the Terai has developed not only into a settlement and immigration area for people from both the mountains and India, it has also become the kingdom's bread-basket. On 42 percent of Nepal's cultivated area, it yields some 77 percent of the rice, 80 percent of the oilseed, 94 percent of the sugar beet, and 94 percent of the tobacco harvests. But reclaiming arable land resulted in massive deforestation of the salwood.

Also situated in the Terai is the main industrialized area outside of the Kath-

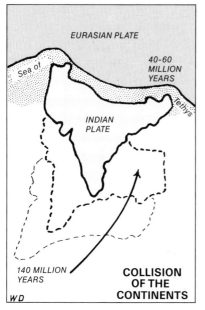

EURASIAN PLATE

40-60 MILLION YEARS

Sea of

Tethys

INDIAN PLATE

140 MILLION YEARS

WD

COLLISION OF THE CONTINENTS

road network. Alongside the old sugar, cigarette and match factories, are new cement factories, metal works, and other industries.

At the Siwaliks, which reach heights of around 1,500 meters, one enters the foreland of the Himalayas. The land here is composed of a very mixture of soft and hard rocks, gravel and sand, highly susceptible to erosion. The area can not be used for agriculture, and is therefore barely inhabited. These forest-covered ranges are broken up by the gravelly beds of larger and smaller Himalayan rivers. They have now become a destination for loggers, and are losing more and more of their protective function – without yielding equivalent usable farmland. As a result of this general deforestation, the seasonal flooding in the Terai is becoming evermore catastrophic.

Those parts of the Terai which are enclosed by the Siwalik hills and the Ganges Plain, and which form shallow basins, are referred to as the Terai's interior. To this area belongs, for example, the eastern Rapti Valley, which also contains the Chitwan National Park. Here one finds protected jungle with wild game, as well as systematically planned settlement zones. The Dang Valley and the valleys of Sindhuli and Udaipur in the East are also in inner Terai.

The flora and fauna include many considered endangered species. In southern Nepal, up to an altitude of 1,000 meters, plant life is dominated by shorea trees and limbas, bamboos, canes and reed species, and gallery forests with umbrella acacias.

Besides birds and butterflies, there are also large mammals such as elephants, the Indian rhinoceros, Bengali tigers, wild cattle, and various kinds of deer and apes. Many of these are being deprived of their natural homes as a result of the continuing expansion of human colonization and will have to be protected in national parks and wildlife reservations.

mandu Valley. The border cities and their populations are: Biratnagar (131,000), Birganj (70,000), Nepalganj (42,000), and Bhairahawa (40,000) – which has more recently been named Siddharthanagar. In addition, Janakpur (44,000) which is known for its temple, is the goal of many religious pilgrims. These cities make the most use of the nearby, little controlled border, and located just across it, the terminus of the Indian railroad network. The small industrial cities of Dharan (50,000), Hetauda (40,000), and Butwal (30,000) are located at the feet of the northern chain of hills known as the Churia Mountains or Siwaliks.

The cities of the Terai, which were at one time oriented exclusively towards either India or the Kathmandu Valley, are now connected with each other as a result of an East-West highway, the construction of which is almost completed. Where only a few years ago one had to use the Indian railway and road networks to travel into eastern or western Terai, the same is now possible on the Nepalese

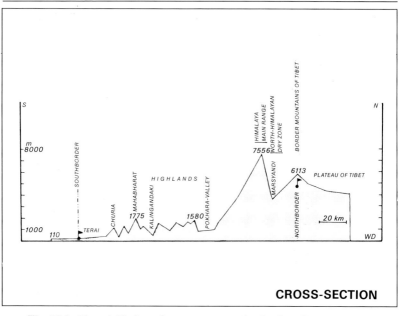

CROSS-SECTION

The Mahabharat Chain and the Highlands

The Mahabarat chain is the pre-Himalayan mountain range which runs north of the Siwaliks over the entire length of the country. Its peaks range in height between 2,000 and 3,000 meters. With them we enter into an old Nepalese settlement area, which is protected from the south by fever-swamps, and from the north by the main range of the Himalayas. It was therefore excellently suited as a retreat area. In fact, enemy armies have hardly ever invaded Nepal, because peaceful coexistence in both the south and the north has always been the rule. The mountain chain consists of crystalline minerals facing conditions of constant weathering and erosion. The river gorges are steep and narrow, offering little space for human settlement. Therefore, people have established themselves on the flanks of the valleys, where they cut down the forests and dug out terraces for their agriculture. Flying over the Mahabhrat range, the density of human habitation is clear from the degree of deforestation and terracing. But, also obvious is the physical threat of the landscape from soil erosion and landslides.

The highland stretching from the north of the Mahabharat range to the actual high range of the Himalayas is called the *pahar* in Nepali. This is the living area of the Nepalese where we find the valleys of Kathmandu and Pokhara with significant urban settlements. The extensively deforested slopes and valley pastures contain many district governmental seats, villages and scattered towns. Here the various ethnic groups of Nepal live together. Over many centuries farming the land enabled them to be self-sufficient, until the population pressure on the land became too great, with soil erosion and the departure of some people as the inevitable result. In the 1960s, this area still provided almost two-thirds of the national population with economic survival. The highlands, which stretch from the eastern to western borders, are between 50 and 100 kilometers in width. They are, in fact, the continuation of the main range of the Himalayas, which run in a north-south direction and in places reach heights of 4,500 meters. The rivers follow the chain until they are forced by the Mahabharat range into a west-easterly direction and they manage to break through the mountains.

This zone, which was originally covered with thick deciduous forests of chilaune, mock chestnut, rhododendron, oak and alder became, in the course of time, a preferred logging area, and finally a land of small private and tenant farmers. To protect the deforested grounds, in certain areas the inclines are terraced into true staircases, which testify to the almost super-human efforts of many generations.

The crops cultivated here include rice up to about 2,000 meters, millet up to 2,350 meters, corn – the main crop of the highlands – up to 2,500 meters, and wheat to 2,800 meters. Around the mostly very attractive farmsteads one finds fruit-trees, and growing in their gardens are leafy and root vegetables. Because of the extensive destruction of the mountain forests in many areas, the collection of fuel wood, the most important energy source, is becoming increasingly difficult. The increase in soil erosion and landslides, which often carry entire villages into the depths, shows that the young, unstable mountains cannot withstand the further increasing population pressures much longer, and catastrophe draws ever nearer. Nevertheless, every year the cultivated areas expand ever further. The land has been decreasing in productivity for years, and the inhabitants lead a poor existence. 60 percent of them live below the poverty line as measured by Nepalese standards. 47 of the 55 highland districts are unable to feed themselves and must buy their food from outside – mostly from the Terai. Only a few roads suitable for motor traffic penetrate

the area, so the greater part of goods transport is done on the backs of carriers or on pack animals.

Erosion of the forests has severely confined wildlife's living space however in the remaining groves and glades there are still supposed to be snow leopards, wild boars, muntjak or barking deer, the blue sheep and the red panda.

Himalaya Main Range

The main range of the Himalayas rises rather abruptly out of the highlands. Above the snow line, which is on average around 5,200 meters in altitude, the peaks are covered with permanent snowfields. The glaciers, which are resupplemented with snow during the monsoons, feed the larger rivers. Eight of the ten highest peaks in the world are in this region, including Sagarmartha (Mt. Everest) at 8,846 meters. The high mountains have only a few habitable places, and these are only sparsely populated. The Sherpas are the most well-known folk here. Their summer settlements range up to 4,500 meters and even higher, where their natural pastures are. More recently, they have offered their seasonal services to mountain climbing expeditions. There are reports of settlements as high as 4,900 meters in some places. Naturally, the altitude of the settlements depends on the growing altitude of their crops; potatoes grow at over 4,200 meters, barley at 4,500. The tree-line is generally around 4,200 meters, however all of these figures depend upon the exposure of the cliffs and other micro-climatic conditions. Among the most important tree species here are maple and birch, firs and stonepines, before scrub and brush take over.

The Himalayas play a significant role as a climatic boundary. They separate the monsoon-wet lands to their south from the dry continental climate of the Tibetan plateau. Paleo-climatic research has

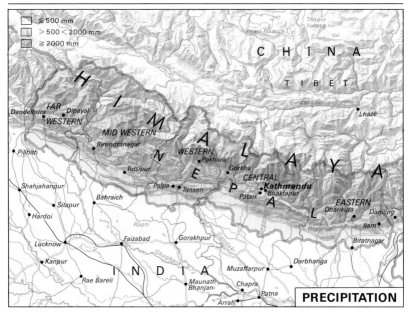

PRECIPITATION

shown that before the raising of the Himalayas the climate of Old Tibet was substantially wetter. This explains the fact that several Nepalese rivers have sources in Tibet, before they break through the main range. The traverse valleys of Kali Gandaki, the Arun, and as well the Buri Gandaki and the Karnali are some very impressive examples. The average annual precipitation in the Pokhara valley is more than 3,800 mm, whereas Jomosom – only 70 kilometers to the northwest – receives less than 250 mm. This shows the dramatic shielding effect of the Annapurna range – with peaks higher than 7,000 meters – which lies between the two areas.

The north-Himalayan dry zone includes a part of Nepal's national territory because in the West the northern border lies 50 to 60 kilometers north of where the main range expires. In this area, referred to as the Himalayan Interior, we find the highlying, sparsely populated area of Nepal, where agriculture is limited to watered oases and sheep breed-

ing on wild pastures is of particular importance. These are found in the districts of Mustang, Dolpo, Jumla and Humla – to the extent that they are protected by the Main Range of the Himalayas. From the north, this area is surrounded by the old Tibetan border range, which is not even 7,000 meters high. It is uninhabited and can only be crossed by a few trading paths which are little-used today. The wild pastures continue into Tibet and are traditionally used by both peoples.

The primary vegetation of the high mountains – juniper, rhododendrons and birches – is reduced here to grasses and rushes, and low, often thorny species. The animal world includes mountain goats, yaks, foxes, wolves and rabbits.

The kingdom of Nepal, now the home of 22,000,000 people of various cultures, is a place with a wealth of life-forms and species; a landscape unequalled in its variety and beauty. But it faces difficult problems: The fragility of the natural world places extraordinary demands on future development planning.

19

LEGEND
AND REALITY

The cradle of Nepal's artistic and cultural evolution is the present-day Kathmandu Valley. Its history is closely connected with the Newar ethnic group, which also gave the country its name. The Newar were the original occupants of the valley. They gradually mixed with other ethnic groups and finally, partly as a result of the introduction of the caste system from India developed an independent and unparalleled culture.

The country bears the stamp of the teachings of a variety of religious orientations and their orthodox rules. Important among these are Hinduism and Buddhism, as well as numerous sects and their cults within the spectrum of the larger religions; for example Shaktiism, Tantric Buddhism and the specifically Nepalese Shiva-Linga cult.

This variety of religious influences, combined with the somewhat unique folk-beliefs, has provided painters, sculptors, architects, gold-, silver-, and coppersmiths, woodcutters and stonecutters with a profusion of motifs.

Nepal is the only Hindu kingdom in the modern world. In addition to substantial influences from Tibet, it has been shaped above all by the socio-political, religious and cultural influence of India. However, in spite of all this, Nepal has managed to retain its own identity. Over centuries, from this exceedingly complex ethnic inheritance, a state of many peoples has steadily developed which, when viewed from outside, appears relatively homogeneous.

In 1768, King Prithvi Narayan Shah brought the various disjointed princi-

Left: The Newar have perfected the art of wood-carving in the Kathmandu Valley.

palities and kingdoms together into one country. At that time the so-called Gurkha Authority was instituted, whose ascendancy has endured since then up to the present day.

Through the centuries various events have, of course, altered the fate of the country, but the Nepalese rhythm of life has changed little.

The Origin of the Valley

Conditioned by factors such as the weather, agriculture and especially by religious beliefs, legends and myths have held up especially well, in a land ruled by natural forces and gods. A myth tells of the origin of the Kathmandu Valley. According to this myth the valley was originally a lake without an outlet, in the middle of which a lotus flower grew upwards. On this blossom appeared the original Buddha – the so-called Adi-Buddha – as Svayambhu, or " he who exists through himself."

Then the Bodhisattvsa Manjushri came from China, and, as a sacrificial offering, split open the ridge at the south of the lake. The water flowed out of this opening and the valley could then be populated. A visible sign of of this sword-stroke today is the Chobar Gorge, through which the holy Bagmati River, the primary stream of the valley flows. It then flows on to North India, where it empties into the Ganges.

According to tradition, Manjushri stayed in the valley until the first settlement of farmers from the surrounding area was established. This stretched from the Hill of Svayambhu to the area of what is today the Pashupatinath Temple.

Manjushri's escort Dharmakara was the first king of this city, which was named after the Bodhisattva Manjupattana. To this day, the highest being – the original or Adi-Buddha – is worshipped by Buddhist believers on the Hill of Svayambhu.

Early Rulers

It is frequently difficult for historians to determine the value of such legends. There is a great deal of source material available concerning the ruling houses in the Kathmandu Valley. First of all in Sanskrit or Newari, and then later in Nepalese, the histories were written down by Pandits or Brahmans or Buddhist Vajracharyas. In these cases it is no simple task to differentiate between legend and reality. The earliest inscriptions, which date back to A.D. 464, were made on a Garuda column in the temple area of Changu Narayan. They refer to the then ruling house of the Licchavi.

One can only speculate about earlier times. It is not certain whether the Gopala (cowherds) or the Kirata ought to be considered as the first ruling house in the

Above: The Adi Buddha first revealed himself in Svayambunath. Right: Traditional prayer wheels in Nepal with the sacred mantra: Om mani padme hum.

Kathmandu Valley. According to uncertain sources, the Kiratas probably ruled over the valley for almost a millenium before they were displaced by the Licchavis. During the Kiratas' rule, Gautama Buddha, as the son of a prince, is supposed to have lived in Lumbini in the south of present-day Nepal around the sixth century B.C.

Ashoka – the Indian Maurya ruler – is also linked with the Kiratas. It is not proven whether (as reported in legends) he really came to the Kathmandu Valley around 250 B.C. in order to erect four stupas in Patan. On the basis of the inscriptions on one of the stone columns in Lumbini named after him, we know only that Ashoka sought out these places, in order to worship Buddha at what is believed to be Buddha's birthplace.

To be sure, the Kirata are mentioned in both of the great Indian epics, the *Mahabarata* and the *Ramayana*. It is assumed that they advanced into the Kathmandu Valley out of the northeastern mountainous region somewhere between 1500

and 1000 B.C. The Rai and Limbu, who live today in the east of Nepal, are believed to be connected with them. Finally, the Kirata probably took up residence in Gokarna.

The Licchavi Dynasty

The Licchavis, who are supposed to have governed the Kathmandu Valley for some five centuries (A.D. 464-897), originated with greatest probability in the north of India. They may well have been threatened by the expansion of their neighbors, and therefore retreated – moving into the Kathmandu Valley, which was conveniently situated for commerce. Because the valley has always been a thoroughfare between Tibet, China and Indias' cultural areas of influence, the population there was constantly under new cultural influences. As a result, their art and handicrafts developed a thoroughly unique character.

This cultural exchange encouraged the powerful Tibetan King Songtsen Gampo

to have a trade route extended over the Himalayas through the Kathmandu Valley and on to India; he also married a Licchavi princess. She then brought along, as a gift, some Buddhist cult-illustrations. Still today, the Nepalese Princess Brikuti is revered as much in Tibet as in Nepal as the so-called "Green Tara," and is thought to have contributed spreading Buddhism to Tibet.

Another spouse of the Tibetan King Songtsen Gampo was the Chinese princess Wen-Cheng, who is revered today as the "White Tara." Through this double marriage, the positions of Tibet and Nepal as independent thoroughfare countries between India and China were established. Since then the trade routes have been considered the best connection over the Himalayas, and are later thought to have played a role in the cultural blooming of Nepal.

The Chinese pilgrim Hsüan-Tsang described the everyday life of the Licchavi period, and gave an impressive account of the artistic talents of the Newar in the

23

use of metal, stone, wood and paint. A number of temple complexes which still have great religious significance today were already in existence at that time. Among them are the Shiva sanctuary of Pashupatinath and the temple of Changu Narayan, which is dedicated to Vishnu, as well as the stupas of Svayambunath and Bodnath.

During the Licchavi period, the rulers showed tolerance toward the various religious practices of the valley population, even though they had a particular leaning in the direction of Hinduism. Buddhism was widely disseminated. While the people spoke a variety of dialects, above all Newari, Sanskrit was the language of the royal courts, which also represented the center of cultural activities. But scientists, theologians, astrologers and men of medicine also made their appearances there. Art historians classify this period as a Golden Age, but that is by no means all. At that time, the Indian common calendar was replaced by the Nepalese system, which is still in use today.

Thakuri Period

There is a shortage of documentation in connection with what is generally referred to as the Thakuri period (ca. A.D. 879-1200 – some see the beginning of the Thakuri era already from A.D. 602). "Thakuri," a word from Sanskrit, means "distinguished ruler" and was used as a title of honor. According to written sources, during this period the valley was ruled by various houses of Indian princes – mostly Rajputan – and just as the political conditions were confused, many writings in Sanskrit and in the Newari language testify to a similarly animated religious and cultural atmosphere.

Since the eighth century, the secret or Tantric Vajrayana Buddhism had been

Right: The statue of Bhupatindra Malla in Bhaktapur, all aglow.

promulgated in Tibet by the Indian master Padmasambhava; it now made its entrance into Nepal. It had an especially attractive character due to its magical practices and secret teachings – which were connected primarily with elements of pre-Buddhist and pre-Hindu folk-religions, shamanism and the various cults of fertility.

The so-called "matrikas," maternal forms, are revered in Nepal. They are put on the same level as the primeval powers that influence all processes of becoming; one must please or assuage them with sacrificial offerings. Incalculable numbers of natural forces – mostly associated with demons and gods – can be banned through the use of certain magical incantations – the so-called *mantras*. An ever-increasing importance was attributed to the cult rituals.

The representations of eroticism that one comes across in the artistic creation of sculptures and temple ornamentation often have their origins in the imagery of Tantrism, which tought that earthly and spiritual well-being could be achieved through rites that included sexual practices. Tibetan and Indian monks came to the Kathmandu Valley in order to take up the new religious teachings, or to carry them further into the other religious centers of India, Tibet and China.

It has frequently been said that in the Kathmandu Valley, questions of caste and differences in notions concerning religious beliefs have very rarely led to war or violent conflicts. However, someone really familiar with the source material will be aware that times have not always been without conflicts. For example, it is known that around A.D. 800 the Indian scholar and yogi Shankara ordered Buddhist writings burned in many places in Nepal, and so contributed to the progress of Hinduism in Nepal. Even more frequently it was discovered that Buddhist monks had been forced to marry Buddhist nuns.

Obviously, religious tolerance was not always the order of the day, as this example proves. At that time numerous monks sought refuge in Tibet, only making their return to Nepal after the tide of authoritarian violence had ebbed – carrying with them a new set of religious ideas, namely Tantric Buddhism.

The Malla Dynasty

The power of the Thakuri dynasty ended in the year 1182, and – barring occasional changes of power – the Mallas proclaimed themselves the rulers of the Kathmandu Valley from that time onward. They would dominate the history of the country for over 500 years – until 1768. In its literal translation from the Sanskrit, the name Malla means "wrestler." Once again, according to a legend, the first Malla prince of the Kathmandu Valley is said to have received tidings of the birth of his son during a wrestling match, which is where he earned this surname.

Already in the time of Gautama Buddha – in the sixth century B.C. – this name appears in connection with a royal dynasty, and during the Licchavi reign (5th-9th century) Malla princes were already living in western Nepal.

It is probable that after the invasion of India by the Moslem Moguls – at the beginning of the 13th century – many of the relatives of this lineage fled to Nepal, in order to build a new existence there.

However, later on Nepal was not to remain spared from the invaders either. For a short time in 1349, the Moguls under the rule of Shams-ud-din Ilyas took over the Kathmandu Valley, and there destroyed temples and monasteries, particularly the Pashupatinath sanctuary. Soon afterwards the Moguls withdrew.

The Malla epoch is divided into two periods – from 1200 to 1482 and from this time up to 1768, the year of the conquest of Prithvi Narayan Shah. Both periods were of great importance for the social, religious and cultural development of the valley. There is now a tend-

ency to consider these periods of history as the age of blossoming – another Golden Age if you will – of the Kathmandu Valley. During the second part of this period, the three royal cities – Patan, Bhaktapur and Kathmandu – gradually developed their present incomparable splendor. At any rate there were also some darker times for the population of the valley, which people prefer to overlook. For example, in 1255 an earthquake left the valley in ruins. One third of the population fell victim to Mother nature, including the King Abhayamalla. Somewhat later, beginning in 1288, the princes of Jumla (in present-day western Nepal), who number among the Khas, plundered the valley over and over again. In the middle of the 14th century, the unity of the valley was shattered, as local noble families proclaimed themselves inde-

Above: This modern painting by Jagdish Chitrakar shows Bhaktapur of old. Right: A farmer from the Bhaktapur area brings in his harvest.

pendent and started to rule arbitrarily in such localities as Pharping, Patan and even some neighboring valleys, among them Nuvakot and Banepa.

With the reign of Jayasthiti Malla, which lasted from 1382 until 1395, some transformations were instituted. The inhabitants of the valley were classified into different castes, following the Indian system of orthodox Hinduism. The entire structure of the country was reorganized, a change which held up to the 18th century. The previous, – to an extent – chaotic conditions were stringently regimented through a rigorous process of "Hinduization," with rather overwhelming results. Jayasthiti Malla transformed an, as it were, open society, which was always ready to assimilate newly arrived groups, into one which was closed. He was rather skeptical when it came to the looser forms of the Tantric cult. By the introduction of the caste system he hoped to save the old order whose existence and indeed continued development was also being threatened by the Moguls.

In 1482, a successor of Jaya Malla allocated the cities of Bhaktapur, Patan and Kathmandu to his sons as autonomous dominions. At that time, the Mallas probably stood under the nominal rule of the Moguls. This influence showed itself, for instance, in the clothing and hair-styles of the Mallas and in the fact that they openly maintained court harems. Under their artistic influence numerous miniatures were painted. In mural painting, a vast array of superficial ornamentation became fashionable with poor results. In spite of all this, the Kathmandu Valley was able to keep its Hindu inheritance intact through all those years because of its relatively safe geographical situation.

Another great period of artistic blossoming was spawned by the rivalry between the city-kings. The three capitals were enlarged and ornamented. Stonecutters, woodcarvers and thangka-painters (*thangkas* are religious cult paintings) from the Newar ethnic group created extraordinary artworks. A variety of cults were in existence, for example

the Kumari cult. Even though the northern (Buddhist) and the southern (Islamic) influences were quite significant, the art of the Malla period still possessed a strong sense of individual creativity and power of expression.

Critics today characterize the later Malla era as a period of extravagance at the cost of the Nepalese people. The life of luxury exhausted the state treasuries of the three monarchs who, during this period, even compared themselves to god-kings. High tax revenues became necessary in order to finance the pomp and splendor of the palaces. The personal quarrelling among the three parallel dynasties – and their vying with each other for power and magnificence – on the one hand ate up their treasuries, but also encouraged an enormous amount of artistic activity. Never had there been so much pure gold, silver and precious stones worked on as in this epoch. State-subsidized art came to symbolize status and power, as was also true later during the Rana period. Unfortunately, we know

little about the artists themselves, as they worked for religious purposes, not for their own fortunes. According to legend, in Kathmandu under Jayaprakash Malla relations with foreign rulers deteriorated so badly that the king was even forced to sell jewels and temple treasures – including those of Pashupatinath – in order to afford to recruit troops for his military.

Shah Rulership

This situation was changed by Prithvi Narayan Shah, who began taking over the valley in 1769. It took him 25 years before he succeeded in the conquest of the three royal cities from the mountain city of Kirtipur.

Angered by the bitter resistance put up by the inhabitants of Kirtipur, he ordered

Above: A guard of honor at the Hanuman Dhoka during the Dasain festival. Right: The portrait of King Birendra on a processional float.

the noses of the town's men be cut off as a warning. The army unit of the British East Indian company, which Kathmandu appealed to for help in its defense, was unable to prevent the conquering of the valley.

Prithvi's ancestors probably originated in Rajasthan, and in the 15th century took refuge in the village of Gurkha, which lies west of Kathmandu. There, they united the various surrounding principalities and small kingdoms of the local ethnic groups. The legislative structure which they founded played an important part in the later unification of the country under Prithri Narayan Shah.

Their attention was directed toward the development of a new nation – the unification of the western and eastern sections of what is present-day Nepal. The close relationship of the Shah with Tibet, China and the British is thought by historians to have been of great significance to the further development of artistic handcrafts and pictorial art connected with the later Rana period. Over and over again,

armed confrontations over trade resources erupted with Tibet, which was at the time under the subjugation of the Chinese Manchu dynasty.

After the establishment of peace pacts with the Tibetans – and with that the Chinese, direct contacts developed with Peking, which gave the Shah a certain security against the increasing activity of the British in India, who had been there since the end of the 18th century. The Shah maintained a very cautious relationship with the British, not only because he feared having to share various trade privileges with them, but also because he had a rather low opinion of people who didn't worship their gods. He did, however, open up trade with British-occupied India as early as 1792.

In 1814, border difficulties led finally to war between the Nepalese and the British. In 1816 the Treaty of Segauli was signed, which above all stipulated that from then on the British could recruit the Gurkha soldiers into the British army, and that in Kathmandu a British embassy

would be opened. Despite the reservations and recalcitrance of the Shah, the British continued gaining influence as a result of their various trade advantages.

In addition, the royal family became weakened through intrigue. Cultural life during this turbulent political period was seriously neglected. In spite of this, the legacy of traditional and religious art survived, but it degenerated to a rather folkloric level. In matters concerning religion, the Shah showed none of the country's traditional tolerance. He permitted only the teachings of Hinduism and Buddhism. Muslims and Christians, whose presence and religious activities had experienced no limitations whatsoever under the Mallas, were now banished from the land.

Rana Oligarchy

In 1846, a commander of the Shah army, Jang Bahadur Kunwar (later Rana) brought the intrigue in the court of the Shahs to a bloody conclusion, and built up a family oligarchy that would last for more than a century. With tight administration and new legislation, the Rana premiers hoped to secure their collection of tax revenues and maintain law and order. Moreover, the family also managed to undermine the economy, while the royal family of the Shah was degraded to a shadow existence. After Jang Bahadur Rana made himself the Maharaja of Kaski (Pokhara area) and Lamjung, he was an equal to the King and so was able to take such measures. This title was particularly important for marriage. To the present day the Shahs and Ranas are allied in this manner. For example, today's King Birendra Dev Bikram Shah is married to the Rana Princess Lakshmi Devi.

In order to have an ally in the event of danger and to prevent an uprising of the opposition which was exiled in India, the Ranas cultivated a close relationship with the British and even visited Great Britain. In 1857, Jang Bahadur sent the English 8,000 Gurkha soldiers to put down the Sepoy uprising in India. Closely interwoven trading relationships developed with India, which had experienced drastic industrialization and urbanization under British occupation. Nepal exported more than it imported, and the earnings flowed to the Ranas.

From 1854-1856, J. B. Rana fought a victorious war with Tibet, which as a result had to agree to an annual payment of tributes, the establishment of a trade mission, and the elimination of tolls on goods.

Nepal's first industrialization came under the Rana ruler Chandra Shamser (1901-1929). He had a diesel power plant built and erected a cable railway for the transport of heavy loads. He also abolished slavery in 1924.

The Ranas gave support to traditional art and culture, but also to art movements of European inspiration. The Nepalese aristocracy developed an ever-increasing taste for western culture and consumer goods. Their ostentatious palaces, built in pseudo-baroque style, are still to be found in Kathmandu.

Only the Rana families and their favorites enjoyed the benefit of schools and higher education. Their despotism went so far that normal households, whose appartments stood across from a Rana house, had to keep their windows closed. It was exactly this sort of behavior that smoothed the way for opposition to the Rana regime. The independence movement in India gave this anti-Rana movement impetus. It was not surprising that in the year 1936 the followers of the Shah royal family and the opposition made off to neighbouring India, where they united into a sort of anti-Rana movement, which later developed into the Nepali Congress Party.

After India won back its independence from the British in 1947 it was only a question of time before the Ranas eventually gave up. In 1951, after King Tribhuvan fled to India, the Ranas were forced to agree to a coalition government between representatives of the royal family, supporters of the Nepali Congress Party and the Rana families. Nepal, until then hermetically sealed off, opened up to the world.

Lately the king's power has increasingly been jeopardized. Corruption and exploitation drove the people into the streets. Mass demonstrations in Kathmandu in February 1990 resulted in clashes with dead and many wounded. The Panchayat system fell, the hardliners were removed and the opposition movement gained ground, political parties were admitted. The Newar Man Singh became the most popular politician. The king had to reconise the constitutional monarchy. In 1994 the united communists won the elections ahead of the Nepali Congress Party.

Right: A Garuda statue in Bhaktapur.

THE PEOPLE

OF NEPAL

The Himalayan Range acts as a tremendous natural barrier between South and Central Asia, but for thousands of years its passes have provided a place for encounters between the Mongolian groups of Tibeto-Burmese speakers, who adhere to Tibetan Buddhism and numerous natural religions; and members of the Caucasian peoples speaking with Indo-Aryan languages and practicing Hinduism as their religion.

Different worlds met here in military expeditions, migrations and trading relationships as well. These led to such a profound combination of cultural and social, economic and political forms, that there is no such thing as a unified, homogenous, "Nepalese" culture. Or is heterogeneity the very essence of that culture?

The area populated by the peoples of Nepal climbs, from south to north, from about 150 meters in altitude to around 5,000 meters in the direction of Tibet. The Mongoloid groups live primarily in the northern sections; the Indo-Nepalese mostly in the southern half of the country. Since agriculture is insufficient to support life in the high mountains, the Mongoloid groups have bred yaks, goats and sheep for centuries. They have also run an active barter of Tibetan salt and wool for Nepalese grain, using the high Himalayan passes between the two countries. A by-product of this trade has been long-term contact with Tibetan culture. In recent decades, however, volume has decreased sharply, because of the situation in Tibet (which has been occupied by China since 1950), and competition from Indian goods.

Left: A woman from the Kathmandu Valley in Dakshin Kali with her sacrificial offering.

The Indo-Nepalese in flat, bountiful Terai had been producing – in step with the fight against malaria – agricultural surpluses, which they brought to market in the closer and more easily accessible Indian markets. In the 1980s, though, the needs of the locals for their own agricultural products increased dramatically, leading to a substantial decline in the export of these goods.

Mongoloid and Indo-Nepalese groups have contact with each other principally in the third main region of Nepal, the central mountains, which in English is referred to – not exactly fittingly – as the "hill region." Here, on carefully terraced fields between 500 and 2,000 meters altitude, rice and other grains are cultivated. But production is insufficient to support the local population, hence there is substantial migration notably to serve in Ghurka troops. Around 60 % of the total population of Nepal lives in the hill region and till about 30% of the total land area, whereas in the Terai – with only 30 % of the population – almost 70% of the land is arable.

When trying to assign individual ethnic groups to particular geographical regions, one must realize that these regions are extremely varied. Individual ethnic groups, for example the Tamang, have to be very flexible when it comes to adapting to their surroundings. And they must accept legwork as a fact of life. They plant rice on fields 700 meters in altitude; They cultivate potatoes, wheat, buckwheat, millet and corn at around 2,500 meters, and they go up to 4,500 meters to bring their livestock to pasture.

The Terai and the Hill Region

The main ethnic groups represented in the Terai include the Tharu, the Darai, the Kumhal, the Danuwar and the Majhi, as well as the Hindu population with its roots in India. These groups speak primarily Nepalese and northern Indian dia-

33

lects. They live from agriculture, mostly as tenant farmers on private estates, which they were unable to register for in time, thus losing their land. In addition, the Majhi are employed as drivers, the Kumhal as potters, and the Danuwar as fishermen.

In the hill region, numerous ethnic groups are settled in the neighborhood of the Hindu population. Progressing from west to east one finds the Magar, the Gurung, the Tamang, the Newar, the Sunuwar, the Rai and the Limbu. Numbered among the smaller groups are the Thakali, the Chantel, the Chepang, the Raaji, the Pahari (Pahi), the Thami, the Haayu, and the Dhimal. A major part of these groups belong linguistically to the Bodic group of the Sino-Tibetan language family; the Dhimal, the Newar, and the Pahari can be placed between the Bodic and Burmese language groups. Several of these groups were previously hunter-ga-

therers. Only the Newar have brought forth an urbanized culture.

The Northern Region

In the far north live – among others – the Sherpa, the Dolpo-pa, the Baragaonli, the Manangi and the Lopa. They usually earn a living as guides and carriers for mountain climbing expeditions, as high mountain farmers, and as yak and sheep breeders. They are linguistically – as well as culturally – connected to Tibet. In general, they are often referred to as *Bhotiyas*. The previously mentioned traders are recruited from these groups in particular. Also to be counted among them are the Humli-Khyampa, who subsist as nomadic traders in the westernmost section of the country.

During the cold winter months several of these groups set off on trading expeditions to the south of the country, where they sell the products of their homelands – herbs and spices – so that they can purchase the products of the south. Some

Above: Despite their hard work, often as porters, the Nepalese are usually friendly.

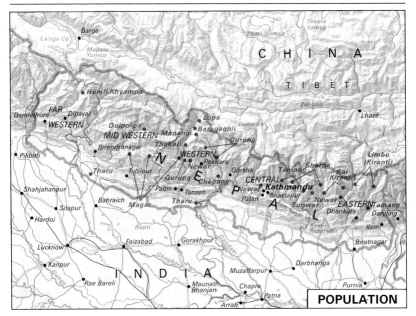

POPULATION

Bhotiyas even travel as far as Bangkok and Hong Kong to conduct their business on a larger scale.

Altogether, the Nepalese ethnic groups make up approximately half of the population. Because no single one of these ethnic groups add up to more than 4% of the combined population of Nepal, they are considered to be minorities. In comparison to this, 45% of Nepal's population are so-called Hindus, who, undifferentiated in their various origins, present themselves as a single cultural unit. They owe the security of their key position in the national government to this sense of unity.

There is precious little clarity concerning the origins and migration processes of the various ethnic groups in present-day Nepal. The Khas have had a rather unique "career." They came from a region of India (Kumaon) to the far west of Nepal as a relatively lowly-placed group in the Hindu caste system. There they built up their position substantially, and were able to step upwards within the Ne-

palese caste hierarchy. A portion of today's Chetri are recruited from this ethnic group.

Kiranti and Tamang Peoples

As a rule, the Kiranti (predecessors of the Limbu, Rai, Sunawar and other ethnic groups that live today in Nepal) are considered to be the oldest inhabitants of central and eastern Nepal. Numerous myths exist about their origins and role in the process of history. It is questionable whether the Kiranti had in reality stayed part in Benares, part in Lhasa and part in the Kathmandu Valley in "early" times, as is portrayed in their myths.

It is also difficult to verify the myths of other ethnic groups, with their supposed glorious pasts as kings and high dignitaries. Their origins, the time of their arrival in Nepal, and their political development are all difficult to research.

Owing to changing circumstances (subjugation to various princes, integration into a united Nepalese kingdom,

35

economic changes, etc.) the ethnic borders in Nepal were redrawn and the culture altered. Individual groups and ethnic clans have, as a result, received names only in the last century. For example, the Tamang, who were settled to the north and east of the Kathmandu Valley, first received their name from the Nepalese rulers in the middle of the 19th century, as the latter proclaimed the first civil legislation. Thus the Tamang, today generally considered to be of one ethnic group, are composed of exceptionally heterogenous sub-groups, with substantially different languages, cultural lore and social customs.

The generally ascertainable mobility of the Nepalese population can, most probably, be traced back to economic transformation and the historical processes of adaptation to the customs of the respective power groups. To this comes the mobility of the modern world.

Above: Brahman woman in festive garb.
Right: Father and son playing.

Ethnic Diversity in the Kathmandu Valley

The colorful mixture of peoples presents itself to the traveler directly on arrival in the Kathmandu Valley. In just the last few years, the social influx from other parts of the country has increased substantially. One encounters people from every region; the city's architectural character is stamped primarily, however, with the imprint of one particular ethnic group: The first encounter with Nepal in the Kathmandu Valley is, to a certain degree, an encounter with the culture of the Newar. This group governed the valley for centuries, which was rather wealthy, thanks to its fertile soil and strategically important position as a trade center between India and China. This resulted in a rich and fascinating secular and religious architecture.

Worthy of note are Hindu as well as Buddhist places, since the Newar managed to integrate both religions to an exceptional degree, even though the expansion of Hinduism sometimes filled the adherents of Buddhism with bitterness in the process.

The Newar were the only group in Nepal that were able to develop an urban culture, but they were also successful in agriculture. At harvest time the connection between life in the cities and agriculture is especially visible. At these times every free spot in the plazas, and sometimes even in the streets, is used to dry the harvested crops. The Newar – as administrators, farmers and craftsmen – have played a key role in commerce over centuries, which has encouraged the flourishing of craftsmanship.

Today many Newar are still good tradespeople, running anything from small tea-shops to middle-sized textile businesses, or even large import-export outfits. Newar families who had resided in the valley for hundreds of years, were ordered by local rulers to travel to remote and underdeveloped parts of Nepal to develop trade.

Although the presence of the Newar is still strongly felt in the Kathmandu Valley especially through their art and craftwork, their role in politics has considerably diminished, although they do occupy a portion of the official positions. Since the Newar kings of the Malla dynasty were overthrown by the Gurkha rulership in the second half of the 18th century, the power and jurisdiction of this primarily high-caste Indo-Nepalese group has decreased. Some among their ranks were recruited to the Shah dynasty, which is still in power today. During the consolidation of Shah power, a period referred to as the unification of Nepal (1744-1814), a large number of these upper caste families moved to the valley where they made their influence felt.

The notion of a "national culture," often mentioned nowadays, is associated in the first place with those cultural elements, values and norms that are manifested particularly in the Indo-Aryan lan-

guage derived from Sanskrit and called "Nepalese" (earlier called *Khas kura*). It is today the lingua franca of this diverse nation. Only half of the population speaks it as their native language; but it is the sole language used in education. This does not please the Newar, for example, who value their writings in "Newari" highly, and occasionally rouses them to vehement resistance. The Nepalese-speaking upper caste Hindus have achieved key roles in the economic process, thanks in part to their political and social dominance. They are the prime choice when it comes to occupying the top positions in the political and administrative apparatus; and they are also the owners of the extensive landed estates. Their influence is not only felt in Kathmandu itself, but also in the provinces.

Only a few members of the original non-Hindu ethnic groups have been able to engage themselves in the central political processes. One way to make contact with members of these ethnic communities is quite simply to go shopping

or visit a travel agent. Groups from the far north – particularly the Sherpas, the Thakali and the Manangi – have made little niches for themselves in these two economic sectors. These groups have made profitable use of the fact that they live at the thoroughfare passes between Nepal and Tibet, and that rulers had to rely upon their services for the collection of tolls.

Many families have succeeded in achieving great affluence, and have expanded their business activities in every direction. Especially since the partial closure of the northern border, which occured as a result of China's annexation of Tibet in 1950, they have been shifting their residences and businesses to the southern regions of Nepal (in particular to the Terai and the Kathmandu Valley). Here, they have been able to use their capital and their flair for business to set themselves up quite successfully. With

Above: Fast asleep on mother's shoulder.
Right: A pilgrim from Mustang.

their retail and travel businesses and factories they have attained considerable influence, which they share only with the Newar and several Tibetan families. The latter, after their traumatic exodus from Tibet, first lived in refugee centers, where they were given the task of weaving Tibetan carpets, which have now become well-known. Today this business is flourishing, and it has therefore been "borrowed" by other groups, among them the Sherpas. The Tibetan religious centers have proven to be a great attraction for practicing western Buddhists, who seek out Nepal to study meditation under the instruction of famous lamas. None of the other groups that reside in Nepal have been able to establish such strong bonds with the West as the Tibetans.

The men who entered the Gurkha troops as mercenaries in service to the British have become rather cosmopolitan. Whether in Italy during the Second World War, South-East Asia during the battles for independence, or more recently in the British-Argentinian conflict over the Falkland Islands, the Nepalese Gurkhas have distinguished themselves everywhere with their courage and endurance as hired soldiers. In spite of the dangers, service in the Gurkha regiments – well-paid by the British – has always been held in high regard. Members of a variety of ethnic groups, particularly the Gurung and the Magar, have been able to eradicate their debts and enlarge their properties with saved up wages and pension benefits.

Prospects and Problems

It is not only the well-to-do who seek out the area around the Kathmandu Valley. Carriers, ricksha drivers, waiters, hotel workers, servants of various rank and janitors are recruited from the stream of migrants, who come in increasing numbers in search of work in the Kathmandu Valley, because there is less and

less land available in the surrounding Hill Region. The population of every ethnic group is confronted with this problem, whether Tamang or Rai, Magar or Chepang. They must take on the most difficult, lowest levels of employment in society, since they usually lack extensive vocational training. Competition is becoming increasingly tough. The level of unemployment has increased to such an extent that, paradoxically, people who stand on higher rungs in the Hindu caste system are struggling to get work normally relegated to the Untouchables – street sweeping, for example.

The city – with its increasing modernization; with its chaos of automobiles, tourists, cacaphonous radios, landing aircraft, and with unimagined opportunities naturally exerts a strong attraction on many young people. Even without economic pressure they are turning their backs on agrarian existence, which they consider to be both boring and burdensome. They are leaving the lands of their fathers, even rejecting service as teachers in their local schools, in order to hurry to the city and be willingly hired for the most inferior positions. Wealthier farmers now complain of the lack of workers, and are confronted with major problems. Alone the hiring of farm workers costs money. The older heads of households must also accept their loss of authority over the younger generations of males.

The disintegration of family relationships is being generally decried in Nepal. As regards the youth who have emigrated to the city, they are just about exhausted by the hard working conditions, loss of status, and general loss of identity. No matter how colorful and quiet they appear, the Nepalese people faces numerous difficult problems.

While the government has already drawn up many ambitious plans for the year 2000, the population of Nepal looks to an uncertain future of environmental destruction, increasing economic difficulties, and weak leadership of the political elite.

RELIGIONS

OF NEPAL

If you were to ask a Nepali whether he is Hindu or Buddhist, he might well answer you simply and with a perfectly straight face – "Yes." Did he misunderstand the question or was it incorrectly put? In the majority of cases, both would be true. A Nepali, especially a Newar, can worship both Buddha and Shiva without falling into a conflict of beliefs. He is reluctant to fall out of favor with any of the gods, and so, just to be on the safe side, he rather worships all of them. Many pilgrims who seek out a temple during a festival strew their offerings (flowers, grains of rice, powdered cinnabar or coins) at all sorts of shrines and holy sanctuaries. There might even be a fire hydrant deprived of its normal function, just because it has the proper phallic form of a linga.

Officially, Nepal is the only Hindu kingdom in the world. That being so, Hinduism has been declared the national religion and other religions are viewed as sub-forms of Hinduism. However, the statistical computation of religious membership is difficult, if not impossible. According to the government census of 1991, almost 86.2% of the population are Hindus. Small in comparison, the figures for the other religions are 7.8% Buddhists, 3.8% Moslems, 0.2% Christians, and 2.0% other religions.

At the main national holy sanctuary, Pashupatinath temple, – as at many other temples –, a sign forbids entrance to non-Hindus. In principle, however, only foreigners are not admitted. Since in Hinduism Buddha is considered to be a

Left: Vishnu and his mount Garuda in Changu Narayan are found on every ten rupee note.

manifestation of Vishnu, Buddhists are allowed entrance.

Frequently in rituals and religious festivals, especially in myths, the distinction between the gods is consciously blurred. Once a year, the linga in the then overcrowded Pashupatinath temple is worshipped as Avalokiteshvara. During the ritual, the linga is adorned with the crown of the Bodhisattvas.

Shiva and his Company

Hindus worship two major gods, Shiva and Vishnu, together with their accompanying hosts. While Shiva appears as a wild, fear-inspiring god – in classical myths he is often the destroyer of the world – Vishnu has a mild, more world-protecting character. The third god in the old Hindu divine trinity is named Brahma and scarcely plays a role in the temple cult today.

Shiva (also referred to as Maheshvar or Mahadev) is worshipped most frequently as a linga. This might be quite a plain and unpretentious abstract phallic symbol, but it may also have the four-sided face of the manifestations of the god. A temple to Shiva is rarely without his riding mount – the bull Nandi – or his weapon, the three-pronged Trishul.

In the classical myths of India, Shiva appears on the one hand as evil and dangerous, and on the other, kindly and benevolent. In Nepal, however, he is a peaceful god, to whom one goes seeking support and assistance. Thus, many votive temples have been erected in his name. In the Kathmandu Valley it is more common to meet gods who are dangerous and require appeasement. These divine creatures are even capable of subjugating powerful Shiva, as can be seen in one particular festival which the Newar celebrate in springtime, mainly in Kathmandu. This festival is held in March or April. The courtyards of houses are carefully cleaned of garbage and other debris.

In the process, a small linga is dug out from under the piles of garbage, which is worshipped in the night. This linga is named *Lukumahadyo*, which means literally "hidden Mahadev" (= Shiva). According to the unwritten traditions, Shiva had sought protection here because he was threatened by wild goddesses, evil demons or even ignorant Buddhists, depending on who's telling the story.

The degree to which Shiva himself has been superimposed on local gods is seen in the god Nasadyo. Newar musicians have a god of protection whose course one dare not hinder. Therefore, there are slits in many walls and specialized shrines, through which the god may pass without having to make any detours.

Originally, neither the cult nor the manifestation had anything in common with Shiva. But in the high tradition of

India, Shiva is also the god of dance (Nateshvar or Nataraja). So, it was an easy step to connect the two gods, especially as it also meant a definite increase in the musicians' status. The god of protection then received the name Nasadyo, the Newari version of Nateshvar ("god of dance").

Although in Hindu mythology the elephant-headed god Ganesha (another name is Vinyaka) is thought of as the son of Shiva, he has a character all his own in Nepal. Pre-Hinduist traits have been connected with this beloved Indian god as well. For example, he receives blood sacrifices and gifts of alcohol much more frequently than in India. Ganesha not only watches over each quarter of the city, but also watches over the entire Kathmandu Valley from Bhaktapur, Chaba, Kathmandu und Chobar.

Coarse, unhewn stones are also used to signify Ganesha, who is otherwise represented with an obvious elephant's head. In any case, one can recognize Ganesha in the sculptures with enough imagin-

Above: The elephant god Ganesha is especially popular in Nepal. Right: The goddess Taleju enthroned on the "golden gate" in Bhaktapur.

ation. Even Bhairava (in classical Hinduism a fear-inspiring form of Shiva) is not always represented as a mask or statue, but often only as a simple stone. In these phenomena there is clear evidence of pre-Hindu divinities, which in the process of Nepal's Hinduization were promoted, so to speak, by being given prestigious Sanskrit names.

Goddesses

Occasionally, Shiva is accompanied by his female companion in her benevolent aspects. Parvathi ("mountain daughter"), Uma ("sunrise" or the "rose of dawn") or Gauri ("golden") are her most frequent names. She may appear either in isolation, as, for example, the great Gauri-stone in the Bagmati River north of the Pashupatinath Temple, or together with Shiva. The image is then usually named Umamaheshvara and portrays the couple in a peaceful embrace.

Shiva's female companion can also appear as wild and threatening. She is then referred to as Shakti, or the embodiment of Shiva's feminine cosmic energy. The connection with Shiva is often very blurred. Then the pre-Hindu traits of such goddesses are only hinted at. In the Kathmandu Valley their names and manifestations, as well as their temples and shrines, are virtually countless.

One of the more frequent motifs is that of the Mahisha-killing demon Durga (often called Bhagavati in Nepal). It appears over and over again, especially on arches above the entrances to temples or on elaborately carved wooden roof-beams. On these, Durga is usually portrayed standing on the demon, who has assumed the form of an untameable buffalo. Durga then impales the demon with a long spear. This motif is repeated in real life in the Dasain Festival, which is dedicated to Durga, among others, and when the heads of hundreds of small water buffaloes are hewn off at the Hanuman Dhoka in gruesome ceremony.

The manifestation of the goddess as Taleju is of great significance. She then functions as one of the goddesses of protection of the Malla reign, who is worshipped in secret rituals, and whose Mantra (a magical incantation for protection) is supposed to guarantee the power of the king. In all three royal cities of the Kathmandu Valley, the most magnificent temples are dedicated to Taleju.

In less prominent places, the goddess is known under a varity of other names. Frequently her temple or shrine is located outside the settlement, from where she should protect the inhabitants. As a rule a movable idol for her worship is kept in the city. It is taken out on special festivals and led down very precisely pre-determined paths.

It is clear that in the cults, the mythology, the forms of worship and the iconography in fact always revolve around one goddess, who appears in a variety of manifestations. Certain groups of goddesses arranged in cosmic diagrams (mandalas) are also basically representations of the one and the same supreme goddess.

So, we frequently find either the Eight Mothers (Asthamatrika) or the Nine Durgas (Navadurga), whose task it is to surround a village or a temple. The most common grouping consists of the eight goddesses Brahmani, Mahesvari, Kaumari, Vaishnavi, Vahari, Indrani, Camunda, and Mahalaki. They can also be joined by a ninth manifestation.

Not only can a goddess have several different names, but a goddess may be represented in several different ways under the same name. For example, the goddess Lakshmi has no temple of her own, but she is portrayed on many representations of Vishnu as his female companion. Her likeness is also worshipped in many private houses as the completely independant goddess Shri who is supposed to care for wealth and well-being.

Right: Procession of Buddhist Theravada monks in Pokhara.

And finally, she appears in Tantric rituals as Vishnu's Shakti and as Vaishnavi, one figure from the Eight Mothers.

The situation is similar with Sarasvati, who is worshiped as the goddess of the arts and sciences. She is seen as both Vishnu's female companion and that of the *bodhisattva* Manjushri (the concept of the bodhisattva is explained later in "The Buddhist World". But she also appears in Tantric rituals – which often refer to the Dark or Blue Sarasvati as opposed to the White Sarasvati.

Vishnu, Rama and Krishna

In contrast to Shiva and his linga, Vishnu, who is also frequently called Narayan, is rarely represented symbolically or abstractly. The plainest form of his artistic manifestation besides the black ammonite are his stylized feet (Vishnupadaka).

More frequently, Vishnu is represented as a human or animal figure. Thus he appears at times as Budhanilkantha, as he reposes on a snake in the primeval waters; at times as Narasimha ("half man, half lion"), as he conquers the adversaries of the gods; at times as a boar (Vahara); and at times as a dwarf (Vamana).

According to mythology, Vishnu appears on the earth in nine manifestations (Avataras) altogether. His tenth manifestation, the horse Kalki (a rider of the Apocalypse?) will only appear at the destruction of the world, at the end of the present Age of Kaliyuga.

Several of the sculptures on which such scenes are portrayed are among the earliest artworks of Nepal. From new revelations it appears, that in the first half of the first millenium A.D. Vishnuism was far more widely disseminated than had been previously assumed.

Vishnu's attributes, the conch – or shells – and his weapon, the discus, *(cakra)* are not infrequently placed on particular columns in front of temples to

Vishnu. They usually surround Vishnu's mount, the mythical bird *Garuda*.

Hanuman, a god in the shape of an ape, also appears in many Vishnuist holy places. He is especially beloved, since he helped a further manifestation of Vishnu, namely the heroic god Rama, in many emergencies. Shrines dedicated to Rama are found less frequently in the Kathmandu Valley, most are in Bhaktapur, which calls itself the city of Rama, and in Deopatan.

Patan, a city which bears a strong spiritual and material imprint from Buddhism, is a center for the worship of Krishna. There are many beautiful temples and shrines to this well-loved god. Krishna is a god with many pastoral and heroic traits. But his widespread popularity is based above all on his romantic love-relationship with Radha. In the worship of Krishna and also of Rama such devotion is of great importance. One prays intimately to them and sings of them with poems and songs that are full of ardor and love for the gods.

The Buddhist World

As is well known, the historical Buddha was born in the middle of the sixth century B.C. in what is today an area of Nepal, more exactly in Lumbini on the southern foothills of the Himalayas. It took more than a thousand years for the first ascertainable relics to be left behind in the Kathmandu Valley. These include early statues of the Buddha Shakyamuni, which are named after Buddha's family name.

The original Buddhism is a teaching of salvation, but in Nepal only a little of this content still remains. Here, primarily Vajrayana Buddhism is still alive. This is a form of Mahayana Buddhism that bears a strong imprint from Tantric rituals.

With this "Great Course" of Buddhism the conception arose that anyone could become bodhisattva. Bodhisattvas are beings who have received enlightenment, but have chosen to refuse the reward – namely entrance into Nirvana, so that they might remain to assist others on their

45

paths toward enlightenment. In Nepal, the bodhisattvas have become regular gods in their own right, and are worshipped in temples with lavish and partially secret rituals. The bodhisattvas are also thought of as offspring or emanations of the Dhyana-Buddha. They are mystical-transcendental Buddhas who also embody the five basic elements of ether, air, water, fire and earth. Feminine aspects are also associated with them, namely the Buddhashaktis. One of the most well-known bodhisattvas throughout Nepal is Padmapani-Avalokiteshvara (also called Lokeshvara or Lokanatha, "Emperor of the World"), who is at the same time Tibet's patron saint.

Avalokiteshvara means literally "the god who gazes downward," an expression of the compassion by which this bodhisattva is primarily characterized.

Above: A Hindu ascetic on a pilgrimage to Pashupati, a manifestation of Shiva. Right: Tibetan musicians playing at a Puja in a Nyingma monastery near Mustang.

Another Buddhist name, Karunamaya, also means "the compassionate." His character shows itself primarily in the sagas of the Macchendranath cult, in which, after a long period of drought, he brings much needed rain to the sorely tried people. In this cult, an originally pre-Hindu and pre-Buddhist deity by the name of Bungadyo (literally "the god from Bunga," a village that is today named Bungamati), joined with gods from both pantheons. For Avalokiteshvara is Macchendranath for the Hindus, for whom there is a variety of local manifestations. For instance, the village of Chobar knows one such god; Kathmandu a White Macchendranath; and Patan a Red Macchendranath and a Minanatha, who sometimes appears as a child, sometimes as other forms of Macchendranath's manifestations. In spite of these various names and forms, there is scarcely a god in the great Buddhist pantheon who is so consistently worshipped across many population groups as the Red Macchendranath in Patan.

Another bodhisattva, Manjushri, has become closely associated with a Hindu deity, namely the goddess Sarasvati. In Vajrayana Buddhism, for example, she is seen as Manjushri's spouse. They are both gods of knowledge and the arts, and it is astounding that in this case, even in spite of their differing sexual indentities, they are treated as equals.

Religious Tolerance

Just as Buddhist deities can become manifestations of Hinduism, so Newaric Buddhism also takes, for example, Shiva and Vishnu as bodhisattvas into its pantheon. In general, however, Hinduism is the more widely embracing religion. The reasons for this lay, in part, in the fact that the kings were closer to the Hindu gods and therefore encouraged Hinduism. For the majority of the Newar, these distinctions are insignificant. They worship almost all of the gods – either Buddhist or Hindu – to the same degree. Therefore, one finds Hindu gods being worshipped

in the main sanctuaries of Buddhist monasteries. Conversely, Hindus include Buddha in their pantheon as a manifestation of Vishnu. Only the orthodox priests occasionally lay emphasis on their membership of one religion and decline attendance to the festivals and temples of the other religious community.

It is unusual – but typical of Newaric Buddhism – that, strictly speaking, there no longer exists a real order of monks. Instead of this there are two groups of "married monks" *vajracaryas*, who are Buddhist priests, and *shakyabhikus*, a grouping which traces its ancestral roots back to Buddha's familial name. Each male member of this caste is a monk for only four days during his initiation. Afterward, however, he remains an active member of his cloister community for the rest of his life, even when he has long since been married. Both in beliefs and in religious viewpoints, there is much tolerance. It is a matter of family tradition which god should be worshipped for protection. And it is up to the individual to

47

choose which god he declares as his or her personal god. For the most part it is also left to the individual whether he or she goes to the temple daily, or sings religious songs at night, or whether he pursues and obtains religious distinctions.

Rituals and Festivals

The situation is completely different when it comes to the essential rituals and festivals of the family, caste or community. Then there is little freedom, as the priests, participants, timing, completion, and materials are all strictly determined and codified.

Thus, important events and changes in life, such as birth, coming of age, marriage and death must be secured by priests with traditional religious ceremonies, to insure that disaster and ritual impurification do not befall the clan or

Above: For Hindus, death requires special purification ceremonies.

family. For this purpose, one calls the family priest, a Hindu Brahman or a Buddhist Vajracarya from the vicinity. Only people of low castes or members of ethnic minorities have their own priests, but these also often try to win over a Brahman for themselves, in order to increase their status.

The birth of a child is an event which carries with it ritual impurification not only for the mother, but instead for the entire house. It therefore requires particular purification rituals. These include prayer as well as washing and dietary restrictions. A more cheerful ceremony is the first feeding of boiled rice to the baby at the age of about six months. This is a festive occasion, and many relativves come together to celebrate the well-being, present and future, of the child.

During ceremonial initiation rites for the higher castes, boys receive the holy cord. They are then for the first time considered to be fully fledged and marriagable members of their castes. The Buddhist groups also celebrate a similar coming-of-age ceremony, at which time the candidates are formally taken into their orders.

Marriage is the most elaborate ritual. Not only must the majority of relatives be invited, but the marriage partner must also be chosen according to genealogy and caste-specific criteria. For the higher castes a wedding can be very expensive. The family of the bride "pays" with both gifts and money in order to find the most suitable possible bridegroom.

Death is the most impure event. It affects the entire group of relatives to varying degrees, but most of all the oldest son. He is responsible for carrying out the cremation ceremony, and furthermore he must have his head shaven, and is sometimes required to dress only in white for an entire year. Years afterward, a ritual must still be performed for the deceased on the anniversary of his death, and no significant event can be begun without distinctly commemorating one's ancestors.

While most of the rituals surrounding the important events of life are limited to relatives, in many festivals the caste or even the entire community of the settlement comes together to take part in the feast. This applies especially when the towns hold the main festival for their gods of protection. The worship of these gods at regular intervals is especially important in order to appease the gods of bad harvests, epidemics, earthquakes and other catastrophes.

Nevertheless, the organization of these festivals lies mostly in the hands of a few specialists, who are often united in a religious association called a *guthi*. One can only become a member of a guthi on the basis of religious specialization, caste membership and place of residence. A guthi exists for almost every ritual obligation; for the payment of sacrificial materials, for the provision of sacrificial animals or for the construction of processional floats.

While the city or town festivals which are devoted to the goddesses are obligatory as a rule, with other festivals it remains up to the individual whether and in what manner he participates. This is the case, for example, with the crowd of participants in the Shivaratri, which is by far the largest festival in Nepal. On this day an especially large number of pilgrims – from India as well – seek out the Pashupatinath temple to worship Shiva with fasting and night-time vigils.

A substantial difference exists between the two types of festival: The town festivals are held for the well-being of the community, and in these festivals the gods are carried around the community. The other festivals are celebrated for personal well-being, and during these festivals, one must go to the gods. The town festivals are bound to certain dates on the calendar, which have much to do with the harvest cycles. In contrast, with family festivals and the taking of religious vows, the best dates for them are determined by certain auspicious or lucky days of the week or according to the personal horoscope of each individual.

Modes of Worship

Just as with the festivals, the methods by which the gods are worshipped are also differentiated by ritual. The most common way to demonstrate one's respect is the *puja*. This form of worship can take place very modestly, sometimes as a simple bow with hands clasped together, or perhaps by the strewing of rice grains. But the Puja can also be an elaborate ritual, in which flowers, incense, water, lights, powdered cinnobar, food (rice, sweets or fruits), coins, cloth or small umbrellas are brought to the god as offerings.

The gifts must be unused, when possible even new, and above all undamaged. The rice grains should also be unbroken and not yet hulled. The donator

larly festival, the *bhai tika*, older sisters, proffer various honors on their younger brothers. Here it becomes even more clear that in Hindu South Asia, status at the individual level depends not only on age and caste membership, but also on one's gender.

Only certain gods accept animal sacrifices and alcohol. Among these one finds many manifestations of the goddesses, particularly the Eight Mothers and the Nine Durgas, Bhairava, Ganesha and Bhimsen. It would be considered a serious sacrilege to make such offerings to Shiva or the bodhisattvas. Goats, sheep, chickens, ducks, and in special cases water-buffaloes are used as sacrificial animals. These should also be flawless and, when possible, of male gender. The sacrifices must be taken "of their own free will," attested to by a shake of the head. In this way the animal expresses its wish to be reincarnated as a higher being. Generally, however, the beast is prompted by having a bit of water dribbled in its ear, which naturally causes it to shake its head.

Only men from the slaughtering-caste kill the animals, not, however, the priests or donors. While the head is intended for the deities and – afterwards – the priests, the sanctified torso is returned to the donor, who then prepares the meat for a feast. The rituals that accompany the animal sacrifice usually follow carefully worked-out rules from Tantrism. The sacrifice cannot be carried out at all until the participants have received a secret consecration (*diksha*). It is seen as life-threatening to organize a sacrifice if one has not been initiated into the cult of the deity concerned.

In one Tantric ritual, an effigy of a deity is placed on a specially purified spot (*asana*), after which the priest calls upon the deity to occupy it. Then, a likeness of the deity featuring its most notable characteristics is created, and during this activity the priest places numerous

usually receives the edible offerings back from the priest. With this the subordination of the believer in relation to the god is expressed, for as a rule one may only receive (cooked) nourishment from a superior. The priest also gives back a portion of the cinnobar, at which time he puts a small red point, the *tika*, on the forehead of the temple visitor. In addition, a sacred blossom is popularly placed behind the right ear. All offerings must be protected from impurity. Among things considered impure are, for example, bodily secretions (excrement, saliva, menstrual blood), liver, dogs, and, of course, members of the untouchable caste.

The puja is a sign of respect but it also implies a plea for protection and prosperity. It is offered not only to deities, but also to elders, priests, gurus, a monk or an ascetic. Furthermore in one particu-

Above: Bell and sword – indispensable in Tantric ceremonies. Right: Sacrifices to the Durga at the Dasain festival.

offerings on ritual diagrams (*yantra*) and with changing hand-gestures *(mudra)* murmers certain secret incantations. Afterwards, the animal is sacrificed, and with the blood that sprays out, the slaughterer makes a magical circle around the sacrifice place.

Following this, the priests distribute offerings to the people who have made the sacrifice, and these in turn give the priests payment, mostly in the form of money. Finally, the place of sacrifice is ritually broken down and the deity again released. Such rituals occasionally extend through the entire night.

As members of the higher castes one can also be privately initiated into the cult of a Tantric deity. Only then does one have the right to worship them directly – that is, without the intermediary of priests. In addition, there are secret teachings on how one can come as close as possible to the higher nature of a deity. These teachings are connected not only with the correct offerings and the way they are presented, but also with the con-

trol of the body – especially breathing – and with the esoteric sexual interpretations of the cult.

Among the popular forms of religious expression are special vows, which are particularly popular amongst women. These are taken to achieve religious merit, to secure the blessings of the gods for this and the next lives, or to put a god into a merciful mood through particularly obliging behavior. Sometimes one fasts for only a day, or one might decide to go on a long pilgrimage.

In addition, an elaborate fire-sacrifice (*homa, yajna*) might be held, or a feast offered for the glorification of a god. It is also possible to organize – rather than merely participate in – the recitation of holy texts or songs.

The entire diversity of rituals and forms of worship in the Kathmandu Valley is, however, not simply a ritual mixture of religions, but rather an expression of the fact that there are many gods – and that several quite different paths can lead to religious salvation.

THE CASTE SYSTEM

Since the beginning of this millenium, the Nepalese Hill Region has experienced the immigration of Hindu groups, under whose influence the local ethnic communities have taken on a part of Hinduism with its norms and value systems. The co-existence of Hindu groups and non-Hindu tribes has resulted in the development of its own specific caste system, which is however still based largely on Indian tradition.

The member of the different castes and ethnic groups live – given some variations from area to area – either in their own hamlets or in mixed settlements. At first glance you can't distinguish one group from the other. People from different groups meet each other in the same businesses; children from the different castes sit on the same benches in the schools and outdoors or play together, people who are members of different castes seem to associate freely with each other. Only an experienced observer would notice that their seemingly uninhibited behavior is actually directed by a great many rules and regulations.

For indeed, the inhabitants of the Nepalese Hill Region are organized into a strict hierarchy. They are classified into superior and subordinate groups, and their rank descends according to their level of ritual purity. At the top of this stratification is the *Tagadhari* caste – ritually the purest Hindus – whose male members wear the "holy cord." They are also designated the "twice-born" caste, because after their physical birth they come into the world once again through elaborate rituals of initiation, this time as

Left: A Newar from Kathmandu wearing the tika, a religious mark, on his forehead.

full social members of their caste. The *Brahmans* and *Chetris* are numbered among these. The conducting of Hindu rituals is incumbent upon the Brahmans; the Chetris are predisposed to being warriors and governors – their rank corresponds to that of the Indian *Kshatriya* rank. Subordinate to these two castes are the Matawali groups – literally: "the alcohol-drinking castes" to which the non-Hindu ethnic communities belong. From the viewpoint of Hinduism all ethnic groups are considered to be castes. However, the members of ethnic groups only see themselves as castes after they have become largely "Hinduized."

The majority of groups have come into such close contact with the Hindus that they have taken on several of their rules. Only a few ethnic groups have been able to withstand the continuing process of Hinduization; in general the rule applies that the Hindu influence decreases from south to north. The various populations living in northern Nepal are located in the sphere of influence of another "great tradition," namely that of Tibet and especially Tibetan Buddhism.

The Northern Peoples

Far away from the religious and political centers of the Hindus, isolated in remote valleys, the people living in the North have mostly entertained relations with the Tibetan population and Tibetan institutions, and their culture exhibits a wide range of Tibetan characteristics. Some of the Magar ethnic group could be classified among the strongly Hinduized groups (not including, however, the Kham-Magar); the Tamang and Gurung find themselves under the influence of both traditions, while the renowned Sherpas have by and large retained the Tibetan Buddhist beliefs and cultural elements. But the cultural practices and religious assumptions within one ethnic group can vary considerably from region

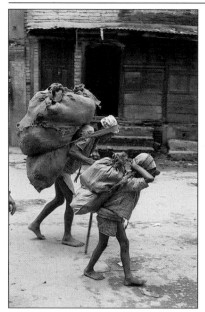

to region. The Newar, who, in an urban milieu, particularly in the Kathmandu Valley, have developed their own caste system are considered to be a separate caste in the scattered villages of the Hill Region where they live.

The Caste of the Untouchables

The Untouchable castes stand on the very lowest rung of the Hindu caste system; these are the *Kami* (smiths), the *Sarki* (shoemakers), and the *Damai*, who practice two occupations, one secular one quasi-religious. They are tailors and musicians and accompany many of the significant Hindu festivals with their music. These three groups form the majority of the Untouchable castes in the Nepalese Hill Region. In the urban environment as

Above: Both father and son are porters. Right: A spicemonger in front of his shop. Far right: Brahmans are not allowed to eat chicken because they are regarded as impure.

well as in the southern Terai strip there is a much larger diversity of ritual specialists or religious healers (*Jhankri*) who are considered Untouchables. In the Kathmandu Valley many of the impure occupations are carried out by Untouchables of Newar ethnicity. Many different Indian castes have settled in the Terai. It is a local peculiarity of the Nepalese Hill Region that the high-caste Hindus also perform occupations that are seen in India as being ritually impure.

Rules and Regulations

The hierarchal structure is founded on the concept of ritual purity. Every person and practically every article and each deed is classified according to this principal. This strict hierarchy has resulted in certain sequestrations. In villages where several castes live side by side, the houses are built a certain distance away from each other. Only members of the same caste occasionally live closer together.

Even slight differences in the appearance of a farmstead can reveal the caste membership of its occupants. Color is no indication of caste membership. Villages where white paint is scarce and expensive will only suggest something about the relative affluence of a household. Only in the farmsteads of the higher castes do you find the clay pedestals with the holy *tulasi* plant. The holy images which hang over the house entrances are also primarily found among the high castes. The view into the houses of the high castes is prohibited and therefore blocked. Thus, the entrances are never constructed directly on the footpaths, which, in contrast, is a common practice among the lower castes. You can also recognize the caste membership of a house's occupants by their domestic animals, because as a rule, animals are not kept unless one is allowed to eat their flesh. The presence of chickens in a yard permits the assumption that the house's occupants do not belong to the highest caste, because the Brahmans do not eat chicken, meat or eggs. Only in most recent times have the Brahman women begun to supplement their private income with chicken breeding, which, however, runs up against the determined resitance of the traditional Hindus. Castes that rank higher than the Magar are not allowed to keep pigs in their yards. These are ritually impure for those of higher caste.

The wells from which people draw their water to wash themselves, are from time to time accessible only to certain specific groups. The Untouchables are not allowed to use the wells of the higher castes at all. They are even prohibited from entering the houses of the higher castes. They are only permitted to stay on the shady verandas, or – if there are already persons of higher caste present – they must sit further away. In many places the Untouchables are also not allowed to set foot into the tea shops.

The rules of ritual purity are expressed in many additional regulations. The purest Brahmans, for example, are not allowed to plow. For the cultivation of

their fields they must employ people of lower castes. Similarly, the higher castes may not carry the sedan chairs of the bride and bridegroom. These tasks are fulfilled by lower, but still touchable castes. The ideas of ritual purity are also expressed in the regulations governing food, especially during the transfer of boiled rice, which can only be passed along from a member of higher caste to another of equal birth or lower-caste person. At larger festivals, when members of a variety of castes are gathered, the rice is only prepared by Brahman cooks for this reason. The rice is then served first to the Brahmans. Only after this may the remaining castes eat. Whereas the high-caste Hindus have to change their clothing before eating, the Untouchables eat in their everyday clothes. The Untouchables

Above: The tika is not only a religious sign, women also wear it as decoration. Right: Only the knowledgeable ovserver could tell whether these men belong to the same caste.

must also keep their distance when other groups are eating. If they are invited to eat at the house of a higher caste person, they must eat outside in front of the door.

The regulations of ritual purity are also manifested during smoking which has all the trappings of a religious ceremony. In the Nepalese Hill Region, frequently several men smoke from one cigarette. Since the saliva of a person from a lower caste is impure, the cigarettes are passed from the higher to the progressively lower caste members. Also during the smoking of the waterpipe, the purity commandments are observed. The entire pipe can only be used by its owner and the members of the same caste. Lower caste people must first remove the wooden mouth piece.

Hindu Rites

Veneration towards those of higher castes is expressed by bowing. One bows down low – to the hands of the person of higher standing. One bows down to the

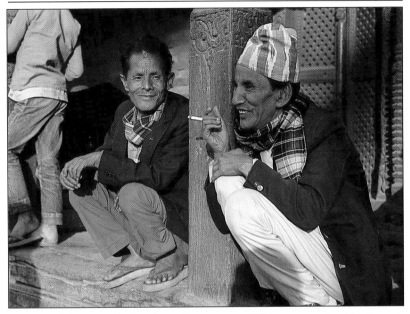

feet of religious dignitaries; in earlier times such a bow was also made to the big landowners.

The beliefs of Hinduism are manifested in a multiplicity of ceremonies, which are conducted by the Brahman priests; the better-educated *Pandits* and the less-learned *Purohits*. Some examples of these ceremonies include purifying rituals such as the *Om*, annual cycle ceremonies like the Dasain festival, or life-cycle ceremonies such as initiation and marriage (both of these rituals can only be conducted by Brahman priests for members of the "twice born" castes), as well as death rituals.

Sacrifice is also a part of some Hindu rituals – according to the deity who is called upon. The Hindus ascribe an especially purifying effect to the taking of a bath in a holy river. For the residents of villages, the religious festivals – which frequently last all night long – are the main occasions for meeting each other.

Children are not recognized as full members of the higher castes. The first years of life are not regulated by the caste prescriptions. Only after their initiations do the young boys become full members of the caste – "born" for the second time. They may not be married until after this ritual; marriages generally take place within the same caste.

For women, marriage is the equivalent of an initiation. After this ceremony, the bride separates from her parents. She is then adopted by the family of her husband. In the family of the husband, the daughter-in-law has at first a reduced status; conversely, in relation to her family of birth she achieves a "holy" status as a result of the merit that her parents and other blood relatives acquire by the "gift of the virgin" (*kannya dan*) to the family of the bridegroom. This "holy" status is manifested, for example, on the occasion of the brother's day, during which sisters visit their brothers and ritually honor them with a tika.

The marital status of women is visible from their appearance. Married women wear a chain around their neck as well as red powder (*sindur*) in their hair partings or on their forehead. Even those who are still single may wear a red "beauty-spot." Widows may not wear any red clothing, no marriage chain and also may not apply a beauty-spot.

Caste and Profession

In contrast to the Indian caste society, the caste structure of the Nepalese Hill Region does not know a strict classification of professions. Traditionally, the only time caste and profession are still intertwined is in the case of Brahman priests and Untouchable handcraftsmen. The majority of the residents of the Hill Region make their living from agriculture. The remaining professions – for example the maintaining of a tea shop or woodworking and other crafts – is performed by members of various castes.

Particularly the higher castes are feeling the winds of change. So, for example, young Brahmans, who have of course learned Sanskrit and are able to direct religious rituals, prefer to work in the modern world as teachers. Other high caste men like to occupy political posts. Within one family one can encounter men with different orientations. In spite of social upheavals in Nepal, the fact remains that the dominance of the high-caste Hindus (Indo-Nepalese) in relation to the rest of the population persists.

Myth and Reality

No genuine Hindu believer would doubt that the system of castes has existed since the beginning of time, and that it is to be traced back to the creation of the gods. However, there are significant points of reference which allow us to assume that it first came into existence during the Vedic period (1500-500 B.C.);

Right: Bathing in the holy Bagmati River is said to have a purifying effect.

the older Vedic writings – holy Hindu books – do not even exhibit all of the so-called Varna names – the main categories of the Hindu caste ordering. The origins of the Indian as well as the Nepalese caste systems are today (still) shrouded in darkness. Most would also agree, that, in relation to Hindu Nepal, it is quite impossible to speak of a single caste system.

Considering the diversity of the origins and customs among the Nepalese population, one can indeed speak of several caste systems; that of the Hindus in the Hill Region; that of the Hindus of the Terai; that of the Newar – where one can make yet a further distinction between the Hindus and the Buddhists – and that of the Moslem population, whose religious orientation certainly stresses equality, but has undergone a strong adaptation to the customs of Hinduism. At any rate, the Moslems as a group rate low within the Hindu hierarchy. The principles and regulations covering ritual purity described above apply – barring certain theoretical and practical deviations of course – for all of the systems already listed here.

When the membership of the high Nepalese castes (Hill Region) speak of the Nepalese society as "one" caste system, they are actually emphasizing their own political, economic and ritual dominance which they have been able to establish in the course of a millenium-long historical process. The cradle of the caste system within the Indo-Nepalese population group is today generally considered among scientists to be the Karnali region in distant western Nepal. It is very probable that three migration streams met each other there at the beginning of this millenium: 1) Hindus from the northern Indian plain – as is the assertion of a number of myths, and to which can be traced the origins of Nepal's caste of warriors from the ruling houses in Rajasthan; 2) the Khas, who came here from the west, as well as 3) members of a variety

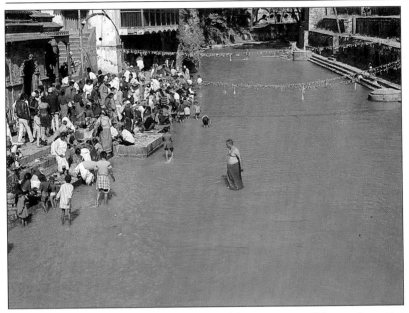

of different ethnic groups which emigrated from Tibet. The Khas are considered the founders of the Jumla Empire (12th-14th century); evidently under their rulership the transition from Buddhism to Hinduism went trough its final stages and a caste system peculiar to the region was established. Furthermore, it is of great significance that groups that had established their dominance in the Jumla Empire after its collapse, gradually continued to conquer surrounding areas, and in the process established a great number of principalities between the 14th and 16th centuries.

Among the conquerors were the Gurkhas, whose skillful battalions conquered not only the western territories including Kumaon and Garhwal (which belongs today to India) in the mid-18th century, but also the kingdoms of the Kathmandu Valley, the eastern regions up to the Mechi River, and the southern Terai region. In 1814, the British East India Company decided that the Gurkha expansion had gone far enough for its taste,

and it sent an expeditionary force that succeeded in forcing them to the negotiating table. The borders of Nepal were drawn between the Kali and Mechi Rivers. Several wars with Tibet in the middle of the 19th century resulted in the determination of the country's long northern frontier.

It is of great significance for the development of the Hindu caste system in Nepal, that the rulers of such a "unified" empire, who traced their origins back to the above-mentioned houses of the western principalities, achieved political power over the other ruling noble families, in particular the Malla rulers of the kingdoms of the Kathmandu Valley. It was the Gurkha rulers who determined which among the ethnic groups were to be set free in the course of the 19th century.

Contrary to widely held opinion, the caste system was not completely eliminated in the year 1963 – even if modern legislation treats all Nepalese citizens as being of equal birth.

ROYAL CITIES IN THE KATHMANDU VALLEY

KATHMANDU
PATAN
BHAKTAPUR
KATHMANDU VALLEY

KATHMANDU

According to the local chronicles, Kathmandu was founded in the tenth century by King Gunakamadeva. However, in this case one must speak rather of a new religious order being introduced into a settlement, which was already in existence – but not yet organized. At any rate, it led to the establishment of additional shrines and sanctuaries.

Legends tell how Gunakamadeva had a dream in which the goddess Malakshmi appeared. She charged him with the task of founding the city of Kantipur (an old name for Kathmandu) at the place where the Vishnumati and Bagmati Rivers flow together. The city was to have the shape of a sword (an attribute of the goddess). The king undertook his task as he had been ordered, and for protection he placed all the important gods around and about the city.

The actual layout of the old city stems from the 16th century, a time when Kathmandu gained greater significance with respect to the older city of Bhaktapur. The rulers Mahendra Malla (1560–1574) and Pratapa Malla (1641–1674) encour-

Preceding pages: Annapurna II and IV. Nighttime on Durbar Square. Left: The Kathmandu pottery market.

aged a number of construction projects, and the city grew and grew.

The limits of the old city are no longer marked everywhere by the old defensive wall, however, the enclosed heart of the city has been by and large extensively preserved. The **New Road** was only constructed after the catastrophic earthquake of January 15, 1934, to make the widest possible approach – suitable for parades – to the palace area.

Today, the capital city Kathmandu attracts ever larger portions of the population from the whole country. Nonetheless, the city still hasn't suffered the fate of many other large Asian cities, which are in danger of suffocating from the sheer masses of humanity, traffic, slums and hectic construction activities. Kathmandu has no underground sewer system, no adequate water supply, only a few properly paved streets – but above all, it has no money. It may be that this last factor alone has hindered the complete re-shaping of such a traditional city, which has already succumbed to the automobile and is criss-crossed with electricity and telephone wires. Fashionable concrete buildings and cheap corrugated tin roofs already disfigure the city enough as is, but even so, the old city centers of the Kathmandu Valley have forfeited none of their fascination.

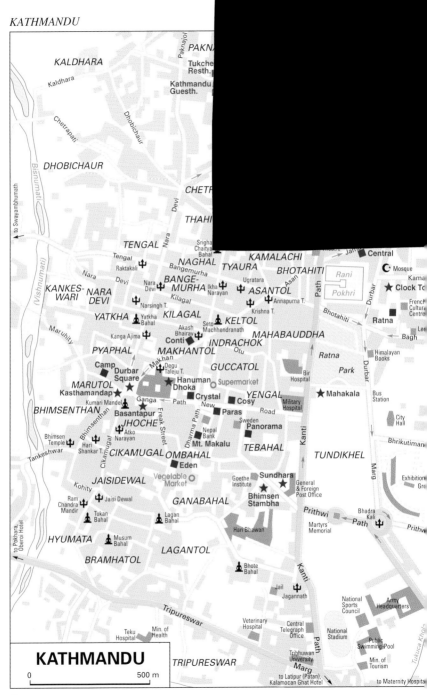

KALDHARA

Kaldhara

Chetrapati

Paknajol

PAKNA

Tukche
Resth.

Kathmandu
Guesth.

Dhobichaur

DHOBICHAUR

CHETR

THAHI

Bisnumati

to Swayambhunath

(Vishnumati)

TENGAL

Tengal

Raktakali

Nara
Devi

NAGHAL

Bangemurha

Srigha
Chaitya
Bahal

KAMALACHI

TYAURA

BHOTAHITI

Central

Mosque

Kama

Clock To

KANKES-
WARI

NARA
DEVI

Devi

Nara

Nara
Devi

BANGE-
MURHA

Ikha
Narayan

Kilagal

ASANTOL

Ugratara

Asan

Annapurna T.

Rani

Pokhri

Durbar

Path

Bhotahiti

Ratna

French
Cultura
Centre

Lee

YATKHA

Yatkha
Bahal

Narsingh T.

KILAGAL

Akash
Bhairav

Kanga Ajima

Conti

Seto
Machhendranath

KELTOL

Krishna T.

INDRACHOK

Otu

MAHABAUDDHA

Ratna

Durbar

Bagh

Himalayan
Books

Maruhity

PYAPHAL

MAKHANTOL

Makhan

Degu
Taleju T.

GUCCATOL

Bir
Hospital

Park

Bus
Station

Camp

Durbar
Square

Kumari Mandel

Kasthamandap

MARUTOL

BHIMSENTHAN

Basantapur

Ganga

Path

New

Hanuman
Dhoka

Crystal

Paras

Supermarket

Cosy

YENGAL

Road

Mahakala

City
Hall

MarutolBhimsenthan

Bhimsenthan

Bhimsen
Temple

Hari
Shankar T.

JHOCHE

Atko
Narayan

Nepal
Bank

Sweden

Mt. Makalu

Panorama

Military
Hospital

Bhrikutiman

Tankeshwar

CIKAMUGAL

OMBAHAL

Eden

TEBAHAL

TUNDIKHEL

JAISIDEWAL

Kohity

Vegetable
Market

GANABAHAL

Goethe
Institute

Sundhara

General
& Foreign
Post Office

Exhibition
Gro

Ram
Chandra
Mandir

Jaisi Dewal

Tukan
Bahal

Lagan
Bahal

Bhimsen
Stambha

Prithwi

Bhadra
Kali

Path

Prithw

HYUMATA

Musum
Bahal

LAGANTOL

Hari Bhawan

Martyrs'
Memorial

BRAMHATOL

Bhote
Bahal

Kanti

to Pokhara,
Oberoi Hotel

Tripureswar

Jail

Jagannath

National
Sports
Council

Army
Headquarters

Teku
Hospital

Min. of
Health

Veterinary
Hospital

Central
Telegraph
Office

National
Stadium

Public
Swimming-Pool

Min. of
Tourism

Tukuca Khc

Tribhuwan
University

Marg

to Latipur (Patan),
Kalamocan Ghat Hotel

to Maternity Hospita

KATHMANDU

0   500 m

TRIPURESWAR

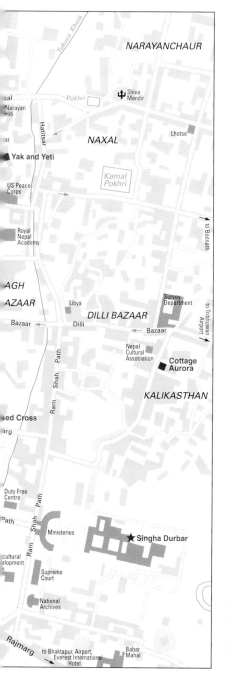

The Palace and the Durbar Square

One point of attraction of all three royal cities of the Kathmandu Valley is their respective palace areas. In Kathmandu the palace is particularly sprawling. It was rebuilt in 1975 in its present form with the assistance of UNESCO on the occasion of the crowning of King Birendra Shah. This **Durbar Square** illustrates the full richness of Nepalese religiosity and culture, and it clearly shows the various types of Nepalese art and architecture. The oldest part of the palace, with its courtyards and numerous auxiliary buildings, was first designed by Mahendra Malla (1560–1574) and since then it has been expanded and reconstructed several times. Both of the interior courtyards, **Mul Chowk** and **Sundhara Chowk** (off-limits to foreigners), as well as the Palace Garden (**Bhandarkbal**), go back to the rule of Pratapa Malla (1641–1674). In 1672, he also had the huge statue of Hanuman placed next to the entrance gate, which is perpetually smeared with cinnobar powder and covered with a red cloth. This god, who is shaped like an ape, is supposed to protect the palace from ghosts and illnesses, and his name is used to describe the whole area **Hanuman Dhoka**.

Pratapa Malla was a cosmopolitan ruler. Evidence of this is borne out by the stone tablet on the main face of the palace, on which the goddess Kalika is revered in 15 languages. One can admire the ruler himself on the columns in the front plaza, erected in 1670, as well as on the **Rani Pokhri**. Similar columns in Patan and Bhaktapur were in fact modeled after these columns.

Nepal's rulers, like the rich and powerful the world round, like to immortalize themselves with statues. Eight equestrian statues more or less define the boundaries of **Tundhikhel Square**, and standing in between is a memorial to the martyrs of Rana rule, as documentation of the protests against this despotic period of Nepal's history. Several Shah-kings, among them the first one, Prithvi Narayan (1769–1775), Tribhuvan (1911–1915), and Mahendra (1955–1972), are represented by imposing bronze statues.

Undoubtedly the most prestigious testimonial to the Rana period is the **Singha Durbar**, which was constructed in 1903 in a pseudo-Baroque, western style for the then prime minister. Later, the Shah government took over the building. All but the main wing burned down in 1973. It has only gradually been reconstructed. Since the end of the 19th century, the king himself has lived in the **Narayan Miti Palace** on the northern edge of the old city. The older buildings of the palace were constructed by the Rana princes, the new section in 1969 by Mahendra Shah. The Shah and Rana rulers left behind great monuments in the old King's Palace in Kathmandu. It is an original nine-storied palace tower on the southern edge of the palace grounds, and features especially richly carved window frames – behind which the queens are supposed to have once observed the goings-on at the **Basantpur Plaza** from an aristocratic distance.

Nearby is the **Gaddi Baithak**, a long throne hall which the Premier Chandra Shamsher Rana had constructed and luxuriously appointed in 1908. He had been inspired by a trip to London.

The Votive Temples

The rulers of Nepal have not only immortalized themselves in palaces and statues, but they also built temples to the gods to commemorate themselves or their close relatives. These were built mostly from contributions and gifts of land to the primarily private communities – the so-called *guthis*. However, since the introduction of a new law which places the guthis under the guardianship of the state, this traditional system has been almost completely destroyed, with the net result that many temples are no longer taken care of.

The Durbar Square is filled with these votive temples. The Trailokya Mohan Mandir (also called the **Narayan Temple**) which is dedicated to Vishnu, was ordered built by King Parthivendra Malla (1680 to 1687) in memory of his brother Nripendra Malla. In 1689, Riddhilakshmi, the widow of Parthivendra, donated an impressive **Garuda Figure**, which is a copy of another statue dating from the eighth century.

Riddhilakshmi's highly influential minister was involved with this, and he also donated – in memory of himself – a three-roofed **Shiva Temple** in **Jaisi Devai**, a copy of which, the **Maju Deval**, Queen Riddhilakshmi had built in the Durbar Square in 1692.

Another such votive temple is to be found in the immediate neighborhood. The elongated **Shiva Parvati Temple** is named thus because this god-couple leans out from the wooden windows of its highest floor. In its interior, the temple which was founded by Rana Bahadur Shah (1777–1790) shelters the Nine Durga Goddesses.

One of the oldest temples in the Hanuman Dhoka is the **Jagannath Temple**, which was also founded by Rana Bahadur Shah in 1797. It is particularly famous for the erotic wood-carvings in its roof buttresses. The Nepalese sometimes offer a cute explanation for these sexual scenes. Out of shame, the goddess "Lightning" would spare this wooden temple. But, no doubt, the actual reason for these carvings is to be found in the old fertility cults and in the religion of Tantrism.

One further **Jagannath Temple** was founded in the same year by Rana Bahadur Shah. This stands of all places in the city prison, and is only one of many votive temples outside the old quarter of Kathmandu.

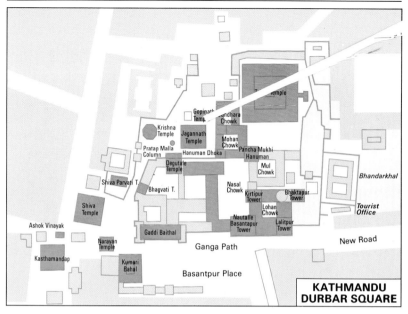

Gopinath Temp.
Krishna Temple
Jagannath Temple
andhara Chowk
Mohan Chowk
Pratap Malla Column
Hanuman Dhoka
Pancha Mukhi Hanuman
Degutale Temple
Mul Chowk
Shiva Parvati T.
Bhagvati T.
Nasal Chowk
Bhandarkhal
Kirtipur Tower
Bhaktapur Tower
Shiva Temple
Lohan Chowk
Tourist Office
Ashok Vinayak
Nautalle Basantapur Tower
Lalitpur Tower
Gaddi Baithal
Narayan Temple
New Road
Kasthamandap
Kumari Bahal
Ganga Path
Basantpur Place

KATHMANDU DURBAR SQUARE

The Seats of the Goddesses

Besides the votive temples, which are mostly dedicated to Shiva or Vishnu, the rulers also secured the assistance of the goddesses, who are so powerful in Nepal. Towering over the northern side of the Durbar Square is the **Taleju Temple**, the largest and tallest temple in the entire Kathmandu Valley. The goddess Taleju, a manifestation of Durga, was the goddess of the Malla kings, who worshipped her with blood sacrifices. She does have another residence on the Durbar Square, but she is worshipped as a family deity here: The three-storied **Degutale Temple**, which was erected by Shivasimha Malla (1578–1619), but completely renovated by Pratapa Malla (1641–1674). According to the chronicles, Ratna Malla (1484–1520), the youngest son of Yaksha Malla, is supposed to have brought a magical diagram from Bhaktapur to Kathmandu, in order to obtain power there with its help. Mahendra Malla (1560–1574) had the temple expanded.

In the process he gave it three roofs and placed it on a five-stepped pedestal, so that the goddess would be visible to neighboring cities.

In addition, a living goddess bestows authority on the King. She is the Kumari, a maiden who is seen as a manifestation of Durga. Every year during the Indrajatra festival, the King is ritually confirmed again in his office. This child-goddess lives the whole year round on the first floor of the **Kumari Bahal**, a Buddhist monastery, richly decorated with wood carvings. It was constructed in 1757 by Jayaprakasha Malla (1735–1768). The Kumari at the Palace of Kathmandu is the most prominent of the many living goddesses in the Kathmandu Valley. They are all chosen from particular, mostly Buddhist castes and must appear especially fearless. In order to determine their force of character, they are locked in a dark room or they are shown horrible masks of demons, and if they don't cry, this is considered one of several signs of their divine predilection. Once they are

69

chosen, the girls continue to be Kumaris until puberty. They do not all lead as isolated a life as the Royal Kumaris in Kathmandu, who must be carried during their few "excursions" outside of the Kumari Bahal, in order not to touch impure ground. Later the Kumaris receive a pension from the state or their village council. They rarely marry, for it brings bad luck to marry an ex-goddess.

Taleju and Kumari are representatives of the numerous goddesses in the Kathmandu Valley who must be worshipped with blood sacrifices and alcohol. They frequently appear in small groups as in, for example, the Eight Mothers (Ashthamatrika) or the Nine Durgas (Navadurga), and have their temples on the edges of the cities, where they can protect the communities. They are frequently associated with stories of human sacrifice.

Above: Town festivals are particularly important for the inhabitants of Kathmandu Valley. Right: Statues of Buddha Shakyamuni, the "wise man of the Shakya family".

Some of the temples are spoken of only with a shudder, as they are thought of as places where murderous demons lurk. Among these are the three-storied temple of Naradevi (also referred to as Shvetakali), where the goddess thrones on two people, and the residence of Luti-Ajima (also called Indrani), which is located amidst the northern cremation sites on the Vishnumati River.

Many holy places of the goddess seem insignificant, because their sanctuaries – that of Raktakali in the **Tangal** quarter of the city, for example – often shelter only an uncarved stone. However, these temples and shrines typically host more festivals and rituals than many a monumental commemorative temple for a more peaceful god. Of Bhadrakali it is said that she transformed bread into gold, as was the case when she assumed the form of a crying child, and a farmer gave her his loaf of bread. The **Lumarhi Temple**, once between fields and meadows, is now located on a busy traffic island south of the Tundikhel Square.

The Little Big Gods

Yet another highly worshipped deity has become a victim of street traffic on Kathmandu's parade ground: Mahakala, whose shrine is located across from the military hospital. The god is venerated by Buddhists as protector of the monastery, and by Hindus as Bhairava (Shiva in his most fear-inspiring aspect, but also a fully independent god).

Scarcely an automobile driver fails to greet this god as he drives past, especially on Saturdays, when multitudes of believers make their pilgrimages there. The reason for this is that at one time a priest is supposed to have tried to capture the god in the stone statue forever. Mahakala, however, resisted this idea, because he, as "Great Time"- the meaning of his name – must endlessly circle around the earth. Finally though, he agreed that he would live in the stone each Saturday.

Bhairava is a very popular god in the Kathmandu Valley. His function ist primarily a protective one. He also accepts blood sacrifices. At the Hanuman Dhoka are two of his most famous effigies: the **Kala ("Black") Bhairava**, a five-meter-high statue, and, a couple of steps further south, the **Sveta Bhairava**. The origin and age of the Kala Bhairava sculpture are uncertain, but it was transported to Durbar Square by order of Pratapa Malla in the 17th century. In front of the large, colorfully painted statue, officers of the court had, at one time, to swear their oaths of loyalty and witnesses attest to the truth of their statements.

The **Sveta ("White") Bhairava** (also mistakenly referred to as Akash Bhairava) is in the form of a large, gilded head, mostly hidden behind a grating which is only removed during the Indrajatra festival. At this time rice beer sometimes streams from his mouth. The statue was donated by Rana Bahadur Shah in 1795 on the occasion of the Indrajatra. Likewise, the huge mask of **Akasha** ("air, sky") **Bhairava** is fetched from the temple of the same name, which lies near from the turbulent Indra Chowk.

71

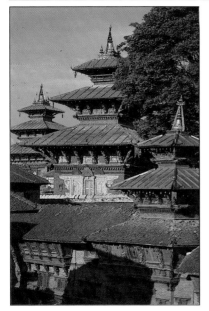

every household also has its own little shrine which is there to demonstrate reverence for ones ancestors.

As is true of all Newar cities, the old city of Kathmandu is composed of small blocks of houses (called *tol* in Nepali), in which the people live in brick houses, some with elaborately carved wooden window-frames and terracotta roofs that have become overgrown with moss. They are, of course, separated according to family and caste. Only very gradually did these blocks of houses grow together into today's densely-packed urban structure. However, in the numerous city festivals the old lines of separation are still recognizable, notably between the upper and lower sections of the city.

Each and every *tol* has its protective Ganesh shrine, where now and then the elephant-headed god is summoned for very special purposes. An expecially memorable example of this is the "**Toothache Ganesh**," where one can pound in a nail to alleviate the pain. The **Ashoka Vinyaka** or **Maru Ganesh** on the Durbar Square is a small shrine which is worshipped by almost all passers-by in order to ease some problem in life.

A wild festival, at which much blood and alcohol flows, is held for **Pacali Bhairava** in southern Kathmandu. On the fifth day of Dasain he is brought by farm-boys – in the form of a large urn of rice beer – from the old city to his open shrine, where he is symbolized by a black stone. Next to that is a life-size *betal* (demon) made of bronze, which lies on the ground. Pacali Bhairava is supposed to have hidden himself there after he was caught spending a passionate night with the daughter of a slaughterman of lowly caste.

These small shrines play a major role in the hearts of the local residents. For example, almost every house worships a stone deity made of plaster – kept standing in front of the threshold – in order to ward off demonic dangers and for the elimination of ritual impurities. Almost

The individual quarters of the city are mostly connected by very narrow streets in which even a riksha can block up the traffic. Only one large street crosses the old city: The trade route between India and Tibet, along which traders cluster their businesses, peddling anything the market demands – from aromatic spices and rusty old nails to souvenirs for the tourists.

The narrow character of the city is relieved only in the public places. Especially on the **Indra Chowk** and in **Asan Tol**, where the old north-south road crosses a smaller street, a riot of color always dominates the scene. Also in Asan Tol stands the **Annapurna Temple**, which received its present form in 1839 from Rajendra Bikram Shah. This revered mother-goddess is portrayed here

*Above: Bhagavati Mandir on Durbar Square.
Right: The inner courtyard of the Kumari Chowk.*

as a silver pitcher wrapped in snakes – a symbol of fertility, on which the farmers, who spread out their goods before the temple, are particularly dependent.

On the plazas one finds numerous rest-houses (called *sattal* or *pati* in Nepali) for pilgrims and traveling traders. These buildings, which open onto the street, were also funded by the well-to-do. On the **Maru Tol** alone – southeast of the Hanuman Dhoka – one finds four such *sattals*: **Simhaa Sattal, Lakshmi-Na-rayana Sattal, Nasa** or **Kavindrapura Sattal** (erected around 1672 by Pratapa Malla for the dance-god Nasadyo) and **Maru Sattal**. This latter resting-house is better-known by its original Sanskrit name, for which verification exists dating from A.D. 1143: **Kasthamandapa**, which literally means "wooden hall," after which Kathmandu is named. The cubic, three-story building shelters at its center a statue of the saint Gorakhnath and also serves as an abode for the cult of his followers, the so-called Kanphatta ascetics.

Water Installations

In Hinduism, a bath cleanses one not only of dirt, but also of ritual impurities. It was therefore of religious merit to found such bathing places. The largest water installation in Kathmandu is the rectangular **Rani Pokhri**, the artificial "Sea of the Kings" which Pratapa Malla had constructed to help his wife to get over the loss of a beloved son. In the center of the pond he placed a Shiva temple that was renovated after the devastating earthquake of 1934. Another especially wide and beautiful water installation is located just behind the post office. It was named **Sundhara** because the water flows into it through gilded spouts in the stylized form of a mythical water-dragon (*sun* means "gold" in Nepali). The installation was built around 1825 by Bhimsen Thapa at the wish of Queen Tripurasundari. This prime minister also had the nearby tower **Dharahara**, also known as **Bhimsenstambha,** erected in the style of a Mogul minaret. This construction work

73

also came crashing down in the earthquake of 1934, but was later reconstructed – albeit a bit smaller.

The bathing places on the Bagmati and Vishnumati Rivers originated largely during the Shah and Rana periods. Both on the **Kalamocan Ghat** and in the Tripureshva section of the city, the Rana princes had them extended and embellished with numerous votive temples. In front of the **Hema Narayan Temple**, the most prominent of these, Jang Bahadur Rana, is to be seen on a column which dates back to 1874.

Buddhist Monasteries and Sanctuaries

Buddhist monasteries are also extant throughout the old town of Kathmandu, but in contrast to the temples devoted to Hinduism, they are tucked away from the

Above: Brahmans at a purification ceremony. Right: Street scene in the center of Kathmandu.

hustle and bustle in interior courtyards. Among their distinguishing features is a Buddha Shakyamuni statue, at least one Caitya cult object and frequently, up on the first floor, a secret deity from tantric worship. Besides these, the temples rarely lack statues of Mahakala or Ganesha and Nasadyo – the god of dance – who is mostly represented as only a hole or slit in a wall. The entrances are frequently ornamented with artistic carvings or wrought metal, and on the roofs there is often a sort of bell-tower *(gajura)* visible from a good distance.

The more than 50 monasteries in Kathmandu – called *baha* in Newari (in Nepali: *bahal*) or bahi, according to their size – are differentiated by the type of building, caste and function with which they are associated. The ostentatious monastery buildings, which have lent their names to many sections of the city, no longer shelter any monks, but serve rather as temples and centers for the ritual life of Buddhist groups. Many of the monastery buildings conceal art treas-

ures, such as rare statues, buttresses and roof pillars (for example the **Yatkha Baha** from the 14th century) or stupas and caityas. These cultic edifices, often privately donated, characteristically have a vertical shaft in their interiors which represents the Buddha, his teachings and the creation of the world. In the **Dhoka Baha** is one of the oldest known votive caityas, dating from the seventh century and including sculptures of Shakyamuni, Avalokiteshvara and others. The **Sighah Baha** (also called **Srigha Caitya** or **Kathesimbhu**) has become well-known because it is a replica of Svayambhunath Stupa. In **Tukan Baha** in the south of Kathmandu is a caitya with Licchavi statues.

In the **Jana Baha** between Indra Chowk and Asan Tol there is a sanctuary of a special sort, the **Seto** ("white") **Matsyendranath Temple**, which is watched over by two lion sculptures. It is also named **Sanu** ("smaller") **Matsyendranath** in order to distingush it from the larger **Rato** ("red") **Matsyendranath** located in Patan. Both gods have a lot in common, particularly in that they are also worshipped as Padmapani Avalokiteshvara (an especially popular guardian deity among the Buddhists) and during a festival lasting several days, at which the gods are carried on procession wagons to a neighboring village. However, everything about the Seto Matsyendranath is smaller, so that one is inclined to believe the legend that the cult in Kathmandu is at least partly an imitation of those in Patan and Bungamati.

PATAN

In contrast to the Hindu-Buddhist Kathmandu and the dominantly Hindu Bhaktapur, **Patan** is pre-eminently Buddhist. This is especially obvious in the legends that recount its founding. According to these, Patan is supposed to have been founded by the Buddhist emperor Ashoka (268–233 B.C.) and his daughter Carumati. The legend has it that Ashoka laid a central stupa and four additional stupas as the corner stones of the city. In fact, four of these stupas are indeed located around the old quarter. They indicate the four points of the compass, at the end of the two streets that intersect and extend through Patan. The fifth, central stupa is believed to be in the interior of the **Patuko Blocks** northeast of the palace grounds, at the very spot where today one finds a great mound of earth nearly ten meters high.

It is unlikely that the origins of these so-called **Ashoka Stupas** can really be traced to the great Indian ruler. At any rate, their unadorned forms make anything approaching an exact dating very difficult, and to date excavations are not permitted. They consist merely of a hemispheric pile of earth with a superstructure added during the 19th century. The exception is the northern stupa, which has been encased in mortar.

To the present day, little more is known about the history of Patan. The city first became the independent seat of a king under King Siddhi Narashima Malla (1620–1661). Under this king and his successors – Shrinivasa Malla (1661–1684) and Yoganendra Malla (1684–1705) – Patan experienced an architectural renascence whose beauty still shines through the great temples and especially in the palace area. The conqueror of the Kathmandu Valley, King Prithvi Narayan Shah, laid the city open to plundering, so that numerous valuable art treasures were stolen. The earthquake of 1934 also caused heavy damage to the city.

Monastery Complexes

The original Buddhist character of Patan shows itself especially in its more than 150 former monasteries. Nearly every fourth courtyard entrance leads into one such monastery building. In the majority of cases these are not shelters for Buddhist monks but secular living-space for Newar families. These are called *vajracharya* (literally "master of the Vajra") or, after the name of the historical Buddha, *Shakya*. The monasteries represent the center of the religious community (*sangha*).

In the 14th century, Jayastithi Malla introduced – more or less by force – a system of castes. Also in Patan the ruling families were Hindu, although they tolerated the Buddhist population. However, the influence of Hinduism led to a situation in which the different groups of Buddhists also cut themselves off from one another. This ultimately meant that the membership of a monastery was increasingly decided by relatives, and not by the wish to lead the life of an alms-seeking monk. In fact, membership in a *sangha* means only that one of one's forefathers was initiated as a monk in the monastery. Of course, one only remains a monk during the few days of the iniatiation rites, but one stays a member of the congregation and monastery for the rest of one's life.

As in Kathmandu, tradition also differentiates between the 18 main monasteries *(baha)* and numerous secondary monasteries *(bahi)*. One of the most well-known monasteries – and the most significant one of the main monasteries in Patan – is the **Kva Baha** or **Hiranya Varna Mahavihar**. It has not only the largest congregation, with over 2,000 initiated members, it also has an especially rich endowment. Many inscriptions on the monastery walls, the earliest dating from the end of the 14th century, bear witness to the numerous donations it has received.

As soon as you step into the inner courtyard, you will see why the monastery has also been called the "**Golden Temple**." Many of the statues and the three copper roofs of the main shrine have been gilded. The carved wooden window frames of the temple are also worth closer examination. The gods here are also the principal deity Akshobhya

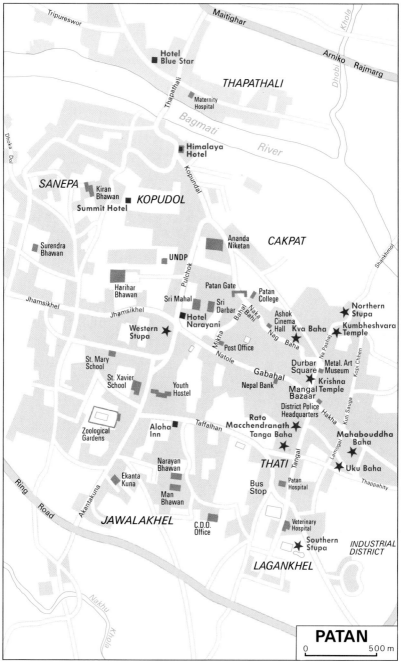

PATAN

0   500 m

(one of the five transcendental Buddhas) and Buddha Shakyamuni, Buddha in his basic stance, i.e., touching the earth. They are both frequently portrayed with the same iconographic features, so that it is not always possible to tell one from the other, all the more so when – as is also true in Kva Baha – the statue is covered with decorative objects, so that it is no longer clearly identifiable.

In the center of the courtyard stands yet another temple with a gilded roof. This is a shrine to the clan-deity of the congregation, a Caitya from the Licchavi period. The courtyard is surrounded by a corridor lit by oil lamps, and decorated with prayer wheels and many sanctuaries, among them four life-size bodhisattva statues in the corners. Apart from the periodically changing guards who watch over the gods, nobody lives in the houses that surround the courtyard. Prayers are said here, or it hosts readings of holy texts or the singing of religious songs. Some especially rare and valuable Tibetan frescos adorn the upper floor of the northern wing.

One of the oldest monasteries is the **Uku Baha** (also named **U Baha** or **Rudravarna Mahavihara**). Its courtyard is full of votive Caityas and a variety of statues: Manjushri, a Vajra, pairs of animal figures, a statue of Juddha Shamsher – the prime minister at the time of the 1934 earthquake, who also donated a lot of money for the monastery's renovation – as well as a member of the congregation who, in 1716, had a large statue of himself erected in the courtyard. The highest deity of the broad, two-storied main temple is a statue of the transcendent Buddha Akshobya, which is surrounded by many other Dhyanibuddhas or bodhisattvas. South of the Uku Baha stands the great **Yantarivi Caitya** (also called **Yatalibi Caitya**), in which more than 50

Right: Stone lions keeping watch over King's Palace in Patan.

Buddhist deities are said to reside. It was supposedly privately founded around 1684 by a certain Ratna Simha.

Also associated with the Uku Baha is the **Mahabouddha Baha** with a temple by the same name. It has become known far and wide as the "**Temple of the Thousand Buddhas**," because each of the over 9000 bricks carries a likeness of a transcended Buddha. It is a tall building in the Shikhara style, based on the temple in Bodh Gaya, India, where Buddha experienced his enlightenment

The Mahabouddha Temple is supposed to have been founded by a rich coin-minter, and was first consecrated around 1600. This building was also seriously damaged by the earthquake of 1934, however, it was possible to restore it to its original form with the help of the memory of the local population. In contrast to most of the other monastery complexes, there are no further shrines in the courtyard, which is so narrow that a view of the entire temple is not possible.

On the other hand, the courtyard of the **Tanga Baha** or **Jesthvarna Mahavihara** is completely overflowing with votive Caityas, stone sculptures, prayer wheels and inscriptions. The **Minataha Temple** constitutes the central point of this complex, which is dedicated to Jatadhari Lokeshvara, a form of Padmapani Lokeshvara. This is a richly decorated building in the style of a pagoda, with two roofs. Its age is not precisely known, although the monastery was already mentioned in the 12th century.

The Macchendranath Temple

The nearby **Macchendranath Temple** is also a sanctuary for a god with many names and faces. Macchendranath is also referred to as *Bungadyo*, because one of the numerous legends about him claims that he originated in the small village of Bungamati. Still to this day, during the winter months, a figure of this god is

brought to the village, which is located ten kilometers south of Patan.

At some uncertain time, this village-god was identified with the bodhisattva Padmapani Avalokiteshvara. In the middle of the 18th century he first received the Hindu name Rato ("red") Macchendranath, in order to distinguish him from the Seto ("white") Macchendranath of Kathmandu.

The Macchendranath in Patan has become a major syncretistic national god of Nepal, because he plays an important role in the fertility of the country. He is supposed to have brought a 12-year-long drought to an end, when the great Yogi Gorakhnath meditated on nine snakes, which are considered to be bringers of rain. According to the Buddhists, Gorakhnath had only done this to lure Avalokiteshvara to Nepal, after which, in his immeasurable benevolence (one of his further names is Karunamaya, "the god filled with compassion") he ended the drought. The Hindus explain Gorakhnath's behavior rather differently. Mac-

chendranath is also considered to be Gorakhnath's teacher. At the instruction of the legendary priest Bandhudatta, Macchendranath is supposed to have been brought from Assam to Nepal. Gorakhnath stood up to show respect for his guru and had to allow the snakes to escape.

The significance of Macchendranath as a provider of rain is especially obvious during his huge festival. From the beginning of summer by the Newari calendar (the end of April) until the beginning of the rainy season (in June), Macchendranath is paraded through the city on a wagon over ten meters high. Following him is a smaller temple wagon which is dedicated to Minanatha. At seven precisely determined points in Patan the god-chariots are worshipped by the population. The high point of the festival is reached when the wagons arrive in the **Jawalakhel** quarter on the western side of Patan. Then, in the presence of the king, the priest shows the believers a black shirt belonging to the god. It's an important moment in the ceremony, for at

79

this point it is vital that several drops of rain should fall.

The Durbar Square

The square in front of the former King's Palace exhibits less Buddhist than Hindu features. The Malla rulers also tolerated Buddhist religiosity, but worshipped predominantly Hindu gods themselves. Perhaps the most significant indication of this religious tolerance is to be found in a **gilded window** on the front of the palace. In its center the bodhisattva Avalokiteshvara can be seen, supported by various riding animals, among them Vishnu's Garuda bird, and surrounded by Hindu gods including Ganesh and Shiva-Parvati. This window is removable, and on special occasions, the King himself appears in its instead – representing to a certain extent a combination of Buddha and Vishnu.

Above: The Royal Bath in the Sundri Chowk, decorated with Tantric gods.

The square is divided into two parts: The northern section contains the **Durbar Square** with the royal palace and diverse shrines, the southern part, **Mangal Bazaar**, includes numerous businesses and street vendors. The center-point is also the intersection of both of the major streets that cut across Patan. The impressive, three-level **Degutale Temple** stands in the middle of the old grounds of the royal palace. The Kathmandu King Shivasimha Malla (1578–1619) gave one of his sons the family goddess Degutale (one form of Durga) to bring with him to Patan, and also charged him with the task of erecting a temple modeled after the Degutale Temple in Kathmandu.

Under Siddhinarasimha (1619–1661), the entire royal palace was generously expanded. Included in this work were a number of temples, magnificent building complexes belonging to the royal court *(chowk),* and many gardens, among them the great palace garden **Bhandarkhal** in the southeast. Under Vishnu Malla, the

Durbar Square acquired more or less its present-day form. The Degutale Temple abuts three courtyards. In the north stands the **Manikeshava Chowk**, which was added around 1660. It occupies the site where an old Licchavi palace originally stood. At any rate, that is what an inscription there from A.D. 643 indicates. Today its courtyard accomodates a small **Archeological Museum**.

South of the Degutale Temple, adjoining a corner of the *Mul Chowk,* is the octagonal *Taleju Temple* (whose imposing Taleju Bell on the other side of the street was erected in 1737. Both were built in 1666 by Shivasimha Malla. Finally we find the **Sundari Chowk** which boast quite probably the most beautiful fountain in the Kathmandu Valley. A particularly notable feature here is the old **royal bath** of Shrinivasa Malla (1661–1684). In the perfectly circular walls of the bath are numerous niches which are decorated with reliefs of primarily Tantric gods. The water flows into the pool from the jaws of a Makara dragon.

On the western side of the north-south axis which cuts across the palace grounds are several Vishnuist shrines, which were founded mostly as votive temples by the Malla rulers. In the extreme south end, Princess Yogamati had the octagonal **Krishna Temple** – also called **Cyasing Devai** because of its shape – erected in 1723 in memory of her son Yogaprakasha Malla, who met an early death.

Further north is the three-leveled **Temple of Harishankara** (a combined manifestation of both Vishnu and Shiva). This was also ordered built by Yogamati, this time in memory of her father Yoganarasimha Malla (1684-1705), who in his day had two statues – of himself and his son – put up on a tall column in front of the Degutale Temple in 1693. A similar column, namely that of Pratapa Malla, stands in Kathmandu. Only the King of Bhaktapur, Bhupatindra Malla, had no column to show for himself at the begin-

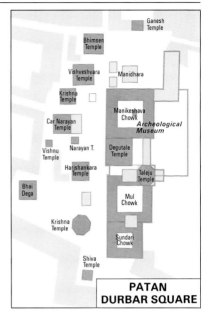

**PATAN
DURBAR SQUARE**

ning of the 18th century. Out of jealousy he is supposed to have killed a son of Yoganarendra Malla by using some secret method – or so it is said in one legend.

The oldest temple on the Durbar Square is the **Car Narayana Temple** from the year 1566. Its roof buttresses, which are decorated with the various manifestations of Vishnu, are particularly impressive.

An unusual building for the Kathmandu Valley is the **Krishna Temple** (also called the **Bala Gopala Temple** after Krishna's child-like manifestation. It was founded in 1637 by King Siddhinarasimha Malla (1619– 1661). It was modeled on the Islamic architecture of the Moguls and on a similar temple in Mathura in northern India. Surrounding a **Shikhara Tower** there are small pavilions on three levels which include columns and built-in arcades. Inside these there are lengthy renderings of scenes in relief from the great Indian epics *Mahabharata* and *Ramayana*. The reliefs are also partly explained in Newari.

The gilded **Garuda Bronze** in front of the temple was also contributed by Siddhinarasimha Malla. This temple is also the highest holy place for the growing number of adherents of Krishna-worship, who distinguish themselves in the singing of their especially devout religious songs. In August and September, the king himself also participates in the extensive celebration of Krishna's birthday.

Besides Vishnu and Krishna, there are also several shrines on the Durbar Square dedicated to Shiva. Again, Siddhinarasimha Malla founded the huge two-storied **Vishvashara** (called **Vishvanath Temple**) in 1627. One of the two riders on the stone elephants at the east entrance is thought to be a representation of the ruler himself.

Many of the buildings in the northern section of the Durbar Square are closely connected with another legend involving

Above: Temple carving in Patan. Right: The wrestlers at the entrance of Nyatapola temple.

the founding of Patan: An ugly grass-cutter from the Lalitvana Forest, who was a worshipper of the goddess Maniyogini, is supposed to have discovered a fountain of youth on this spot. When King Biradeva heard news of this event, he founded the city of **Lalitpur** (= Patan) on the same spot. He also had a pond dug out for the serpents that were reputed to provide man with water, and he had various shrines erected, all of which were named after goddesses whose names begin with "Mani" (literally "jewel" or "precious stone").

In fact, even today several of the buildings and sanctuaries still carry these names. For example, the large fountain across from the Vishveshvara Temple received the name **Manidhara**. On the stairs to those fountains that can be walked on stand two pavilions. The one to the north is assigned a special function. It is the **Manimandapa**, where astrologers gather every year in order to determine the most auspicious moment for the beginning of the Macchendranath procession. One can also see a stone throne in the hall, which Yogendra Malla had built in 1701. This date is indicated by an inscription on the back.

The three-leveled **Bhimsen Temple** in the northern part of the square dates back to the time of Shrinivasa Malla. It is rectangular and was not built on a pedestal, as was frequently the case with temples dedicated to Bhimsen and Bhairava. The temple itself is not placed directly on the ground but is on the first floor. It is in fact a restored version of the original which was almost completely destroyed by fire in 1862.

It is said of Bhimsen that, at the time of Yogendra Malla, he threatened anyone passing by with death. Therefore, the king asked his guru to do whatever he could to appease the god. The holy man declined, and so the King appointed his brother to do the job, and he was able to calm down the god.

Kumbheshvara Temple

The **Kumbheshvara Temple**, in the north of the city, is considered the oldest temple in Patan. Jayasithi Malla (1382–1395) founded the shrine which is dedicated to one of the forms of Shiva. However, since that time the building has been repeatedly expanded, and was increased to five stories in height from its original two. As a result, the Nyatapola temple in Bhaktapur and this Kumbheshvara Temple are the only existing pagodas with five roofs.

Next to this temple an artificial pond – so it is told – is fed with the holy water of Lake Gosainkund in the Himalaya Mountains. At the time of the full moon in the month of Shravana (July-August) a bath in this pool is supposed to be particularly beneficial. On that date, hundreds of pilgrims stream by to worship the four-faced *linga* in the temple. In addition, a small temple is erected in the middle of the pond with another *linga* especially for this occasion. Here, like at the other temples dedicated to Shiva, the men of the higher castes exchange the holy beads which they received at their initiations.

BHAKTAPUR

The third-largest city of the Kathmandu Valley is **Bhaktapur** ("city of the pious"), which is also named **Bhadgaon** ("rice-village"), located 16 kilometers east of Kathmandu on the old trade route between India and Tibet, which is still today a vital artery cutting through the city. There are approximately 50,000 people residing in its heavily-populated old quarter, a large portion of whom are Newari Hindus. The majority of these are farmers, even though they have a rather urban appearance. Of the three royal seats in the valley, Bhaktapur is the least affected by modern life. New buildings have been constructed reluctantly, and motorized traffic generally stays out of the city. As a result, even today Bhaktapur offers a rare glimpse into an almost intact city of the Middle Ages.

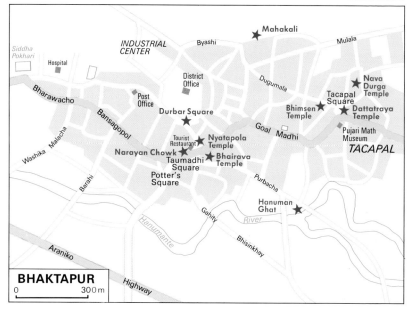

The Nepalese-German **Bhaktapur Development Project** was an influential contributor to the preservation of Bhaktapur's historical character. The Project combines measures for the improvement of the quality of life (water supplies, sewer systems and road construction) with the renovation and restoration of selected buildings. One goal was – and still is – to avoid sacrificing tradition to unnecessary modernization.

According to legend, Bhaktapur is supposed to have been founded by King Anandadeva Malla (1147–1166), after which he turned his sovereignty over Kathmandu and Patan over to his older brother, Narendradeva Malla. In reality, however, Bhaktapur is the product of several small settlements which grew together, and in the course of time expanded. This was especially true during the rules of the Malla Kings Jayasithi (1382–1395), Yaksha (1428–1482), Jitamitra (1673–1696) and Bhupatindra (1696–1722). In 1768, Bhaktapur lost its autonomy, when it could no longer hold

its own after heavy battling with the troops of Prithvi Narayan Shah.

The city is separated into two spacially contrasting areas: The upper city to the east and the lower city to the west. During certain festivals, as, for example, in the *Bisketjatra* in springtime, the people from these areas engage in ritual bouts that can become quite hefty at times. Every year this jousting produces a number of wounded.

Just as in the other Newar cities of the Kathmandu Valley, the public plazas represent the center points of the 24 quarters of the city. In Bhaktapu,r these are especially distinctive and often give the quarters their names. Things are especially lively on, for example, **Potters' Square**, where the potters' wheels spin perpetually and earthenware stands drying before being baked in the kiln.

The Durbar Square

In contrast to Kathmandu and Patan, the old palace is not located in the center of the city, but rather on its northern boundary. As a result, the front plaza is integrated to a lesser degree with the life of the city. The beginnings of the palace complex extend back to Yaksha Malla (1428–1482), however certain individual buildings and sculptures are older (see sketch on p. 86).

One of these is dedicated to Taleju, the goddess of protection of the Malla kings, who had been brought to the city at the beginning of the 14th century. Her seat and temple is in one of the main courts, the *Mul Chowk*. This is closed to non-Hindus, but you can catch a glimpse of the wooden tympanon above the entrance, two golden windows in the interior courtyard, murals that date from the 17th century, and the statue of King Jitamitra Malla alongside his wife dated 1708/9. Surrounding the Mul Chowk are several auxiliary courtyards and the **Nag Pokhri**, the royal bathing pond.

Access to the temple grounds is through a richly ornamented **Golden Gate**, the **Sundhoka**, in the royal palace. It was built into the façade of the palace by the last king, Ranajit Malla, in 1753.

This same ruler also had a life-sized statue erected on a column in front of the gate, which portrays his father **Bhupatindra Malla** kneeling in reverence before Taleju, under the protection of a shield. The basic traits and structure of the palace still goes back to Jaksha Malla, but it was completed under Bhupatindra Malla. The façade of the east wing – which is constructed of red brick and features 55 black, artfully-carved wooden windows – stands in stark contrast to the white-plastered west section, with its Islamic ornamentation and its gate, over which two large lion statues stand watch. The **Bhaktapur Museum** is now accommodated in the west wing. It has a collection of Newaric statues on exhibit and Tibetan scroll-pictures *(thangkas),* as well as mural paintings from the 17th century.

There are comparatively few monuments standing on the front plaza. Earlier drawings show that at one time the plaza was substantially more built up than it is now. Here too, the earthquake of 1934 caused heavy damage and destruction. On the west side of the palace grounds one can see some evidence of this destruction in the only provisionally reconstructed remainder of the **Shiva Temple**, which was originally much larger. In more recent times, a rectangular resting-house has been reconstructed, with German assistance, after its historical model and on its original location.

Among the preserved or restored sanctuaries on the palace plaza is a replica of the Pashupatinath temple in Deopatan – the **Yaksheshvara Temple.** It is named after its founder, Yaksha Malla. He began construction of the temple in 1478, apparently so that he could worship Pashupati without having to travel the long distance to Deopatan. This temple was destroyed by the 1934 earthquake, and wasn't restored until 1968.

Not far from there stands the **Vatsala Temple**, built in the Shikara style. This goddess has her primary seat in the Pashupatinath Temple of Deopatan. Jagatprakasha Malla (1643–1672) had this temple erected in Bhaktapur.

Still two further temples feature the north-Indian Shikara tower: A 1696 temple, probably founded by Bhupatindra Malla, which is believed to be dedicated to the goddess Siddhilakshmi and whose stairs are bordered with various animal statues, and another **Durga Temple**, whose builder and year of construction are unknown. The large double-leveled temple on the extreme west end of the plaza is locally designated as the **Narayan Temple.** However, it actually houses a cultic illustration of Krishna. The constructor and year of founding of this building are unknown, but judging from the style it comes from the later part of the 17th century.

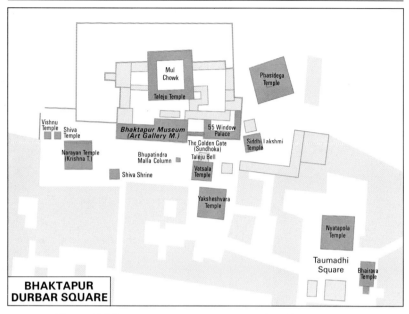

BHAKTAPUR
DURBAR SQUARE

Taumadhi Square

Unlike the Durbar Square, **Taumadhi Square** is located in the center of the city, surrounded by old Newaric residences. Here there is always a colorful riot of traders and passers-by. Two temples dominate the "skyline" of Taumadhi Square: the Nyatapola Temple and the Bhairava Temple.

The **Nyatapola Temple** is the largest temple in Bhaktapur. It stands on a five-stepped pedestal, on the corners of which are four Ganesh shrines. The five-storied pagoda roof, which is over 30 meters high, towers over all the other buildings in the city. Nyatapola was erected in 1703 by king Bhupatindra Malla and dedicated to his own guardian deity. Some say it was a bit of one-upmanship with the great Taleju temple in Kathmandu. No one, with the exception of priests, is allowed to set foot inside its

Right: The magnificent entrance to the Bhaktapur Palace: The "Golden Gate".

sanctuary, in which this goddess is worshipped with Tantric rituals. Accordingly, the temple is not named after the secret goddess, but simply means "five-storied temple."

The ascent to the temple is flanked by pairs of statues representing guardians and deities: First, there are two legendary wrestlers who are supposed to be ten times as strong as ordinary men, then lions, elephants and the mythological lion-clawed griffins. Finally, the series is completed by two Tantric guardian goddesses.

The three-storied **Bhairava Temple** was also founded by Bhupatindra Malla, in 1717. It is a rectangular building, and the god has his seat in the top level. The actual cultic effigy is kept in a part of the building closed to foreigners. However, one can catch a glimpse of a comparable Bhairava mask between the first and second roofs.

One such mask is also taken from the Bhairava Temple and carried in a large processional cart during Bhaktapur's

huge **New Year's Procession**, the *Bisketjatra.* Following this cart is another carring the goddess Bhadrakali. Both of the carts stand on Taumadhi Square on the border between the upper and lower cities. At the beginning of the procession, men from both the city's sections engage in a tug-of-war.

At this point it is not unusual for heavy fighting to break out between the members of the different quarters, which are ridden with old rivalries. Most often, the struggle is won by the men of the higher social strata from the upper city. The new year is ushered in with the ritual erecting of a tall tree, but only when the carts have reached the square in the south, which can last days.

The large, somewhat elevated platforms on Taumadhi Square also suggest the sort of festivals of which Bhaktapur has a good number. Normally, these platforms serve as places for the sale of fruits, vegetables and fowl, however, on certain days they become stages for rituals and religious festivals.

In the southern section of the square there is a single-storied house in which the **Café Nyatapola** has been installed. Originally it was a residence and, in all probability, also the quarters of a local deity. Further south there is an adjoining temple courtyard, the **Narayan Chowk**. In it is located a two-storied pagoda, the **Tilmadhav Temple** (also called the Narayan Temple), which is dedicated to Vishnu. This place of worship was already mentioned in inscriptions dating from 1080, but the present form of the temple originated, as is also true of the Nyatapola and Bhairava Temples, in the early part of the 18th century. In front of the entrance are three pillars featuring attributes of Vishnu, with his mount **Garuda** in the center, and his discus and conch on either side.

The Tacapal Quarter

Another major square is located in the Tacapal Quarter on the eastern section of the old trade route that cuts through

Bhaktapur. The center of this section of the city is undoubtedly the three-storied **Dattatraya Temple**, which originally served as a place for assemblies as well as a wayside rest house. The name of the temple means trinity, and accordingly, its sanctuary houses statues of the trio of gods Brahma, Vishnu and Shiva-Mahadeva.

King Yaksha Malla is supposed to have had this wooden building constructed in the 15th century. It was later restored by one of his successors, Vishva Malla, in the middle of the 16th century. The portico on the western side and the statues of wrestlers flanking the stairs – these are copies of the lower pair of statues in front of the Nyatapola Temple – date from the year 1860, as do the three columns with Garuda, discus and conch.

Another sanctuary, the rectangular two-storied **Bhimsen Temple**, is situated in the west of the square. It is dedicated to the god Bhimasena, who is very popular because of his enormous power. He is the hero idolized in the *Mahabharata* epic, and in Nepal he is also the protective god of many castes of craftsmen. Adjoining the Bhimsen Temple to the rear is one of the largest fountain complexes in Bhaktapur.

Located to the southeast behind the Dattatraya Temple is the **Pujari Math**, a house that originally served for the reception of sectarian pilgrims and the directorate responsible for alterations to temples. However, it was renovated in 1971-72 and transformed into a **Museum for Art Handcrafts**.

The Pujari Math is especially well-known for the rich, finely-nuanced wood-carvings from the 18th century that grace its doors and windows. Particularly beautiful among these is the **Peacock Window,** which faces the alley on the east side of the building.

Right: Entrance to the Dattatraya temple in the Tacapal quarter of Bhaktapur.

Temple Groups

The number of shrines, temples and seats of gods that one also finds in Bhaktapur on thresholds, in every courtyard and at each street intersection is scarcely countable. However, these seemingly insignificant holy places frequently receive more attention than, for example, the great monuments on the Durbar Square.

Every morning each household demonstrates its membership to its section of the city, by sending someone of the household, most frequently a woman, to seek out the nearest seat of the gods in the quarter. This might be a small enclosed shrine, or it might simply be an uncarved stone lying by the side of the road. It may be dedicated to Ganesh, Bhairava, or the Divine Mothers. Prayers are offered to these gods requesting assistance for the day. Fulfilment of some concrete wish – for the birth of a son, success in an examination, or luck in gambling – might also be requested.

In addition, the street deities are also visited for protection against ritual impurity. The Hindus think of events such as birth and death as making one temporarily impure. Only certain gods and demons accept such defiling things as hair clippings, umbilical cords and the clothes of a dead person. These deities reside mostly in the so-called **Chvasa Stones**, which are associated with every household. They can easily be recognized as lotus-shaped stones in the pavement at intersections of public places.

Each quarter of the city is also assigned one of the various cremation places in the south of the city along the **Hanumante River**. When someone dies, his corpse is carried along precisely predetermined "death-paths" through the old city to the cremation place of his caste. At these so-called *ghats*, such as the **Kalighat** and **Hanumanghat**, there are mostly only small shrines to the gods, votive temples and rest houses.

Besides the individual gods for each section of the city there are groups of gods that protect the entire city, notably the Navadurghas and the Asthamatrika. The Nine Durghas have a common house, the **Navadurgha Temple** as it is called, in the eastern part of the old quarter. Masks of the gods are kept here, which are employed by certain castes for rituals that occur mostly at night, always at different spots in and around Bhaktapur. Usually they dance for the protection of the city.

The Asthamatrika – which means "Eight Mothers" – have their shrines scattered around the core of the city. Several of these seats, such as those of Mahakali and Mahalakshmi, have been greatly expanded. The Eight Mothers are also expressions of old protective principles, according to which the gods must protect the cardinal points in order that the world's diversity be subsumed into a greater cosmic context. In autumn during the Dasain Festival, many of the residents of Bhaktapur go to each of the Asthamatrika shrines for eight consecutive days, where they pray to the goddesses for a good rice harvest.

The goddesses do not only have their permanent homes in their shrines at the edges of the city, each has also a *dyoche* – literally god house – inside the city. Statues of the goddesses are kept there to be taken out only during processions. These god houses don't always turn out to be quite as large as the **Mahakali dyoche**, but are often indistinguishable from normal residences.

KATHMANDU VALLEY

The Kathmandu Valley is scarcely bigger than many a medium-sized city: It is 25 kilometers long and about 15 wide. But, thanks to its special geographical location (one could also say geo-strategic), it has for ages been a point of intersection between two of the great cultures of Asia: The Indian and the Tibeto-Chinese. Only all too gladly did pilgrims, monks and traders, or threatened clans from the

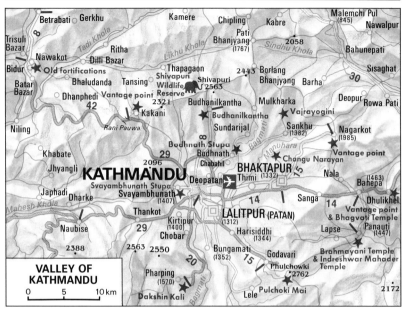

neighboring regions settle in the Valley to wait for the thaw in the north, or to avoid malaria in the swampy lower spurs of the Himalayas during the rainy season. The valley is surrounded by massive mountain chains, offering protection from enemies, and being at an elevation of about 1,400 meters it has a rather pleasantly mild, subtropical climate.

Little is known about the earliest settlements. They must have only been small villages comprising scarcely more than a few houses. They were inhabited by Tibeto-Burmese speaking tribes, the ancestors of the Newar, who now represent the majority of the population in the cities of the Kathmandu Valley.

For a long time the local rulers held power only over small areas. It wasn't until the reigns of Kings Jayasithi Malla (1392–1395) and especially Yaksha Malla (1428–1482) that the Valley was politically united. However, under Yak-

Right: Statues of Dhyanibuddha Akshobhya on Svayambhunath Hill.

sha Malla's sons, the empire again broke up into the three kingdoms of Kathmandu, Patan and Bhaktapur. With this came the beginning of a great period of cultural blossoming in the history of Nepal, to which we owe a number of extraordinary monuments and priceless works of art.

What is found in Kathmandu, Patan and Bhaktapur in concentrated form appears again in the other towns which are scattered throughout the entire valley. The smaller villages are for the most part not as diverse as the old royal cities. Their significance lies rather in a single sanctuary, a particular caste structure, or their special location. Such is the case in, for example, **Banepa**, which was still a politically important city during the Malla period, and now only has a couple of small Vishnu temples and a temple to Candeshvari to show for itself. In the village of **Chapagaon**, the Vajravahari Temple continues to attract believers. It is dedicated to a manifestation of Vishnu as a boar. Its actual object of reverence,

which is, naturally, shaped like a boar, is thought to date from the fifth century.

In **Harisiddhi**, the temple of a goddess by the same name, who allegedly demands human sacifice, and the seat of the goddess Vajrayogini, on a mountain near **Sankhu**, both have a special force of attraction, which extends far beyond the village limits.

Thimi, however, is wrongly referred to only as the "City of Potters". Although this caste has achieved an outstanding status there, the city, which is located between Kathmandu and Bhaktapur, offers a most extremely complex combination of religious edifices, among them a ritually important Balkumari temple from the 16th century.

Many of the hamlets on the cliffs or on the surrounding mountains have become well-known less because of their religious significance than for their location. They offer a rewarding view of the Himalayan mountain-range or over the Kathmandu Valley. From the Newar city of **Dhulikhel** (30 kilometers away from Kathmandu) you can gaze over the entire areas of Langtang, Helambu and also toward the east out to Makalu. The view from **Nagarkot** (15 kilometers northeast of Bhaktapur) also provides the beholder with an overwhelming panorama including mountains like the Annapurna Massif, the Ganesh Himal and the Lhotse. In springtime, when the tree-high rhododendrons are in bloom, it's worth a climb to the **Shivapuri** (2,563 meters) to the north of Kathmandu, or to **Phulchowki** to the south which is accessible to traffic and from where one can overlook the entire Kathmandu Valley. The southern **Godavari** is also worth a day-trip just for its botanical gardens.

Svayambhunath

The fame of the **Svayambhunath**, the Kathmandu Valley's most significant stupa, which rises up over the valley basin on a hill to the west of the capital, reaches as far as Tibet. According to the legend, Manjushri – a bodhisattva and

god of wisdom – found a lotus flower there as he was cutting through the surrounding mountains with his sword in order to drain the lake which once covered the valley. A Manjushri Temple, which the Hindus worship as the seat of Sarasvati – the goddess of wisdom and art – is located west of Svayambunath.

Even though the earliest inscription is dated A.D. 1129, which is quite recent, the Svayambhunath stupa must be considered one of the oldest religious places of the Valley. It has been renovated over and over again, but particularly after its partial destruction, suffered during the Islamic invasion in the mid-14th century. This is recorded in an inscription from A.D. 1372. The overall look of the stupa today reflects this period. The best approach to the stupa is from the east, up a staircase with 365 steps, which is bordered by several votive Caityas and Akshobhya statues from the early Shah

Above: Young Tibetan monks in front of the Bodhnath stupa.

period. When you have reached the top, you will find yourself observed by one of the eyes of Buddha, which are painted on all four sides of the stupa's tower. They are a part of the complex symbolism of this religious building. A leveled-off hemisphere arises from a rectangular base, a symbol of Buddha and his completeness. Surrounding the cupola is a balustrade with 211 prayer wheels, each of which carry the holy mantra *Om mani padme hum* (Oh, you jewel in the lotus blossom).

The five Dhyanibuddhas or Tathagathas are also inserted alongside watchful riding animals in the recesses of the stupas: In the east are Akshobya on an elephant as well as Vajrocana on a lion; in the south Ratnasambhava on a horse, in the west Amytabha, who is the most worshipped of these, riding a peacock; and in the north, Amoghasiddhi on the heavenly bird Garuda. Between these transcendental Buddhas, who also represent the five cosmic elements of earth, water, fire, wind and ether, are niches for their four assigned female traits, the so-called *Buddhashaktis*.

A series of 13 shields, donated by the monasteries in the area, project from the tower. They are the rejuvenating discs, which symbolize steps on the way to perfection and enlightenment. A central element of the stupa is a wooden post in the interior, which must be renewed regularly in great rituals. The stupa is surrounded by pilgrimage amenities: Rest houses for pilgrims, souvenir shops, Tibetan monasteries (*gompas*) from which prayers and muffled fanfares emanate; and five special shrines, which represent three elements (wind, earth and fire) as well as two mystical snakes. Among the larger buildings there is also a much-attended temple which is dedicated to a goddess who gives protection from smallpox and childhood illnesses: Hariti, or, as she is called by the Hindus, Sitala.

Again, it was King Pratapa Malla whose influence was decisive in laying out the grounds. From him came the large bronzen *Vajra* (Tibetan *Dorje*) dated 1667, which is on a large mandala to the east of the stupa. A *Vajra* is, in the mythology of Hinduism, a thunderbolt weapon of the gods. However, the Buddhists regard it as a diamond scepter and as a symbol of the absolute. Pratapa Malla also erected two sacred buildings in the style of the Hinduistic Shikara temple: **Pratapapura** and **Anantapura**, which, of course, are named after himself and his favorite wife. They are dedicated to the goddesses of Vajrayana Buddhism.

The countless votive Caityas and sculptures which surround the Svayambhunath are evidence of the popularity of the stupa. They are for the most part not very old; in contrast to the equally popular Hinduist Pashupatinath sanctuary, astoundingly few holy places originated during the Licchavi period. Even the three life-size **Dipankara statues** were probably not erected before the late Malla period.

Bodhnath

Next to the Svayambhunath stupa, that of **Bodhnath** (also called "**Baudha**") is the most significant Buddhist sanctuary of the Kathmandu Valley. With both a diameter and height of 40 meters, the **Bodhnath stupa** is also the largest religious structure of its kind in the valley. It is located about eight kilometers north-east of Kathmandu on the old trade and pilgrimage road between Tibet and India. A pair of Buddha's eyes painted on the stupa's tower can be seen from a good distance. However, the stupa is becoming increasingly hidden by tall houses which have been settled in primarily by Tibetans who have been forced into exile over the past decades.

An increasing number of Tibetan monasteries have also been founded in the recent past. Residing in one of these is the *Cini Lama* – after the Dalai Lama and the Panchen Lama the third-highest dignitary of the Tibetans. In general, the Bodnath stupa is a place of worship predominantly for Tibetans and Sherpas, rarely for the Newar Buddhists.

From the point of view of architectural history, the three-leveled substructure on which the hemisphere and the thirteen shields are raised is worthy of note. Its builders were clearly attempting to unite two cosmological ideals: The scalar way up the mountain and the hemisphere.

There is another stupa located not far from the Bodnath Stupa in the village of **Chabahil**. It is substantially smaller, with a diameter of 14 meters. This stupa has become famous because of a legend: The Indian Emperor Ashoka (3rd century B.C.) and his daughter Carumati are supposed to have founded it. However, its true age is just as uncertain as that of the stupa in Bodhnath.

In terms of ritual, the Chabahil Stupa has become largely insignificant, but in the village itself there is a highly worshipped **Ganesh Temple**, surrounded by

several very old sculptures and relics from the Licchavi period.

Pashupatinath

Pashupati, one of the manifestations of Shiva, was already a protective god for rulers according to the earliest written documents of Nepalese history. Even today, the king closes the speeches he makes from his throne with the declaration: "May the god Pashupati protect us!"

The **Pashupati Temple**, in the small, idyllically situated city of **Deopatan** on the west bank of the Bagmati River, has therefore become the most significant holy sanctuary of Hinduism. Mornings and evenings, numerous believers stream into Deopatan, vendors of devotionalia peddle pictures of gods, flowers or pieces of incense, and offer lodgings for pil-

Above: Two ascetics, devotees of Shiva, in front of the Pashupati Temple. Right: The Pashupatinath ghats are always brimming with life.

grims. Additionally there are the *ghats* – bathing grounds on the banks of the Bagmati – where corpses are also cremated.

According to a popular myth, this is where Shiva, in the guise of a gazelle, took refuge from his spouse Parvati and the other gods. This act threatened the safety of the world, and so everyone looked for Shiva. When Parvati finally found him in the **Mrigasthali Grove** on the east bank of the Bagmati, he attemped to flee across the river, whereupon his horn broke into four pieces. So he stayed where he was and was henceforth worshipped as "Master of Animals" (Pashupati) and as the four-faced *linga* (phallic symbol and sign of Shiva).

The main temple is closed off to non-Hindus, but from the western road and from the other side of the river on the Mrigasthali Hill, you can get a glimpse of the temple courtyard: The pagoda-shaped Pashupati Temple was reconstructed at the end of the 17th century by King Bhupalendra Malla, after the previous building was completely consumed by ter-

mites. In front of it, on the western side, stand two large bronze **Nandis** (Shiva's bull and riding-mount).

In the vicinity of this two-storied temple, countless further temples have been erected. Kings, aristocrats and wealthy merchants always seek to immortalize themselves with votive **lingas** near the country's patron god. Particularly outstanding among these are the grounds of the **Pancadevala Temple** of the kings, south of the Pashupati Temple, but the Rana rulers also left behind their traces: A chain of *linga*-shrines stands on the east bank of the Bagmati; south of these there is a predominantly Vishnuist temple complex with a **Ram Temple** from the 14th century; located in the **Mrigasthali Grove** there are over 60 additional small *linga*-templets. The grove is also the site of the Shikara Temple of Goraknath (a foundation of the Kanphata Sekt), around which apes play.

The temples and shrines of the goddesses are even older and ritually more significant. The **Seat of the Guh-yeshvari** in the northeast is mentioned as early as the 11th century in handwritten manuscripts, though the temple standing there today was first laid out by Pratapa Malla (1641-1674). According to the legend, Parvati had thrown herself on a sacrificial fire after her father harshly rejected Shiva's request for her hand in marriage. Shiva then traveled throughout the country carrying his beloved Parvati on his shoulder, whereby, parts of her corps fell to the ground. Her *guhya* – literally the "hidden" or "concealed", but also "anus" or "vulva" – is supposed to have landed in Guhyeshvari.

The **Temple of the Goddess Vatsaladevi**, which is located west of both bridges over the Bagmati, also enjoys great popularity. It is usually associated with human sacrifice. Frescos are painted onto the exterior walls of the temple, and on the east side jackals are even pictured with human limbs sticking out of their maws.

Each year in March and April, Vatsala is carried in a huge city-wide procession to the Pashupati Temple, where they then ram the temple with her processional chest: It is said that Shiva (Pashupati) refuses her because in her rituals she accepts alcohol and blood offerings. Nowhere else in the Kathmandu Valley is the latent conflict between the pure, vegetarian and the more savage atavistic Tantric Hinduism more openly contested than here.

Roughly 150 meters further south stands the temple of the Nine Durgas, the **Rajarajeshvari Temple** from the early 15th century (on the way there you will find one of the oldest **Buddha Shakyamuni statues** of the Kathmandu Valley, dating from the 7th century).

In the west of the city, on the other side of the Ring Road, there is another shrine to a goddess: the **Jayavagishvari Temple**. Painted on its north side is a large portrait of Bhairava, which must be renewed every twelve years.

Changu Narayan and Budhanilakantha

Just as Svayambhunath and Bodhnath are centers of Buddhism and the Pashupatinath is the focus of Shivaism, Changu Narayan and Budhanilakantha represent the cultural and historical high-point of Vishnuism.

Changu Narayan (also named **Dolagiri**) stands on a hill roughly four kilometers north of Bhaktapur. This location was already mentioned in A.D. 464 on a column inscription before the main temple – the oldest remaining inscription in Nepal. The content of the inscription is most informative: The son of the king Manadeva dissuades his mother from joining her deceased husband on the funeral pyre.

The temple itself in its present form originated at the beginning of the 18th

Right: Changu Narayan, the oldest Vishnu shrine in the Kathmandu Valley.

century. Located on the west side are bronze portraits of the founder, Queen Riddhilakshmi, and her young son Bhupalendra Malla (1687-1700). However, the son was no longer there in 1704 for the festive dedication of the temple. Its cultic symbol shows Vishnu (Narayan is another name for Vishnu) riding on the heavenly bird Garuda.

This sculpture, from the fourth century A.D., is not always visible since the temple is usually closed, but facsimiles are located all over the Kathmandu Valley, starting already with the statue on the ninth-century forecourt. The life-size Garuda in the form of a human being on the west side is quite probably a portrait of King Manadeva.

The temple, which is surrounded by rest houses and a number of more recent votive shrines with *lingas* and Vishnuist sculptures (Krishna and his female companion Lakshmi) is the repository of precious treasures of Nepalese sculptures. One **Vishnu Trivikrama statue** from the 8th century represents Vishnu as a midget: When the demon Bali promised him as much land as he could measure out in three (*tri*) strides (*vikamra*), Vishnu grew to the size of a giant and stepped through the underworld, the earth and heaven.

Apparently originating from the same atelier is the nearby **Vishvarupa Statue**, which represents Vishnu as the Emperor of the World, surrounded by his spouse and a host of accompanying figures. One **Narasimha Statue** from the 13th century portrays Vishnu as "half man, half lion," a disguise in which he killed a demon who was terrorizing the whole world.

In the north of Kathmandu, a Vishnuist religious symbol known under the name **Budhanilakantha** is worshipped even more than Changu Narayan. It shows Vishnu in the middle of an ocean – symbolized by a pool of water – sleeping on a coiled snake. This is also the form that Vishnu rests in after each cyclical de-

struction of the universe. He also slumbers, however, during the four hottest months of summer. When he wakes up in the autumn, thousands of devotees stream to Budhanilakantha in order to greet him with flowers and fruits.

The king, who is considered an incarnation of Vishnu, is refused entrance to Budhanilakantha. The five-meter-long picture – of which there are several facsimiles in the Kathmandu Valley – is supposed to have been dedicated by Vishnugupta in the 7th century.

Dakshin Kali

One of the most popular goddesses in the Kathmandu Valley is Kali or Camunda; in Nepal, the two are iconographically difficult to tell apart. This goddess of death is often represented as an emaciated, hollow-eyed and withered figure, with flabby breasts, bejeweled with chains of human bones, snakes around her neck, and dancing on a corpse. She likes to dwell around cremation places or other similarly dark locations outside of settlements.

One of her most popular manifestations is known as "Kali of the South", **Dakshin Kali**, indication from which direction she protects the valley. Her little shrine is hidden in a gorge along a mountain brook, surrounded by statues of other mother goddesses. This was once the seat of a pre-Hindu goddess, who – as is so frequent in the Kathmandu Valley – was only gradually identified with the great goddesses of the Hindu pantheon.

While the remote location of the Dakshin Kali once helped to ensure that she would only be visited by initiates, now every Saturday hundreds of automobiles proceed up the little mountain road from Kathmandu, in order to worship her with bloody animal sacrifices.

On the way there one passes **Kirtipur**, a medieval city with around 10,000 inhabitants; in 1959 it became the seat of the **Tribhuvan University**. It's a place of historic significance: In 1757, the city successfully repelled Prithvi Narayan

97

Shah's first assault. When he finally took the town, he is supposed to have had the noses and ears of all the male inhabitants cut off. Kirtipur offers countless holy places and sanctuaries, notably a three-storied **Bagh-Bhairava Temple** and the **Cilanco Stupa** along with its monastery buildings.

A little further up the road, a short visit to **Pharping** is probably well worth your while. This little mountain village boasts a **Temple of the Goddess Vajrayogini** from the 17th century; a rock sanctuary (named **Sheshnarayan**) with a Vishnu-trivikrama statue from the 14th century and, on the ridge of the hill, a hermitage which is considered by the Hindus as the sanctuary of Gorakhnath (a footprint found in the stone here, typical of this holy man, originated in the year 1390). However, the Tibetans believe this place to be one of Padmasambhava's resting places.

Above: A Newar woman hard at work in the fields near Kirtipur.

Also located on the way to Dakshin-Kali is the village of **Chobar**, which has become famous because of the **Bagmati Gorge**, which the legendary bodhisattva Manjushri is supposed to have chopped out with his sword, in order to let the lake which once covered the Kathmandu Valley flow away.

In the village itself, which is located on a nearby knoll, the **Adinath Temple** from the 16th century is particularly interesting. The main cultic object of the temple consists of an apparently local figure with a red face and wide-open eyes looking a little like the Red Macchend-ranath in Patan. It represents the bodhi-sattva Avalokiteshvara. However, the name "Adinath" is also carried by Shiva, to whom several other sanctuaries in the same location are also dedicated. And so, at the entrance to the Kathmandu Valley, with the many myths and legends which have been woven around it, we find an ever-increasing, magnificient religious diversity and a variety of cultural tradi-tions unparalleled in South Asia.

KATHMANDU

Accommodation
LUXURY: **Soaltee Holiday Inn Crown Plaza**, Tahachal, Tel: 272550. **Yak & Yeti**, Durbar Marg, Tel: 413999. **De l'Annapurna**, Durbar Marg, Tel: 221711. **Sherpa**, Durbar Marg, Tel: 227000. **Everest**, New Baneswor, Tel: 220567. **Shanker**, Lazimpat, Tel: 410151.

MODERATE: **Shangrila**, Lazimpat, Tel: 412999. **Blue Star**, Tripureswor, Tel: 211470. **Malla**, Lekhnath Marg, Tel: 410320. **Dwarika's Village**, Battisputali, Tel: 414770. **Kathmandu**, Maharajgunj, Tel: 418494. **Ambassador**, Lazimpat, Tel: 410432. **Woodlands**, Durbar Marg, Tel: 222683. **Yellow Pagoda**, Kanti Path, Tel: 220337. **Hotel Crystal**, New Road, Tel: 223611. **Vajra**, Bijeswari, Tel: 271545. **Gautam**, Jyatha, Tel: 215014. **Kathmandu Guest House**, Thamel, Tel: 413632. **Mandap**, Thamel, Tel: 413321.

BUDGET: **Lhasa Guest House**, Jyatha, Tel: 211147. **Tushita Rest House**, Kanti Path, Tel: 216913. **New Gajur**, Jyatha, Tel: 212621. **New Ganesh**, Bhote Bahal, Tel: 220296. **Shakti**, Thamel, Tel: 410121. **Sita**, Chhetrapati, Tel: 214978. **Star**, Thamel, Tel: 411000. **Tibet Guest House**, Chhetrapati, Tel: 214383. **Yeti Cottage**, Thamel. **Tara Gaon Resort**, Boudha, Tel: 271545. **Ratna**, Bagh Bazar, Tel: 224809. **Manaslu**, Lazimpat, Tel: 410071. **Blue Diamond**, Jyatha, Tel: 226392. **Mount Makalu**, Dharmapath, Tel: 224616. **Prokla Guest House**, Jyatha, **Tel: 276566. Himalayan View**, Jyatha, Tel: 414770. **Maya Guest House**, Boudha, Tel: 414866.

PATAN

Accommodation
LUXURY: **Himalaya**, Sahid Sukra Marg, Tel: 523900.

MODERATE: **Narayani**, Pulchowk, Tel: 521711. **Summit**, Kopudol, Tel: 521894.

BUDGET: **Oasis**, Patan, Tel: 522746. **Aloha Inn**, Jawalakhel, Tel: 522796.

Restaurants
Cafe de Temple, Durbar Square, Tel: 527172

BHAKTAPUR

Accommodation
BUDGET: **Golden Gate Guest House**, near Durbar Square. **Shiva Guest House**, near Durbar Square.

Restaurants
Cafe Nyatapola, Taumadi Square. **Cafe Soma**, Tacapal Square.

NAGARKOT

Accommodation
MODERATE: **The Fort Resort**, Tel: 290869, city office: 216913. **Flora Hill**, Tel: 223311. **Tara Gaon**, Boudha, Tel: 271545.

BUDGET: **Niva Home**, Tel: 223590.

DHULIKHEL

Accommodation
MODERATE: **Dhulikhel Mountain Resort. Himalayan Horizon.**

BUDGET: **Dhulikhel Lodge**, Tel: 011-61114.

Hospitals
Kalimati Clinic, Tel: 271873. **Bir Hospital** (Kanti Path), Tel: 226963. **CIWEC Clinic** (Baluwatar), Tel: 410983. **Kanti Hospital** (Maharaganj), Tel: 411550. **Maternity Hospital** (Thapathali), Tel: 211243. **Teaching Hospital** (Maharaganj), Tel: 412303. **Teku Hospital**, Tel: 211344. **Nepal International Clinic** (Hitti Durbar), Tel: 412842. **Patan Hospital**, (Lagankhel), Tel: 522266. **Bhaktapur Hospital**, Tel: 610798.

Each embassy has its **doctors' list** – please inquire!

Pharmacies
Several pharmacies on New Road at the Gate. Medications can be obtained without a prescription. They are cheaper than in the West.

Nightlife
Casino Nepal in Hotel Soaltee. Open 24 hours a day all week long. Ask in the hotel about free transport, Tel: 270244/271011. **The Galaxy**, discotheque in the Everest Hotel open every day from 9 pm-2 am, except Mondays. Entrance only for members and guests of the hotel, admission 400 rupees per couple. **The Damaru**, discotheque in Hotel Woodlands. Irregular opening times. Admission 350 rupees per couple.

Culture
Besides performances for the Nepalese in the Royal Nepal Academy and the Rastriya Nach Ghar (National Dance Theater) there are various dance and musical groups in Kathmandu:

The New Himalchuli Culture Group: At the Hotel Shanker, Lazimpat, from seven to eight in the evening. Tel: 410151. Admission 75-100 rupees per person.

The Everest Cultural Society: At the Hotel De l'Annapurna, Durbar Marg, from 7-8 pm. Tel: 220676. Admission 90-150 rupees per person. Nepalese and Indian musical pieces and ghazals are performed in the Everest Hotel, in the Ghar-e-kabab Restaurant, Durbar Marg, and in the Moti Mahal, Durbar Marg. The Soaltee, Yak & Yeti, Everest, Shangrila, Shanker, Himalaya, Vajra, and Kathmandu Hotels as well as K. C.'s Restaurant in Thamel have specially announced programs.

Restaurants

Especially in Kathmandu –, and here and there in Patan – there is something for all tastes. In Bhaktapur as well as in Dhulikhel and Nagarkot you can get Nepalese, European and Chinese dishes in the better-known hotels.

NEPALESE: **Bhanchha Ghar**, Kalamadi (near Durbar Marg). **Nanglo**, Durbar Marg. **Third Eye Restaurant,** Thamel (diagonally opposite the Hotel Star). **Kathmandu Kitchen**, Jamal. **Tushita**, Kanti Path. **Naachgar**, Durbar Marg.

INDIAN: Is especially tasty at the **Ghar-e-kabab**, Durbar Marg. **Third Eye Restaurant** (the chicken chilli is delicious), Thamel. **Everest Hotel**, New Baneswar. **Oberoi**, Tahachal. **Ambassador Hotel** (especially the tandoori dishes), Lazimpat. **Moti Mahal**, Durbar Marg. **Shiva's Sky**, New Road. **Gorkha Palace**, Thamel.

NEWAR: **Thayabbhu**, on the way to the Shanker-Lazimpath hotel.

TIBETAN: The oldest restaurant in Thamel is the **Utse** – Tibetan, Mongolian and Chinese cooking. **New Om**, Chetrapati.

THAI: **Him Thai**, Lazimpat, Tel: 418683. **Rium Thai**, Durbar Marg.

CHINESE: **Nanglo** – Chinese Room, Durbar Marg. **Third Eye Restaurant**, Thamel. **Omei Restaurant**, Jyatha. **Arni Ko Room**, Durbar Marg.

JAPANESE: **Fuji**, Kanti Path (small park). **Koto**, Durbar Marg. **Kushi Fuji**, Durbar Marg. **Himalaya Hotel**, Sahid Sukra Marg. **Kubarayas**, Thamel.

EUROPEAN: **G's Terrace**, Thamel, quiet roof terrace, Tel: 416717. **K.C.'s**, Thamel (steaks, pastries and pizzas). **K.C.'s Consequence**, Balaju (north west of the ringroad, beautiful garden). **Third Eye**, Thamel. **Nanglo**, Durbar Marg (try the tomato soup and sizzlers). **La Dolce Vita**, Thamel (good Italian food). **Rooftop**, Everest Hotel, New Baneswor. **Gorkha Grill Soaltee**, Tahachal. **Cimney Room Yak and Yeti,** Durbar Marg. **Garden Restaurant Summit Hotel**, Patan, Kupondol. **Aloha Inn**, Jwalakhel.

GOOD BREAKFAST RESTAURANTS: **K.C.'s** (fresh waffles). **Mike's Breakfast**, Naxal, near Police Headquarters, quiet sunny garden, with an art gallery. **Nanglo**, Durbar Marg. **Annapurna Coffee Shop**, Durbar Marg, good cappuccino, fresh breads. **Mona Lisa**, Thamel.

Shopping

KATHMANDU: The most important shopping districts are in Thamel, the Durbar Marg, Indra Chowk, New Road and on the Durbar Square. Indian Kashmiris offer leather goods and "silk" rugs. In the various boutiques on the Durbar Marg and in Thamel there are chic designer fashions. Shakun's famous **Wheels-Boutique** near the Hotel Annapurna offers custom made clothing.

BODHNATH: Tibetan every-day items, textiles, jewelry, thangkas (painted religious scrolls), turquoise items and rugs.

BALAJU INDUSTRIAL AREA (near Kathmandu): Factories processing silk and cotton, with their own shops –; they also have especially beautiful Pashimi-shawls and scarves.

SVAYAMBHUNATH: Tibetan articles, thangkas, bronze statues and masks.

PATAN: At the Durbar Square, in Jawalakhel (Tibetan camp with carpet weavery) and in the Industrial Estate, Lagankhel (woodcarvers, bronze and metal casters, precious stones).

BHAKTAPUR: On Taumadhi Tole, the Durbar Square and Dattatraya Plaza (cooperative for the preservation of traditional crafts with beautiful products such as masks, textiles, pottery works and puppets, thangkas).

THIMI (near Bhaktapur): Pottery workshops and mask makers.

KIRTIPUR: Textile workshops, weaveries.

Public / Entertainment Parks

Gokarna-Safari-Park, behind Bodhnath (elephant and horse riding are possible).

Balaju Garden with 22 dragon-headed water-fountains, on the way to Trisuli (with a public swimming pool).

Thankot-Tribuvan-Park, on the road to Pokhara (flower garden).

Godavari Botanical Garden, behind Patan (park-grounds, conservatory and ponds near the Jesuit School, below the Phulchowki Mountains). The zoo in Patan near the Tibetan camp of Jawalakhel.

Museums / Art Galleries

National Museum of Kathmandu: This is located in the quarter of Chhauni near the Svayambhunath Stupa. Weapons, jewelry, bronze statues, metal works from Patan and thangkas. Open daily except Tuesdays and holidays from 10 am to 3.30 pm.

Tribhuvan Museum Kathmandu: This is located in the Hanuman Dhoka Palace at the Durbar Square. The life of King Tribhuvan and his successors is portrayed. In addition there is a coin collection. Beautiful views from Basantapur Tower. Cameras are not permitted. Open daily except Tuesdays from 10 am to 4.30 pm.

Museum of Natural History: Located near Svayambhunath, this museum shows an outstanding collection of the fauna and flora of Nepal. Opening times from 10 am to 4 pm.

Nepal Association of Fine Arts (NAFA): In Naxal, with exhibitions and sale of contemporary Nepalese art. Opening times from 10 am to 5 pm.

Siddhartha Art Gallery: In Kanti Path, with contemporary art especially of Sashi Kala Tiwari, Manohar Man Poon and Jagdish Chitrakar. Opening times are from 12 noon to 7 pm.

The Gallery Palpasa: In Kantipath, with contemporary art; one of the oldest galleries. Opening times from 12 noon to 7 pm, Sunday through Friday.

B.B. Thapa Art Gallery: In the Hotel Soatee Road, Kalamati; with classical and naive paintings of Buddhist themes.

Art Museum in Bhaktapur: This museum is located in the Palace of the Fifty Five Windows at the Durbar Square. With exhibitions of fascinating old sculptures and paintings from the Newar. Opening times from 10 am to 5 pm.

Hermitage Art Gallery and Studio: Situated behind the Bodhnath Stupa; it is a non-profit art center with weekly painting classes and studios.

Indigo Gallery: Tel: 411724 (near Mike's Breakfast).

Festivals

BHAKTAPUR: New-Year's Festival, *Bisket Jatra*, Carriage Festival.

A one week festival in the entire valley. The goddess Bhadrakali and the god Bhairav are paraded through the city on temple carriages – mid-April.

Gai Jatra, Dance of the Dead – mid-August, day after the full moon.

Bhimsen Jatra – end of August, day before the new moon.

Sakimala Punhi – November, full moon, evening.

THIMI: New Year's Festival – mid-April.

PATAN: *Rato Matsyendranath Jatra*, Carriage festival, symbolic ushering in of the rainy season – second half of April until June.

PATAN, KIRTIPUR: *Krishnasthami*, the god Krishna's birthday – end of August.

KATHMANDU VALLEY: *Buddha Jayanti*, Buddha's birthday – May, full moon. *Gai Jatra*, dance of the dead – mid-August, the day after the full moon.

KATHMANDU: *Seto-Matsyendranath-Jatra*, carriage festival in honor of the god by the same name – end of March.

Ghode-Jatra, horse-racing at Tundikhel Square, on the next day a sword-fight takes place, based on the ritual conflict among the goddesses of Kathmandu – March/April, new moon.

Indra-Jatra, festival for Indra, the living goddess Kumari, and the king – September, full moon.

NEWAR TOWNS: *Gathamuga*, spirit exorcism – end of July, the day before the new moon.

Gumla, Buddhist procession month – beginning of August, after the new moon.

PASHUPATINATH: *Tij*, fasting festival of women – August/September.

Shivaratri, big meeting of pilgrims and ascetics in honour of the god Shiva – end of February.

Vatsalajatra, ritual struggle between the godess Vatsala and Shiva – March/April, new moon.

Bala Chaturdasi, night festival of lights for the dead – November/December.

BUDHANILAKANTHA: *Haribodhini*, the awaking of the god Vishnu from his cosmic sleep – October/November.

BODNATH: *Magh Purnima*, festival of the thousand lights – February, full moon.

Lhosar, Tibetan New Year – beginning to middle of February.

Trekking Offices

Asian Encounters, Nagpokhari Nayabato, Tel: 413612. **Ama Dablam Trekking Ltd.**, Thamel, Tel: 415372.

Annapurna Mountaineering and Trekking Pvt. Ltd., Durbar Marg, Tel: 222999. **Bhrikuti Himalayan Treks,** Nagpokhari Nayabato, Tel: 417459 (including mountain bike tours). **Himalayan Rover Trek**, Lazimpat, Tel: 226141. **Himalayan Horizon**, airport area, Pokhara, Tel: 253. **Himalayan Explorer**, Jyatha, Tel: 2-16142. **Lama Excursions**, Durbar Marg, Tel: 220186. **Lukla Treks**, Lazimpat, Tel: 415346. **Natraj Trekking**, Kantipath, Tel: 226644.

Summit Nepal Trekking, Kopundol, Tel: 525408. **Sherpa Trekking Service**, Kalamadi, Ghantaghar, Tel: 220423. **Sherpa Society**, Jyatha, Tel: 470361. **Sagarmatha Trekking**, Thamel, Tel: 225875. **Yeti Trekking Ltd.**, Kantipath, Tel: 225982.

Rafting Agencies

Karnali River Expedition, Thamel, Tel: 225896. **Himalayan River Exploration**, Lazimpat, Tel: 418491. **Journeys White Water Rafting**, Thamel, Tel: 4-10093. **Great Himalayan River**, Durbar Marg, Tel: 410937. **Rapid Adventure**, Thamel, Tel: 416751.

Taxi

Yellow Cab, 414565. **Night Taxi**, 224374

Tourist Information

KATHMANDU: Basantapur, Tel: 220818. Airport, Tel: 470537.

PATAN: Patan Dhoka, Tel: 523692.

1 Far Western
2 Mid Western
3 Western
4 Central
5 Eastern

CHINA

NEPAL

Jumla
Dolpo
Mustang
Annapurna
Pokhara Valley Pokhara
Langtang
Helambu Solu Eastern
Kath.Khumbu Nepal
Kathmandu Valley
Terai

Lucknow

Biratnagar

BANGL.

Patna

Allahabad
Varanasi

INDIA

Rajshahi

SUMMITS AND LAKES

POKHARA

BEGNAS AND RUPA LAKES

POKHARA

The small town of **Pokhara** has a completely different atmosphere than the capital city. Pokhara has about 150,000 inhabitants, and lies in the heart of a 900-meter-high valley by the same name, some 200 kilometers west of Kathmandu. If you want to get some relief from the screeching traffic and restless agitation of the Kathmandu bazaars, then you should come here and set off for the shore of the Phewa, Begna or Rupa Lake, where in clear weather, lying back under banana fronds, you can enjoy a unique mountain panorama. The summits of the Annapurna and Dhaulagiri Massifs are mirrored in the lake; the view of the "Nepalese Matterhorn"– Macchapuchare – is especially impressive. It is also called the fish-tail-mountain because its curiously-shaped peak looks like one, but it can't really be recognized as such until you engage in one of the exhausting but exhilarating treks which start from Pokhara into the interior Himalayan valleys. There were originally seven freshwater lakes – called *pokhari* – located in this valley, from which its name was also derived.

Preceding pages: Macchapuchare and Annapurna seen from Lake Phewa.

The largest of these is the five- kilometer-long **Phewa Lake**, which at its narrowest point measures 100 meters across and at its widest two kilometers. Located at its southernmost side, along the **Pardi** quarter, there is an artificial dam with a hydroelectric generator, which was put back into repair a few years ago.

Picturesque villages, gently rolling chains of hills with terraced fields of rice, subtropical forests and the unique silhouette of the Himalayas, whose gigantic mountains are only 50 kilometers away and seem so close that you could grasp them, are the great attraction of this place: On the left juts the **Dhaulagiri** (8,167 meters), followed by **Annapurna South** (7,219 meters) and **Annapurna I** in the background (8,091 meters), then the pyramid-like tower of **Macchapuchare**, one of the holy mountains, whose peak has never been conquered (6,993 meters), **Annapurna III** (7,555 meters), **Annapurna IV** (7,525 meters), and next to it **Annapurna II** (7,937 meters). Further to the right from there you can also recognize in good weather the **Lamjung Himal** (6,983 meters), east of it the **Manaslu** (8,163 meters) and finally the **Himalchuli** (7,893 meters).

One legend purports that at one time in the place of Phewa Lake there lay a beautiful valley, which was inhabited by gracious and well-to-do people. However, over time they became ever more uncharitable and inhumane. The gods, who didn't want to believe this, sent down to the valley one of their number in the shape of a beggar, in order to test the people there. Nowhere did he receive any charity. Only one poor old couple had compassion for him. Blazing with fury, the gods decided to annihilate the valley. Only the two poor people were warned; they fled to a nearby parcel of high ground. While they were still on their way they became aware of a thunderous din, as huge masses of water deluged into the valley and completely inundated it.

Like so many legends, this story has a real background. In all probability, a tectonic quake, which occur frequently in Nepal – or natural erosion – unleashed a catastrophe about 600 years ago, which led to a glacial lake pouring into the valley and also partially covering the plain with water.

History of Pokhara

In spite of its central location and ideal climate, the valley has never gained the cultural and political significance of Kathmandu and its neighboring cities, although most important trade routes between India and Tibet does pass through here. Rather, Pokhara crystallized in the course of the centuries into a marketplace, for it was the gathering place for the surrounding population, such as the Gurung, Newar and Magar. Especially in late autumn, when the mountain inhabitants from the interior valleys of the Himalayas come here to spend the winter, the mule caravans of the Thakali and the Baragaonli crowd the bazaar streets, and everywhere the Lopa from Mustang hawk dried herbs, spices and fossils from the upper Kali-Gandaki River.

It can be assumed that the first settlers in the valley were Gurung, whose origins are just as unclear as the history of the valley. Like the Magar, it is also said that the Gurung have an astounding ability to adapt themselves to changing religious, geographic and cultural circumstances. They were originally known as goat and sheep herders, and still today many of the Gurung living in the surrounding higher villages often keep a dozen or so goats or sheep. Almost every village has a herd of some 200 to 300 animals. From April to September they are pastured on high-altitude meadows, where the weather is cooler and the variety of grasses and herbs far greater. In October the herds are driven down the hills – sometimes all the way to Terai, in order to sell them profitably for the Dasain festival which occurs in October. Today most of the Gurung people live as farmers and livestock breeders in villages, whose comfortable financial situation comes from the pensions of the men who have served as Gurkha soldiers. As a result, the jewelry of their women is particularly elaborate and sumptuous.

Political impulses brought the Rajputan princes out of India in the 14th century, with whom Chetris and Brahmas fled into the Pokhara Valley. Then, from the little village Kaski-Kot north of Phewa Lake, the fore-fathers of the conquerer Prithvi Narayan Shah pushed onward to Gurkha, from where the Kathmandu Valley would later be conquered. The resulting integration of the Kaski – or Pokhara – region into the Kingdom of Nepal brought an economic revival. Then the Newar from the Kathmandu Valley came and settled in Pokhara, building multi-storied houses and temples and establishing artisan workshops. The one-time settlement took on an increasingly urban character. When the trade route to Tibet was closed off in 1959 after the flight of the Dalai Lama, many of those Thakali employed as middlemen between India and Tibet had to seek a new place of residence. A few of them settled in Pokhara and, being clever businessmen

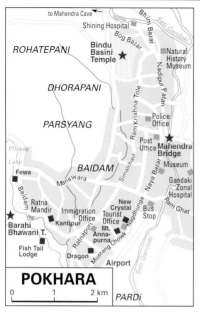

POKHARA

0   1   2 km   PARDi

and hotel owners, they made a decidedly positive contribution to the city's economic development.

The main attractions in Pokhara are the shores of Phewa Lake along the **Baidam** and **Pardi** sections of the city. In contrast to both of the other larger lakes located on the way to Kathmandu – Lakes Begnas and Rupa – this area is accommodating to tourists. Countless little souvenir businesses – primarily owned by Tibetans – restaurants, small hotels and lodges in all price classes; boat, bicycle and more recently wind surf-board rental shops are all to be found here.

Earlier – when Nepal was still the dreamland for hippies rather than trekkers, and Freak-Street in Kathmandu still housed genuine freaks, **Pokhara Lake Side** was *the* secret tip. Only a few little lodges and hotels such as the Swiss Cottage (still in existence) operated at that

Right: The summit of Macchapuchare, one of the sacred mountains of Nepal.

time, and the "long term guests" rented small cottages near the lakeshore for themselves. Today, there is a number of restaurants here, with a varied and tasty cuisine. The more exclusive **Fish Tail Lodge** in quiet, beautiful surroundings, offers excellent buffet meals. The bar of the Fish Tail, with its lovely fireplace, is the right place to celebrate at the end of a successful trek.

The scene around and about the big old "newspaper tree", from which the fast and comfortable Swiss Buses still begin their journey to Kathmandu or the Indian border is the place to get the latest information about the surrounding trekking regions. You will always find somebody who has just arrived back from Manang, or an eyewitness of the fact that the Annapurna Base Camp is overcrowded. Agents at the lake or directly at the airport offer the opportunity to book an organized trekking tour, a bout of river rafting or an excursion into the Chitwan Park at the last minute.

The swimming possibilities all around the lake are really excellent – as long as you don't plunge into the cool water right where the locals wash and do their laundry. But here too, the water was much cleaner ten years ago when there weren't so many tourists!

A rewarding trip might be a brief visit to the little **Barahi Bhawani Temple,** on a small island not far from the lake's edge. Barahi is thought of as a manifestation of the goddess Kali; on festival days animal sacrifices are also offered to her here. If you still have a little more time, you should take a trip to the the other side of the lake and climb up the hill there. About half-way up is a little hut near Gurung peasant houses where mostly fish, but also other delicious titbits are offered. From the top, where there is a new **Peace Stupa**, you can enjoy the overwhelming view over the lake and out to the ice-giants of the Himalayas. A Buddhist temple with a look-out terrace has been

erected near the stupa, with Japanese help.

Be careful during the monsoon season when boating! Within the shortest time, a storm can brew up over the lake, and you should make sure that you can get back to the Baidam shore in time. Also located in the neighborhood of the boat docks is the royal palace with a guest house, strictly shielded from the general hubbub. The medow on the south shore has been transformed into a park.

The departure point for many trekking tours is the former **Shining Hospital**, which can be reached either by taxi or the city bus. The hospital, which had been for a long time the only one within a radius of several days' hiking, has been replaced by the modern Western Regional (Gandak) Hospital in Pokhara. On the large plaza in front of the former Shining Hospital, busses and porters await new customers. One can drive to **Suikhet** or **Lumle** on the recently completed Baglung road. The "classic" Annapurna tours start from Suikhet and Lumle.

Pokhara City

Since the end of the 1960's, this little city has developed rapidly, following the completion of the overland roads from Kathmandu to Pokhara and from there on down to **Sunauli** at the Indian border. Pokhara became the administrative center of the Gandaki zone (one of Nepal's 14 administrative zones). Within the shortest time, schools, hospitals and administration buildings were built. Flights connecting the city with Kathmandu take place several times daily. Since the middle of the 1980s, an additional road to **Baglung** in central Nepal has been built under Chinese management. From a sleepy market spot, Pokhara has developed into a typical bazaar city, unfortunately featuring haphazardly erected high rises, a sure sign of overly-hasty growth.

Pokhara is divided into three zones: The **bazaar**, the area around the **Airport** and **Baidam/Lake Side** on the shore of Phewa lake. The **Tibetan Centers** are

107

particularly interesting and significant in recent history. These were originally conceived as refugee camps for the Tibetans who were driven out of their homeland in 1959 by the Chinese. At that time Nepal put land and building materials at the disposal of the refugees, so that they could build a new home for themselves here.

Three Tibetan settlements are located in the Pokhara area. **Hyengja**, in the north, lies on the trekking route into the mountains, **Chorsanghu** is close to the big bus station, while the Tibetan village of **Tashiling** is in the south, behind the airport and is known for its carpet weaveries, other craft workshops, schools and health station.

In the meantime, many of the Tibetans who have settled here have managed to achieve a moderate degree of prosperity through skill and hard work. Some of

Above: A young girl from the Pokhara Valley. Right: Women setting young rice in a paddy.

them have even established their own souvenir businesses. These can primarily be found along the lakeshore in Baidam and Pardi.

The **Seti Gorge** numbers among the particular natural beauties in this area. At its narrowest point it is only 4.5 meters in width. Here, in the course of millenia, the Seti River has gnawed its way to a depth of 45 meters into the valley floor. You can get a good view into the gorge from the **Mahendra Bridge** (Mahendra Pul) in the Pokhara Bazaar. The 1,590-meter-high **Kanhu Danda Hill** stands in the northeast of Pokhara; it can be reached from the Bazaar over the Mahendra Bridge.

About seven kilometers north of the Bazaar you can get to the **Mahendra Cave,** a stalagmite cave which to date has been only incompletely explored and is therefore only partially accessible. Take care: It is unlit.

In the Bazaar itself you might take a rewarding little excursion to the **Bindu Basini Temple**, located on the northern

edge of the city. Sundays and Tuesdays an enthusiastic crowd gathers here to offer their sacrifices to a goddess – an incarnation of Parvati, the spouse of Shiva.

There is a striking difference between the tourist-populated lakeshore promenade of Phewa Lake, and the Bazaar section of the city, which has now become relatively hectic. It is almost impossible to imagine that until 1961 even primitive ox-carts were unknown here and, at first, had to be brought in by airplane.

BEGNAS AND RUPA LAKES

The **Begnas Lake** is not yet so frequented as Phewa Lake, but is just as beautiful. It is picturesquely located at the foot of a hill, nestled in among rice and mustard fields, citrus trees and papaya groves. You can get there by public bus in a half-hour ride from Pokhara over the road to Kathmandu – the **Prithvi Rajmarg**.

From the bus station on the southwestern shore of Begnas lake there are two possibilities to gain access to the terrain. Either you set off to the left and go directly to the lakeshore, where you can cross the lake with a row-boat, or perhaps an indigenous log canoe, or you turn to the right on a hike that takes you past village-like settlements of Chetris and Gurung. After about one and a half hours you arrive at a knoll from which you have a lovely panoramic view over the three-square-kilometer Begnas Lake and the somewhat smaller **Rupa Lake,** which is connected to it. Everywhere along the way, you will meet curious villagers who aren't accustomed to seeing foreigners in this still relatively undiscovered region. There are two possibilities from here: Either choose the same route back, or proceed by way of a medley of twisting paths down to the edge of Begnas Lake.

The residents of this touristically untested area are very helpful and – for an appropriate payment – will gladly row you back across the lake to the exit point near the bus station, which is still far away.

109

POKHARA

Accommodation

LUXURY: **Fish Tail Lodge**, Lakeside Pardi, Tel: 20071. **New Hotel Chrystal**, Airport Nagh Dhunga, Tel: 20035. *MODERATE:* **Dragon Hotel**, Pardi, Tel: 20391; managed by Thakalis, with especially beautiful garden. **Mount Annapurna**, Airport Side, Tel: 20027.
BUDGET: **Fewa**, Lakeside Baidam, Tel: 21051. **Ashok Guest House**, Damside, Tel: 20374. **Garden**, Damside, Tel: 20870. **Mona Lisa**, Damside, Tel: 20836. **Tragopan**, Damside, Tel: 21708. **The Kantipur**, Lakeside-Baidam, Tel: 20887. **The Hungry Eye**, Lakeside-Baidam, Tel: 20908.

Restaurants

Besides the restaurants in the larger hotels, there are countless places to eat in Pardi and Baidam-Lakeside. Try the cakes at **The Hungry Eye**, Baidam-Lakeside. Besides European cuisine, the **Dragon Hotel** offers Nepalese and Indian dishes. In **Mount Annapurna**, ask for the Tibetan momos. The **Rodee-Steak-House** at the damside (views of the lake) offers besides the holy cow, bashfully called "filet" on the menu, delicious tandoor dishes and stuffed nan breads. At the shores of the Baidam, quiet and on the lake, you will find **Fewa Park** and **Boomerang.**

Hospitals

Gandaki Zonal Hospital, in eastern Pokhara, in the quarter of Ranipauwa. However, in case of serious illness, it is advisable to fly to Kathmandu.

Museums

Annapurna Regional Museum: Vivid portrayal of Nepal's plant and animal world. The butterfly collection is especially worth seeing. On the first floor is a presentation on the Annapurna Conservation Area Project. Located in the Prithvi Narayan campus in northern Pokhara. Open daily (except Saturdays) from 10 am to 4 pm. **Regional Museum**: Small museum on the surrounding area. Between the bus station (China Chowk) and Bazaar. Open daily (except Tuesdays) from 10 am to 4 pm.

Telecommunication / Post

The post office is located in the area of Mahendra Pul in the bazaar. Opening times: Sunday to Thursday 10am to 4 pm, Friday 10 am to 3 pm.

Getting There

FLIGHTS: The Royal Nepalese Airline, Necon Air, Everest Air and Nepal Airways offer daily flights from Kathmadu to Pokhara and vice versa. Flying time is ca. 35 minutes. Book well ahead! The RNCA office in Pokhara is right near the airport. With flights from Pokhara to Kathmandu, sit on the left side – because of the mountain view. Daily flights are also offered from Pokhara to Jomosom and Baglung. There are occasional flights to Manang.
BUS: With the Swiss Bus or other private companies you can ride for 250 rupees from Kathmandu to Pokhara in five to seven hours. The boarding point is behind the post office at Bhimsen Tower in Kathmandu. A night bus also departs from there for about 100 rupees. With the local bus (100 rupees), which starts from the central bus station opposite Thundikel Square, the drive takes eight to ten hours. In Pokhara, most of the buses to Kathmandu or to Bhairahava/Butwal on the Nepalese/Indian border depart from the bus station on China Chowk. Tickets can be obtained at hotels or directly at the bus station – buy well ahead!
CARS / TAXI: Taxis to Pokhara cost about US$ 20.

Tourist Information

The **Tourist Office** is located opposite the airport, Tel: 20028. Open from Sunday to Thursday, 9 am to 6 pm, on Friday until 4 pm.

Visa Extensions / Trekking Permits

The **Immigration Office** is reached by going from Baidam along the lakeshore road, turn left at the first big intersection in Pardi. Open Sunday through Thursday from 10 am – 4 pm, in summer until 5 pm, and Friday until 3 pm. *Note*: visa extensions and trekking permits are only handled Sunday to Thursday 10.30 am – 12.30 pm and Friday until 12 noon (see pp. 238, 243)

Shopping

On the lakeshore streets there are countless souvenir shops. There are two larger Tibetan camps with carpet weaveries, where souvenirs are also sold. **Tashi Palkel** is located near Devin's Fall in the south of Pokhara, and **Hyengja** is about an hour's walk north-west of the town. You can also get there by bus or taxi on the new Baglung road.
On the lakeshore and in the bazaar you can buy so-called *saligrams:* these are fossils which are found in the river-bed of the Kali Gandaki. In the bazaar north of the post office you will find the photography

shop Bishwa Shakya – Zenith Photo – where you can buy beautiful posters of Pokhara and its surrounding. Ask in the **Mount Annapurna Hotel** about the Tibetan artist Mr. Lutup. He paints impressive pictures with Tibetan motifs.

Various

Bicycle and Motorcycle Rental: It is possible to rent bicycles and motorcycles along the lakeshore road. Motorcycles can be also rented between China Chowk (bus station) and the bazaar. Repair shops are also located there. However, prices are generally higher in Pokhara than in Kathmandu.

A **camp site** with toilets is located in Baidam-Lakeside directly on the lakeshore.

Boat Rental: A boat costs about 80 NR, with rower ca. 150 NR.

Folk Dancing: In the larger hotels folk-dance groups perform from time to time. Watch for the corresponding announcements. In the Dragon Hotel and in the Fish Tail, in a hall especially devoted to this purpose, the performances are especially impressive (100 NR).

Taxis: Group taxis and taxis drive everywhere. You usually have to dicker about the price.

Ponys: Ponys can be rented at Pony-Trek opposite the airport for ca. 200-300 rupees per day. Tel: 20253.

Buses: A bus goes back and forth between the Bazaar and the lake.

Views: Many hotels have nice roof terraces, from which one can get a lovely view of the mountain panorama. Do not miss the sunrise! In good weather, you can see, from left to right Dhaulagiri (8,167 m) far in the distance, then Annapurna South (7,219 m), Annapurna I (8,091 m), Macchapuchare (fishtail mountain, 6,993 m), Annapurna III (7,556 m), Annapurna IV (7,525 m), Annapurna II (7937 m), further right to the east Lamjung Himal (6,985 m), Mansalu (8,156 m), and way to the right, Himalchuli (7,893 m).

Excursions

Because Pokhara is very sprawling, it is definitely worth renting a bicycle. Besides the **Mahendra Cave** in the north of the town or **Devin's Waterfall** in the south by the dam, you can also reach the **Begnas** and **Rupa Lakes**. From the bus station out to the Begnas Lake it's about thirteen kilometers – first on the road to Kathmandu, then after about ten kilometers turn left on the gravel road that leads directly to the village of Begnas. Then walk the rest of the way to the lake. From there, you can either hike further along the west shore or take a boat trip to the

north shore. From there it takes about thirty minutes to climb **Pachbaya Hill**, from which you have a wonderful view of the Begnas and Rupa Lakes. In two hours you can hike from here back to the village of Begnas. You can also take a taxi or a bus to the Begnas Lake.

Kandu Danda Hill is a 1,560-meter-high mountain with particularly fine views northeast of Pokhara. In good weather, the view of the Dhaulagiri and Annapurna massifs is overwhelming. On the eastern peak of the mountain there is a fortress ruin (**Kanhu Kot**) from the 18th century. The hike up Kanhu Danda Hill takes about four hours there and back. Begin at the Mahendra Bridge (Pul) over the Seti River, and hike eastwards up to the Buddhist monastery which is visible from a long way off. Just short of it, a path to the left leads up to the mountain.

Sarankot is 1,600 meters high, northwest of Pokhara directly above Phewa Lake. A day-trip to this marvellous viewpoint is quite breathtaking, because you have a steep hike up the mountain; however, the view is full compensation for the hardship you must endure to get there. You will also find an old ruin of a fortress and a temple. Restaurants and tea shops edge the trail, which begins in the Pokhara Bazaar at the Bindu Basini Temple. You reach the top in around three hours.

On the way back, you can climb straight down the mountain to Baidam-Lakeside in about two hours, on a beautiful path winding past small settlements, with a great view of Phewa Lake.

GORKHA

Accommodation

MODERATE: **Gorkha Hill Resort**, Tel: 227929 (Reservation in Kathmandu)
BUDGET: **Hotel Gorkha Bisauni** with restaurant.

Getting There

Buses from Kathmandu to the 138-kilometer-distant Gurkha depart daily from the bus station in Kathmandu. The ride takes about six hours and costs ca. 60 rupees. Buses from Gurkha to Pokhara cover the 110 kilometers in about four or five hours. The ride costs 50 rupees.

PALPA / TANSEN

Half-way between Pokhara and the Indian/Nepalese border is the high-altitude village of **Palpa/Tansen**. *MODERATE:* **Hotel Srinagar**, Tel: 20212, with adjoining restaurant.

1 Far Western
2 Mid Western
3 Western
4 Central
5 Eastern

CHINA

Jumla
Dolpo
Mustang

Annapurna
Pokhara Pokhara
Valley
Langtang
NEPAL Helambu Solu
Kath.Khumbu
Kathmandu Valley
Terai
Eastern
Nepal
5

Lucknow

Biratnagar

BANGL.

Patna

Allahabad
Varanasi

INDIA

Rajshahi

ON OLD PILGRIM TRAILS

ANNAPURNA BASE CAMP
JOMOSOM-MUKTINATH TRAIL
MANANG TREKKING

TREKKING IN THE ANNAPURNA REGION

By far the most well-known hiking routes in Nepal among trekking tourists are the Jomosom-Muktinath Trail and the well-trodden path to the **Annapurna Base Camp.** Apart from the beautiful landscape and mountain scenario along the deepest valley on earth, going by the Dhaulaghiri and Annapurna Massifs, the hiker walks for part of the time down one of the oldest trade routes between the Indian subcontinent and trans-Himalayan Tibet.

It is especially interesting to come into contact with the various inhabitants of the central hill regions and the adjoining valleys of the Himalayas. Although the paths here are extremely well beaten – particularly in October and the late spring – and the local residents have been used to foreigners and their apppearance for many years, they still show as great an interest in their foreign guests and their ways of life as they ever did.

There is now an ample selection of small lodges and hotels along both trekking routes and we needn't go into detail

Left: Ulleri on the Muktinath trek marks the end of a long climb.

about them. The *bhatti*-shops, in which one is invited to linger and drink tea, can also be found everywhere along the hiking paths. They are ideal places to learn some local lore. One can carry on conversations in English in most of the villages. Nevertheless it is still advantageous to pick up a few of the most important Nepali words and phrases (see the Guidelines at the end of this book).

Most of the population of this region knows Nepali, although the individual ethnic groups such as the Magar, Gurung, Thakali and the residents of Mustang – the Baragaonlis and the Lopa – speak their own languages.

In spite of the flight from the land which is also to be observed here in Nepal, in the last few years many of the ethnic groups in the Annapurna-Dhaulagiri area have either stayed or come back. To some, the ever-increasing number of tourists is an amusing enough attraction to settle down here; for others, the government or foreign partners have taken pains to provide the population with better living conditions. This must be said in order to make clear to the new arrival that the conditions – in comparison to the past – have improved substantially. There are now several small hydroelectric generating stations in many villages. The electricity they produce has

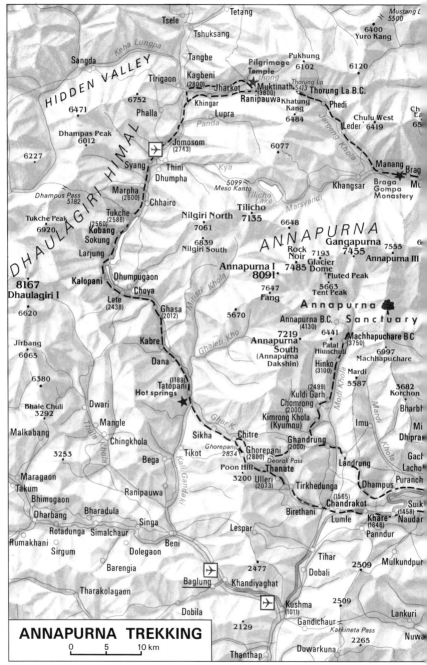

ANNAPURNA TREKKING

0   5   10 km

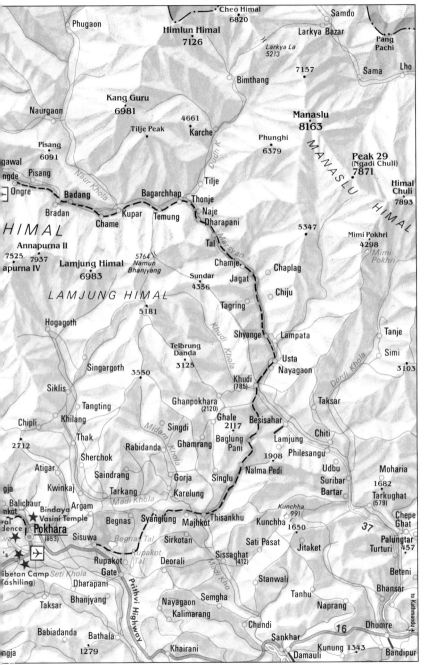

greatly improved the quality of life of the local people.

In those places where there is still no electricity, a plant of appropriate size is at least planned in the next few years or is just under construction. Many Nepalis have a tendency to postpone things of importance. They will generally say: *bholi, bholi* ("tomorrow," which here has the meaning of *soon*) or *khe garne* (what should one do?). However, in the area of **Thak Khola** along the **Kali Gandaki,** where the Thakali live, or in the region of **Ghandrung**, the settlement area of the Gurung, this manner of speaking is less common than elsewhere in Nepal. Improved water facilities, enlarged and shored up hiking trails, supervision of the forests assigned to their villages and more schools make this district stand out

Above: Sometimes trekking requires considerable courage and persistence. Right: Winter landscape on the way to ABC, the Annapurna Base Camp.

visibly from the other rural areas of Nepal.

Organization and Self-Initiative

One contributing element of this is the village communities, which are in part well organized, and ethnic groups, which in general tend to favor not so much Hinduism, but Buddhism and the various ancestor and demon cults, which allow a greater degree of freedom in their personal lives. An organization must also be mentioned which in the last few years has been much talked about as an exemplary project for environmental and cultural protection. The **Annapurna Conservation Area Project,** set up by Dr. Chandra Gurung, has been active since 1986, mainly in the Ghandrung area.

The project is working under the **King Mahendra Trust for Nature Conservation** in Nepal, and – with its planning and individual projects – has made major contributions to the improvement in the quality of life of the population. It is

worth emphasizing here that this is not a governmental institution. As a result, better conditions were created to coordinate planning with the needs of locally affected populations. The intention was not to establish a Nature Reserve, in which the local residents are normally excluded from all considerations, sometimes even re-settled to other another section – or *out* – of their native area altogether.

Trekkers shouldn't be too surprised if they are asked to leave behind a fee for the Annapurna Project when they are at the immigration office in Kathmanu or Pokhara. The money is piped directly to the Project for new kerosene depots, health projects or other efforts. All around the Annapurna trail you will frequently come across information boards which request that you keep the surroundings clean, not only to set a good example for the local residents, but particularly for other hikers!

The Annapurna Conservation Area Project has recently ben extended to the region along the Kali-Gandaki River up to Mustang and beyond the Thorung-La Pass to the area of Manang.

Trekking Routes: Conditions

The treks in the Annapurna region presented here have lost their expeditonary characteristics described very drastically by Maurice Herzog in his classic piece *Annapurna*, about the first ascent. Nowadays you will hike from lodge to lodge. Some of them will even offer a hot shower, almost all of them have simple double rooms and menues offering a wide range of dishes from apple pancakes to Yak cheese pizza. Often, you can chose between several kinds of beer and there is plenty of Khukri rum and Snowland vodka.

If you pack your rucksack cleverly (not more than 12 kg) you can do without a porter. A warm sleeping bag, an anorak, gloves, a cap and climbing boots are absolutely necessary. In case you hire porters to cross the Thorung pass (5,416 m), it is your responsibility, too, that they

have the correct mountain equipment (warm clothing, boots)!

You will actually need a guide for this pass only in winter, and even then you can often join one of the groups with a guide. While occasional landslides and dubious sagging bridges are considered "normal" hazards along the round-Annapurna-trail, the Thorung-La crossing is not without dangers: do not underestimate the possibility of altitude sickness and unexpected snow storms.

The trek around the extended Annapurna massif takes about 20 days. But if you walk the Pokhara-Jomsom-Manang-Dumre route described on page 121 in the opposite direction and start in Dumre, walking up the Marsyandi Valley, the ascent to the Thorung pass will be a bit less exhausing and altitude acclimatisation simpler. If you fly to or from Jomosom (2,743 m), you can make the tour a week

Above: On the ABC trek you cross the timber line at Hinku. Right: Looking toward the summit of Annapurna I from the base camp.

shorter. It is possible to book a charter flight to Manang (STOL landing strip in Hongde, 3,350 m), but not advisable because of the lack of appropriate altitude acclimatisation.

There are busses from the **Tibetan Camp Hyengja** (rug weavery and Tibetan souvenirs) to **Suikhet**, where there are several teahouses. The tarred road to **Baglung** built by the Chinese has been finished, so that you can drive directly to the little village of **Lumle**.

From Suikhet, the climb up to the village of **Naudanda** takes roughly one hour. A beautiful path on the ridge leads parallel to the road westward. The trek in the direction of Jomosom and Muktinath actually begins at this point, for now you have finally taken leave of the Pokhara Valley.

Phewa Lake is located on the other side of the ridge. From there you can get to **Naudanda** in 6 hours, by way of the village of **Sarankot**. This is the long way to Gandrung and the Annapurna Base Camp.

ANNAPURNA BASE CAMP

To take a shorter path into the Annapurna Base Camp you should turn right just after Suikhet (1,100 m), and from there on take the long steep trail up to the opposite mountain ridge to **Dhamphus** (1,700 m), from where IT takes 3 days to reach the village of Chomro. The path leads on to **Landrung** (1,600 m), with the remarkable houses of the Gurung. Here it's worth leaving the straight way to the Base Camp: Descend into the Modi valley, cross over a bridge (1,280 m) and climb steeply up again on steps hewn out of the ground to reach **Gandrung** (2000 m). This village, which is the center of the Annapurna Conservation Area Project, offers an exquisite view of the Annapurna Massif with the great flank of the Annapurna South, the Hiunchuli and the so-called Fish-Tail Mountain – the holy twin summits mountain Macchapuchare (6,993 m).

Gandrung (Gaandruk) is a Gurung village with quite comfortable lodges. You can see the wealth brought by the pensions of British Gurkhas. After about three more hours you progress from Gandrung to **Kimrong Khola** (**Kyumnu**). From there it is only one more hour to **Chomro**, a Gurung village which for some time has also been the location of a major kerosene depot.

In the high tourist season the population consumes almost a thousand liters of kerosene per month for the purpose of cooking. The use of the depot was connected with difficulties in the beginning, because many of the residents thought that using kerosene burners instead of wood stoves would spoil their food. However, once they realized how it could simplify their work in the kitchen the depot began enjoying great popularity among the people of the entire area.

In Chomro you should inquire if the little seasonal lodges along the road and at the Macchapuchare and the Annapurna Base Camp are in service. Otherwise you must be sure to pack sufficient provisions for the next two- to three-day-long tour.

In addition, you should also inquire whether or not there is a danger of avalanches, especially in springtime.

After a three-hour hike from Chomro you reach the mountain pastures of **Kuldi-Garh** (2,500 m). From here on the path continues through dense, humid bamboo rain-forest, and after about five hours you get to **Hinko** (3,100 m), located under an immense cave-like rock overhang. Beyond Hinko comes a stretch where there is danger of avalanches. Ice avalanches tend to break off Hiunchuli, and are often noticed only too late.

From the cave you proceed in a two to three hour long ascent up to the **Macchapuchare Base Camp**, at 3,750 meters altitude, where a cabin is also located. The west flank of Macchapuchare, which up to now has never been ascended, towers above you. A British expedition had failed at Nepal's sacred mountain in 1957, and shortly afterwards a climbing ban was issued. A most intoxicating view of the imposing giant mountains is to be had at the Annapurna Base Camp, which is another two hours away, at 4,130 meters. Those who decide to go still somewhat higher will experience an unforgettable panorama – from left to right the Hiunchuli (6,441 meters), Fang, Annapurna I (8,091 meters), Annapurna III (7,555 meters), Macchapuchare (6,993 meters), the Tent Peak and the Fluted Peak.

Beware of taking your ascents too rapidly. With the slightest hint of nausea you should descend immediately. Altitude sickness – as frequently mentioned in this book – is unpleasant and has already cost some people their lives.

On the return hike you can reach the village of **Ghorepani** (2,800 meters) from Khola and Gandrung by way of a rather indistinct path over the **Deorali Pass**, which lies on the trekking route to Jomosom. Located about half way there

Above: The valley between the Dhaulagiri and Annapurna massifs. Right: Beyond Jomosom the barren landscape is like that of nearby Tibet.

is a guesthouse in **Thante** which is managed by a veteran of the Gurkhas. You should give some consideration to taking a guide with you from Gandrung to Ghorepani. On the next day you can undertake a rewarding one hour ascent from this village onto the 3,200-meter-high **Poon Hill**. From Ghorepani you can get back to Lumle, Naudanda and on to Pokhara in a one or two day hike down the valley via **Birethani**.

JOMOSOM-MUKTINATH TREKKING

You should count on two weeks for the way there and back; for the trek around the Annapurnas a good 20 days. From the 1,458-meter-high **Naudanda** you can reach **Khare** (1,646 meters) in three hours. But thanks to the new Baglung road, you could just take a bus or a taxi from Pokhara all the way to **Lumle** (1,600 m). From there on you continue to **Chandrakot** (1,646 meters), for which you need just short of one and a half

hours. Here you are only one more hour's distance from the first check-post, where you must present your trekking permit. In three hours from there you will reach the village of **Tirkhedunga**, and then the path up begins to get more and more exhausting and burdensome. It will take you at least another hour to get to the little village of **Ulleri** (2,073 meters), and from here on begins the steep ascent to the top of the pass over **Ghorepani** (2,600 meters), which takes at least three hours. From Ghorepani, where primarily Gurung and Magar, but also Chetris and the so-called untouchable castes such as the Damai, Sarki and Kami live, you have a beautiful panoramic view, especially when you climb up **Poon Hill** (see above). The descent from the highest point of the pass can last up to four hours. The road passes by the small inviting village of **Sikha**, and leads on to the river bed of the **Kali Gandaki**, where **Tatopani** (1,189 meters) is located, the village with the hot sulphur springs. It is a pleasure, after the fatiguing descent, to take a

121

bath here. If the forced march should have exhausted you, you will be able to relax a bit in this village and enjoy some pumpkin pie, a local speciality inspired by the Americans, and a delicious variety of citrus fruits.

Here the trek intersects the old traders' path that leads south to the Indian border along the river. Even today you still come across the heavily-loaded mule caravans, or run into a pilgrim on the path to the sanctuary in Muktinath. Tatopani used to be one of the places where the Thakalis from Thak Khola – located further north in the Mustang district – stayed during the winters. Many of them now possess farms and hotels here. Very popular among hikers are the good food and cosy, homelike living-quarters, for which the Thakali people are famous throughout Nepal. However, many of the lodges have suffered when a few years ago a flood – caused by a glacial lake in Tibet which suddenly drained – devastated the

Above: Porters at rest. Right: An encounter between two worlds on the path.

place and destroyed half of the village. Also in **Dana**, the next village – a good hour's distance from Tatopani – the influence of the hospitable Thakalis holds sway. Here there are impressive palatial houses with artistically-carved wooden balconies. Dana was earlier a toll station for traders, which was managed by Thakalis. Today a check-post is located here in order to examine trekking permits. It's a good three hours from Dana to **Ghasa** (2,012 meters), on the way to which you pass by the **Rupse Khola Waterfall** and the little village of **Kabre**.

The climate, which up to now has still been of a pleasant subtropical sort, starts to change here. The landscape, too, undergoes a change from luscious green to dry. Forests of pine replace the deciduous trees, and a different vegetation starts to develop. The human settlements look different as well. Flat, layered-stone buildings border the edges of the trail. This is where the genuine Thakali region begins. And this is also the location, specifically at **Kabre** (1,707 meters), of the most deeply-cut river canyon in the world, through which thunders the Kali Gandaki. It breaks through at a height of 1,700 meters, clamped in between two 8,000-meter peaks of the Himalayas – to the right is the majestic snowcovered Annapurna Massif and to the left the mighty Dhaulagiri.

The area of Thakuri influence extends from Ghasa up to Jomosom here in the southern part of the Mustang district, the capital of which is Jomosom. Following the long, drawn-out village of **Ghasa** along the old pilgrim and trade route to Tibet is the village of **Lete** (2,438 meters) which you can reach in three hours, then **Kalopani, Larjung** and **Kobang** (2,560 meters), two to three hours' distance from Lete, and finally Tukche, at which you arrive after an hour's hike.

As soon as you get behind Kalopani the valley begins to broaden enormously; the Kali Gandaki begins to meander a bit

through an increasingly drier landscape with conifer and pine forests. Now there is no longer a trace of the glorious trader history of the Thakuri to be found. Besides agriculture and livestock breeding they have acted as toll-collecting *subbhas* since the middle of the 19th century, and as traders between Tibet and India. However, the times when one trader's caravan after the other paraded through these villages are over.

Tukche was the main point of re-loading in its day. You can still admire the palatial stone buildings and the carefully attended mani walls of the rich traders of days gone by. But otherwise, there is nothing left of the industrious activity from back then. The mule caravans, which once transported salt and grains out from Tukche, now rapidly leave the village behind them, setting their courses for **Marpha**, which is now the largest and most important village besides Jomosom.

After the closure of the Tibetan-Chinese border in 1959, trading activities suffered badly. A portion of the Thakalis from Tukche and its surroundings emigrated to more southerly regions. As a result, the quaint little town of Marpha (2,600 meters) has since the end of the 1960's become ever more widely renowned for its fruit and vegetable cultivation, thanks in particular to the government-sponsored **Horticulture Farm**. The farm, known throughout Nepal, is especially famous for its *rakshi* (spirits) distillery, which makes use of the apricots, pears and apples that grow in this area. In the meantime there are already two further distilleries, in Tukche as well as in **Syang**, a small village which is located further north.

The Thakali – Masters of the Valley

The influence of Tibet has led – in addition to a distinctive ancestor-cult – to a syncretism of animistic conceptions connected with the Bön tradition and Lamaism in the forms of the Nyingma School (old school) in the region between Ghasa and Jomosom.

123

The Thakali were segmented into the Tamang-Thakali (from Ghasa to Tukche), the Marpha Thakali (in Marpha) and the Yhulkasompa-Thakali (Syang, Chimang, Thini). The Tamang-Thakali were certainly known throughout Nepal. They placed particular emphasis on being the only ones to be named Thakali, for this name was connected with the power and political influence which they used to possess as privileged traders of salt and grain.

To this day their name is connected with their one-time prestige, because after their re-settlement after 1959, the Tamang-Thakali either took over influential posts in the Nepalese administration, or they built up large businesses and hotels. The orientation toward the Nepalese order of society, which is influenced by Hinduism, has, in the meantime, manifested itself above all in the

Above: A Thakali mule caravan passing through Marpha. Right: A happy sadhu at Muktinath, the end of his pilgrimage.

immigrated Thakali in such a way that the role of ancestral worship, which had once been of central importance in the life-cycle of the Tamang-Thakali, receded further into the background. Also, today the Tamang-Thakali are still in competition with both of the other Thakali groups in the Mustang district, who are principally occupied with agriculture including livestock and fruit cultivation.

In contrast to the Tamang-Thakali, the life-style of the Yhulkasompa-Thakali is much more traditional. It is, for example, thoroughly rewarding to deviate from the trekking route in order to seek out the very beautiful village of **Syang** on the path to Jomosom, which can be reached in one or two hours. You will find prayer flags with mantras written on them, mani walls, and *chörten* everywhere. Perhaps you might also – after payment of a small donation – get to take a peek inside the *gompa* (monastery.) Sometimes there is a monk sitting there painting *thangkas* (cult scroll-paintings).

By **Jomosom** (2,743 meters; district capital) at the latest you will have ascertained that the climate is indeed continuously becoming harsher, and that the landscape has the remote quality reminiscent of a desert. The village is divided into several sections. First of all you encounter the airport, which has a variety of accomodations for those unfortunates who must often wait for days for a flight. You frequently hear stories of tourists being stranded here, cursing and mourning their confirmed booking on the flight home out of Kathmandu. At Jomosom Airport, taking off can be extremely difficult for planes after 10 a.m. due to the notoriously strong winds which begin blowing at that time. Adjacent to the airport grounds there are administrative buildings primarily for the army, which is here to secure the border to Tibet and China – a seven days' distance. Also, a recently constructed check-post is located in this area. The actual heart of the village is connected to this section by a bridge over the Kali Gandaki. On the other side of the bridge there are several especially attractive hotels. There is also a small bank next to a hospital.

Muktinath – Goal of the Pilgrims

Through the Kali Gandaki Valley, which becomes increasingly windy during the day (as it is blowing south to north, trekkers really suffer on the way back), the path continues through the gravelly river-bed and then up steep rock ridges. If you are lucky, you might find ammonite fossils millions of years old, but you can also buy them directly from traders. Our goal is the pilgrimage village of Muktinath (3,800 meters), which is around six hours' distance from Jomosom. There are two ways of getting there. You can hike from Jomosom to **Kagbeni** (2,800 meters) in two hours, with a short break in the *eklai bhatti* (the only rest house anywhere in the area). Kagbeni is the last accessible village to foreigners before the restricted area of northern **Mustang**, the kingdom of Lo. From here

we have the fatiguing ascent to the valley of **Baragaon**, in which Muktinath is also located. Another trail leads over a steep knoll behind the *eklai bhatti* directly into the high-altitude valley. Passing the village of **Khingar** (**Khyenghar**) you reach **Ranipauwa**, a small settlement from which it takes only a few minutes to get to the holy village **Muktinath**, which is located in a little poplar forest.

The population here is plainly distinguishable from the Thakali, in both language as well as appearance and living habits. They are named Baragaonlis – people from Baragaon – and are of Tibetan origin, but they prefer to call themselves Gurung. It is assumed that the southernmost outpost of the Tibetan kingdom was once located here. The chequered villages are reminiscent of pueblos, and the red-plaster Buddhist

gompas – visible from quite a distance – exert a magical power of attraction on the visitor. The living conditions here are as harsh as the climate.

Muktinath was already mentioned around 300 years before the era of the *Mahabharata* epic. Hindus as well as Buddhists make pilgrimages to this village, where Brahma – the creator-god of the Hindus – made a sacrifice "by setting a fire on the water." And, in one small Buddhist gompa, you can actually see slender natural gas flames rising from the ground with jets of water. The Buddhists believe that the great master teacher Padmasambhava (eighth century A.D.) – who bought the Tantric Vajrayana Buddhism to Tibet – used to meditate here. They will be happy to show you his alleged foot prints.

MANANG TREKKING

The crossing over the **Thorung Pass** is the only connecting path between the two large valleys of the **Kali Gandaki** and

Above: The village of Jharkot is only a few minutes walk from Muktinath. Right: The Braga Gompa, high and remote in the Marsyandi Valley.

the **Marsyandi Khola**. In March, when even up here at 4,000 meters the fierce winter begins to slowly let up, the first caravans of porters follow the exhausting trail over the pass, still deep in snow. In October, when the heavier snowfalls start, the Thorung La again separates the two valleys.

Out of Muktinath (3,800 m) it is a steep ascent up to the top of the pass to 5,416 meters. Even if you have now gotten accustomed to long hikes, reaching the top still presents quite a challenge. You should be, therefore, more careful and follow the old mountain-climber's rule of "ascending slowly." By the time you have reached Muktinath, you will be in a high-altitude region, where regardless of physical condition, age or other factors, altitude sickness can break out. Headaches are the first sign of this insidious illness, which – if you disregard it – can have deadly results. Spurious heroics are completely out of place here. The only thing to do is descend to a village at lower altitude, in order to become more acclimatized, and then attempt the climb again.

Crossing over the pass requires two days of hiking, primarily because of the great differences in altitude. Thus it is recommended to spend the night either at about 4,200 meters in a little teahouse or at about 4,800 meters on a well located meadow. Beyond here there is a stunning view of the summits of Dhaulagiri and Tukche Peak (6,920 meters). Between the little teahouse and the Thorung La Base Camp there are no established lodging possibilities. In wintertime, for security reasons you should be equipped with a tent, or at least a bivouac sack when crossing the pass. In the past, blizzards and high moutain sickness have claimed victims in the pass. Besides the cold temperatures at night, there is also the sun, which at these altitudes is not to be underestimated. A good pair of sun glasses and sun protection cream are therefore absolute musts in your backpack.

On the next day you arrive – after a steep and laborious ascent – to the 5,416-

meter-high **Thorung La**. From here you have an incredible panorama over the summits of Annapurna, the Chulu and Pisang Mountains, and the Thorung Peak. The descent continues to the huts of **Thorung Phedi Base Camp** (4,470 m), or to a large camping site about two hours further. From this point on you will again find tea-houses and lodges.

On the next day, you will hike along the upper Marsyandi Valley (called Manangboth) and arrive via Leder (4,200 m) in the large village of **Manang** (3,500 m) with its quarrystone houses. The Manangi are famous and infamous traders. They are intrepid travelers, whose routes today often lead them even as far as Hong Kong or Singapore. Their splendid stone houses are decorated with the colorful prayer flags of the Buddhists, which flap gaily in the wind. The view of the gigantic glacier of the **Glacier Dome** (7,193 m) is also very impressive. Furthermore,

Above: A Nepalese kitchen needs little equipment.

its exceedingly slow movement down the mountainside is accompanied by clearly audible sounds. The houses in the next village, **Braga** (3,450 m), picturesquely perched on a cliff, are also entirely made of stone. They have large roof terraces, aligned to the south. In the cold season, the life of the villagers takes place here under the scarce warm sunshine. Braga also possesses a gompa, worth seeing. Its origin can be traced back to the poet and great yogi Milarepa.

From Manang to Pokhara

The path leads on through the Marsyandi Valley, while the mighty ice-giants of the Annapurna group are still in view. The trail leads through pine and juniper forests, passes by the **Manang Airport** (**Hongde**) – to which charter planes fly – and continues further to the large village of **Pisang** (3,200-3,500 m) at the foot of **Pisang Peak** (6,091 meters). It is a "trekking peak" that can be ascended only with a permission liable to a fee. In Novemer 1994 eleven trekkers from Germany and Switzerland perished here.

The following day, the trail leads you further down through the valley along the river, past the former Tibetan Khampa encampment of **Badang** (2,900 m), site of an apple plantation. The next larger settlement is **Chame** (2,680 m). Nearby you wil find hot springs (*tato pani*).

Down from here to the village of **Tal**, the residents are followers of Tibetan Buddhism, and decorate their houses with colorful prayer banners. The next station on this trekking route is **Shyange** or, two hours further, **Khudi** (785 m).

If you don't want to take the dusty path along the road over **Besisahar** to **Dhumre**, you can hike west from Khudi directly to Pokhara in two or three days of walking. This route leads through the villages of **Nalma Pedi**, **Thisanku** and **Dhal Besi**. Through the **Begnas Valley** you finally reach the **Rupa** and **Begnas Lakes**.

ANNAPURNA / MUKINATH

In almost every village you will find very simple accommodation, which is indicated by signs. However, in the **Gandrung** area and with the Thakali in **Tukche**, **Marpha** and **Jomosom**, besides the really good and wide variety of food, the sanitary facilities are also better than elsewhere. To some extent, there is hot water for a delightful bath!

Festivals
In **November** – *Dekhyop* mask-dance in the buddhistic Nyingmapa monasteries of Tukche and Marpha.
In **March** – *Torungla* bow-and-arrow festival among the Thakali in Tukche.
In **August** – *Yartung* riding festival and competition in Muktinath.
In **September** – *Shyopen Lhawa* village festival of the Thakali in Kobang. (The dates vary – inquire.)

Hospitals
In Jomosom, the district capital with an airport, but in case of severe illness one should immediately fly back to Kathmadu.

Backpack Pharmacy
It is recommended to bring along sterile bandages, water disinfection tablets, medications against joint pain and diarrhea illnesses (frequent shygella and amoeba dysentery, and worms), sun protectants, elastic bandages, medications for colds and inflammations, light analgetics, and antibiotics. You must consult your physician beforehand. Don't distribute any medications to the population.

Telecommunication / Post
Radio installation in **Jomosom** (airport, army base). Postal stations in **Gandrung, Tatopani, Tukche**.

Trekking Season
The best times for trekking are in October and November as well as March through May. Because the monsoon rains only partially reach Thak Khola and the Muktinath region, you can have there a very good hike even in the summer. Note: there are leeches in the area of Gandrung and the lower-lying valleys at this time of the year.

Bank
There is a bank in **Jomosom**; teller windows open according to the usual business hours. Attention: Always inquire concerning any forthcoming holidays, because then the bank is closed.

Distilleries
If you hike from **Tukche** to **Marpha**, located shortly before the entrance to the village is a **horticultural** farm where, under the management of the legendary Pasang Sherpa, the widest variety of vegetable and fruit types (pears, apricots, apples) is grown. The Marpha brandy which is produced here is prized throughout Nepal. I

In Tukche, at Nirjal and Mana Sherchan you can get – besides apple and apricot brandy also orange brandy (oranges from Tatopani). In **Syang**, ask after Bishnu Hirachan's distillery.

Shopping
In the Tibetan camp shortly before **Marpha** when coming form Tukche, there are carpets for sale.
In **Jharkot** and **Muktinath**, shawls and scarves produced by the local population out of yak and goat wool are really worthwhile buys.

Various
The center of the Annapurna Conservation Area Project is in **Gandrung**. Hot springs are found in **Tatopani.**
There is an army base in **Jomosom** – in case a helicopter is needed.
Note: from about 10 am there is a strong backwind from Marpha to Muktinath; on the return trip you're walking into it. For this reason, you should get up early. Between Larjung/Kobang and Jomosom there is electricity.

Getting There
An aircraft to **Jomosom** (grass landing strip) flies several times weekly from Pokhara (ca. 30 minutes) and Kathmandu (ca. 50 minutes). These flights are very dependent on the weather and actually very uncertain. Recently, Nepal Air Charter, Nepal Airways, Everest Air and Necon Airways opened flights there as well. Inquire about the most recent departure times and the latest prices at the airline offices in Kathmandu.
To Pokhara from Kathmandu by bus or flight (p. 110). Starting points for Trekkers: in Pokhara from Phewalake or Bindu Basini Temple. Respectively by taxi or bus on to Sarankot, Nandanda or Lumle (Jomosom-Trek) or to Suiket (ABC-Trek).

Worthwhile Trips
Since 1992, **Lo Manthang** (about 4,000 meters altitude) – the capital of the formerly prohibited region of North Mustang – and the border, which is about a day from Lo Manthang, are accessible from **Jomosom** through Kagbeni. See p. 191.
Note: the **North Mustang** route can only be booked through a trekking agency. Furthermore, a daily fee of US$ 70 is levied (as of 1995).
From **Tukche** up the 5,200-meter-high Dhampus Pass; bring along food, fuel, and a tent.
From **Lete** to the Annapurna Base Camp North over a 4,900-meter-high pass (Thulo Bugin).
From **Thini** (Gaon) near Jomosom to the Meso Kanto Pass (5,100 m) where you can see the Tilicho Lake. On all these excursions, it is vital to pay attention to altitude sickness. Be prepared for self-catering.

Poon Hill with observation tower, 300 meters above Ghorepani, 45 minutes ascent.

TRIP INTO THE
MIDDLE AGES

RARA LAKE

DOLPO

JUMLA

Because of the isolated location of the entire Jumla region, flight is the only recommended way to travel. Otherwise you will have to take a wearying bus journey and make the final approach to your destination on foot, which in itself could really qualify as a separate trekking tour. For the flight connections a RNAC 20-seater Twin-Otter aircraft is employed, but it can only fly when the weather is good. There is a direct flight once a week, but the connection via Nepalganj is better. It flies from Kathmandu as well as from Jumla several times daily (except in the monsoon season). You can only fly to Dunai/Juphal via Nepalganj; from Nepalganj to **Juphal** there are two flights a week.

The fastest way to get to Jumla over land is by public bus, from Kathmandu via Nepalganj to **Surkhet**. Be forewarned, however, that this is a trip for adventurous souls. Travel time is about 46 hours, and you can expect the bus to be crowded. From there it takes seven or eight days on foot, via the villages of Dailekh and Kalikot.

The best way to get to **Dunai**, the dis-

Preceding pages: The deep-blue Phoksumdo Lake near Dolpo Pa.

trict capital, is to take the bus to Pokhara (travel time about twelve hours) and from there to take the eight to twelve day hike by way of Baglung, Dhorpatan and Lake Puphal.

The Jumla and Dolpo districts of west Nepal have remained almost completely spared from the ravages of the modern tourist trade, and a visitor might feel – so to speak – transported into the Nepalese Middle Ages. On the one hand this is very attractive. On the other hand, however, the trip requires a lot of preparation. If you do not go on a promoter-organized trekking tour, then in making your travel plans you can count on having to be completely on your own, and accordingly well enough equipped for self-sufficiency. That means you will have to bring along everything from your tent to your toothbrush and soup-cubes.

The accomodation and shopping possibilities in this area are exceedingly limited, and even in the district capitals of Jumla and Dolpo there is hardly anything to be found. During certain seasons even the local population obtains some of its provisions by airplane, because the basic staples on hand – such as rice and wheat – are inadequate for their nourishment and the supply is not always ample.

Do not be misled by such high-sounding names as "hotel" or "lodges." Almost without exception, these worthy establishments offer primitive accommodation which should only be entered into with a healthy dose of pioneer spirit and plenty of insect repellent. The accompanying "restaurants" often serve exclusively tea and *chapatis* (a flattened bread of unleavened dough); at certain times of the year even getting *dhal bhat*, the national dish (rice with lentil sauce, one of the most commonly prepared foods), can become a problem for the traveler.

Once you have left the district capitals, any hope of seeking out a lodge or restaurant will be in vain. Making yourself understood to the local population presents yet another problem. Hardly anybody in this wonderfully secluded region speaks English, so that you would be well advised to pick up a few phrases of Nepali or, among the Dolpo, Tibetan, so that you will be able to conduct at least the most essential conversations.

Note should also be taken of the climatic peculiarities of this region. The imposing Dhaulagiri Massif as well as its western spurs, which separate the region from the Indian low plains, are in effect a weather boundary, by which the influence of the monsoons is substantially reduced. As a result the area is relatively poor in precipitaion, with cold to very cold winters. However, in contrast to most of the other regions of Nepal, this sort of weather can also blow in during the summer. The climate of Dolpo in particular is highly reminiscent of that in Tibet. The best times for travel here are May, September and October. Nevertheless, before you make up your mind to take a tour through the Dolpo region, you must be appropriately acclimatized, because you'll be staying at some very high altitudes. As has already been mentioned in previous chapters, altitude sickness has even forced some very seasoned walkers to make a hasty retreat. Unless you prepare yourself in this manner your life could be in danger.

FROM JUMLA TO RARA LAKE

Jumla (2,347 meters) – which is situated among green fields of grain in the Tila river valley – is, despite its administrative importance, a small and not exactly clean town with no more than 4,000 inhabitants. There is only one lodge and a small number of shops at which the shopping opportunities are primarily limited to the autumn, when, after the harvest, a selection of grains, fruits and vegetables is available.

The population of Jumla consists predominantly of Thakuri, a sub-caste of the Chetri, of which the current king (Birendra Shah) is also a member. As such we are dealing here with Hindus, who, as members of the second-highest caste, are actually not allowed to let us "untouchables" into their houses or offer us other accommodation.

The walk to **Rara Lake** takes about four days. If you should require the services of carriers, they can be hired in Jumla. You should know, however, that they are normally very poorly equipped and are not exactly fluent in the English language. After you have presented your trekking permits to the local police in Jumla, turn eastwards, past the landing strip and on up to the confluence of the Tila with the **Chaudbise** river. From this point on the going gets steep over the village of **Ghursenigaon** (2,590 meters) until **Padmara** (3,017 meters), a village which is reached after a good march of about six hours.

The next day you climb further up the mountains and before long find yourself high above the dense evergreen forests. Shortly after crossing the **Khali-Langna Pass** you will reach a fork in the path. The path that leads up from the south is a faster and more direct connection to Jumla than the other, howeve, it is certainly the more difficult route because it hauls its walkers over the **Danphe Pass** (3,688 meters). Through a dense mixed

CHANGLA HIMAL
6776
5949
5950
6078

Maquan He *(Matsang Tsangpo)* Paryang
5550

C H I N A

CHINA
NEPAL
7062
6712
6562
5660
Langu

Karnali
Rara Lake
Mangri

Shey-Phoksumdo
She – Phoksundo

Gumgarhi
Jahri
Rara
I.N.P.
Siha
Ludku
Pina Chauta Bumrad
4160 (Khali-Lagna Pass
Padmara 3545
Ghursenigaon
Jumla (2347)
Kurari

6596
6883
Kanjiroba
6525

KANJIROBA
HIMAL

Phopagaon
National Park
5931

Tingjegaon

5115
Kagmara Pass Kanjelaruwa
6612
N'akagmah
Pungmo Ringmo
5960

Gothigaon
Kunrigaon
Munigaon
Naphykhona
5459

Chaurikot Rimi
3810
Kaigaon
Lunh

Murikot

Bohngna Pass
Tibrikot

Park
Numla Pass

Do
(4090)
Basia Pass
Rohagaon
Dunai
5264

Kakkotgaon
6581

Tarakot
Khanigaon
(2800)

Dumjala
2637
Jajarkot
2102
Bheri

5922
5382

D H A U L A G I R I
5606

Royal Dhorpatan
4773

7660

8167
Dhaulagiri

H I M A L

Jumlikhalanga
Musikot
Rukumkot

Padmi
4688
Hunting Reserve
Dhorpatan

Bega

2537
Sallyan
2828

Baramelo
3583
Jelbang

Beni

Thapagaon
3531

Baglung

N E P A L
2059

Lawamjula

Khumkhani
2446

Ramkot
2786

Tulsipur

Swargdwar
Pyuthan
2143

Tamghas
2339
2570

Ghorahi

Sandhikharka

955
1818

2277
1688
Tansen

JUMLA DOLPO
TREKKING

0   20 km

forest with imposing birch trees, whose bark has found application in this region as a paper substitute, you hike down to **Sinja Khola**, and, soon after crossing it, arrive at the little village of **Bumrad** (six hours). The next leg of the journey passes through **Chauta** and the **Ghurchi-Lagna Pass** (3,444 meters) in seven hours to the settlement of **Pina** (2438 meters). Shortly after Pina there is another fork in the path. After leaving the main path, which leads to **Gumgarhi**, you turn to the left and come finally to **Rara Lake** after an interesting five-hour-long hike, that takes you through the small village of **Jahri** (2,530 meters).

The entire region surrounding the lake was declared a national park in 1975. Here it is less the panorama of the steep ice-giants that makes the visit seem so rewarding, than the overall beauty of the landscape. Fir trees, spruces, Scotch pines, cedars and rhododendrons form a large and sprawling forest, in which bears, wild-cats, wolves and red deer are still to be found. The most beautiful of the many campsites lie along the southern shore of the lake.

In the process of establishing the national park, the Nepalese government undertook a step which has since given them much cause for regret. The population that was living around Rara Lake was resettled. They were offered land in the Terai – the flat-land in the south of Nepal instead. However, this did not turn out to be to the advantage of the dislocated people. Today they are living in the Terai under somewhat worse conditions than before in Jumla.

Although this region is not a traditional and important destination for pilgrims – such as Muktinath, for example – there are certainly a few stony witnesses to the past. The **Malla Stones** are one such relic, stone pillars with Devanagari inscriptions, which originated in the 12th century, when the Malla kings ruled over western Nepal. Located on the eastern

shore of Rara Lake there are the so-called petrified foot-prints of the god Thakur, who is supposed to have shifted the outlet of the lake from its original location here to the west. To commemorate this occasion, a ceremony occurs each year in July or August.

For the return path to Jumla there is an alternative route which leads west of the one already described. It steers downwards to the **Khatyar Valley** and further over a 3,800-meter mountain ridge to the settlement of **Ghorasain** (3,800 meters, six hours). From here, about four hours separate you from **Sinja** (2,438 meters), which was once a summer residence of the Malla kings. A two-days march with about 16 hours' worth of hiking time are still required at this point to reach Jumla, which will finally be accessed through the **Jaljala Valley**.

FROM JUMLA TO THE DOLPO

At the end of 1988 and in May 1989, a section of a district was opened for tourism by the Nepalese government which is among the most interesting regions of Nepal. This is the **Dolpo**, a region which belongs legally to Nepal, but whose inhabitants, as fas as their descent, culture and language are concerned, are Tibetans. As a result of their isolated location, the approximately 4,500 *Dolpo pa* – as the inhabitants of this plateau (which lies between 3,300 and 4,500 meters in altitude) are named – have been able to preserve their traditional way of life to the present day. One special aspect of their culture is that the ancient and rather animistic rites of *Bön* – the old pre-Buddhist primitive religion of Tibet – are still alive, with their partly shamanistic ceremonies.

The Dolpo was already settled by Tibetans in the tenth century. These gave the land the name *Bä Yül* – "hidden country." Up to about 1800 it belonged to Tibet, but it was obliged to pay tribute to

neighboring Lo and Jumla. It wasn't until after the subjugation of these kingdoms by the Gurkha dynasty that Dolpo became a part of the Nepalese kingdom. Even so, the influence of Kathmandu remained insignificant, and it took until 1963 before the government opened up direct links with the *Dolpo pa.*

Although it only takes two and a half days from Jumla to reach the border of the Dolpo district, it takes seven to push into inner Dolpo, which, as already mentioned, is so especially interesting. Leaving Jumla one turns first to the east and passes the Thakuri settlements of **Gothigaon**, **Kunrigaon** and **Munigaon** (seven hours). Further up-river along the Tila River, which becomes ever narrower, one finally arrives after three hours at **Naphukhona,** the first village with a purely Buddhist population. Make sure you pay

Above: Trekkers and porters need resilience on the journey to Dolpo. Right: A cheerful and serene monk in the monastery at Ringmo.

a visit to the **Nyingma Monastery** above the village!

Through birch, fir and rhododendron forests you then proceed to the **Barbaria-Lagna Pass** (3,810 meters, four hours), which forms the boundary of the Dolpo district. After a steep descent the valley broadens out, and above the **Bheri River** you move along the scattered settlements of **Chaurikot**, **Rimi** and **Kaigaon** (seven hours hiking with only poor camping possibilities).

Those who shy away from the technically easy, but fatiguing and burdensome path over the **Kagmara Pass** (5,115 meters) can cross over the Bheri at **Kaigaon** and reach the Shey Phoksumdo National Park (see p.140) in four or five days by way of the considerably lower **Bolangna Pass**, via the villages of **Tibrikot**, **Dunai** and **Rohagaon.**

If you decide to take the Kagmara Pass anyway, you will make the acquaintance of a splendid mountain panorama, whose view alone is rich compensation for the difficult of the climb. Via **Hurikot** you

hike first of all along the Bheri – in perfectly pristine nature – up to the river's fork. After that the way leads for a short while up the chilly waters of the **Jagdula River**, which you soon cross. Passing by a lonely military station (3,100 meters, four and a half hours) you next come into the **Garpung Valley**. Climbing steadily, you leave the forest region and arrive after about five hours at a wide, 4,100-meter-high plain, which must be crossed. Turning into the last side-valley to the right, you see the Kagmara Pass directly before you.

In springtime it is recommended that you spend the night at the foot of the pass, in order to begin the march very early the next morning, because the snow fields that await you on the other side of the pass must be crossed while they are still frozen hard. It takes two and a half to three hours to reach the top of the pass. From there one has a great view of the ice-giants of the **Kanjiroba Himal** and the Kagmara group with the **Kagmara I** (5,960 meters). With the breathtaking

view of the western walls of **Kanjela-ruwa** (6,612 meters) you start down the easy path into the **Dorjan Khola Valley**. Keep an eye out for the famous blue sheep (*bharal*) and snow grouse which can occasionally be seen along the way!

After five and a half hours you come to regions, at an altitude of 3700 meters, where suitable camping spots can be found. Three hours later you will once again come across the first traces of human civilization – initially in the form of meager, isolated fields and huts, then in the form of houses with their characteristic flat roofs on which cloth is woven, yarn is spun or laundry is washed and dried. Located in the ground floor of these houses are stables and supply rooms which are connected to the living quarters by wooden ladders. These are made of roughly-hewn tree trunks which are sawn through lengthwise and into which steps are then notched. Meeting the first residents you will believe you have really been transported to Tibet: You will be openly and heartily welcomed in **Pungmo**, and everything that seems unusual to them will be touched, ogled and commented on.

The most memorable aspect of these houses are the red and white painted entrance halls and the interior wall-paintings many of which show a strong *Bön* influence. The deities are identical to those of Tibetan Buddhism, only the names are different, and the swastika, with its arms pointing left, one of the symbols of the *Bön* religion, shows up all over the place. You shouldn't neglect participating in a *puja* in the **monastery** of Pungmo – in exchange for a donation you will be allowed to enter.

From Pungmo you will need another hour to reach the entrance of the **Shey-Phoksumdo National Park**, where your trekking permits will first be checked again. There you can also get information about the park, and there is also a small museum devoted to local fauna.

After payment of the appropriate fees you can enter the national park, and, after a three-hour-long hike which includes some very steep climbs, you will come upon the village of **Ringmo**. On the way there are beautiful views of the eroded landscape opposite you, and also of the waterfall which forms the outlet of the Phoksumdo Lake.

This deep-blue lake, located directly below Ringmo, is surrounded by high, glaciated mountains and shelters a small gompa (monastery) on its southeastern shore, which houses an aged monk who still practices the old rites, which are similar to shamanism. In the smoke-blackened prayer chamber there are numerous amulets and dried herbs hanging from the ceiling, which he uses for healing illnesses. His art is based on methods of naturopathy, however, it includes elaborate and secret gesticulations which are of great meaning to the *Dolpo*

Right: Salt is still carried on the backs of resilient goats.

pa. In serious cases the healer visits the patient at night, puts himself into a trance, during which he inhales the smoke of a juniper or rhododendron fire, and besides dispensing the natural medicines he also tries to entice the spirit of the sick person – which had earlier been kidnapped by evil spirits – back into his body, through singing, dancing and prayer. This "treatment" is not without a price, after all, a religious healer doesn't live on fresh air and love alone.

Because of the beautiful view of the **Kanjiroba Himal**, a hike around the lake is strongly recommended. It takes about a day to progress along the western shore toward the northeast section. There is little point in going further in this direction because shortly after the lake you strike upon the boundary of a restricted area, which as a tourist you may not cross. The famous **Shey Monastery** and the **Crystal Mountain** still cannot be visited at the moment.

From Ringmo on you can choose two paths:

Direct Descent to Dunai

First take the same route back to the entrance of the national park. From there you can reach **Dunai** in a two-day march. The path there at first trails along the luxuriant banks of the **Dorjam Khola**, and then, upriver for five to six hours of constant up and down. Finally, you leave the forest zone, and after another five to six hours reach the district capital Dunai, which is located in an open hill territory. When the weather is clear one has a beautiful view of the massive silhouette of the Dhaulagiri Himal.

Over the Basia and Numla Pass

This variation is certainly more interesting, though it takes four or five days longer. It leads from Ringmo in a southeasterly direction up to the **Basia Pass**.

This approximately 5,100-meter-high pass has to be crossed just as does, on the next day, the **Numla Pass** at about the same height. The path is certainly simple enough for the beginner trekker, and offers a lovely view of the Dhaulagiri group, however, because of its altitude, it is very fatiguing, so that the walking times depend very strongly on your physical condition and acclimatization – and the weather. In spring you can count on a lot of snow on the passes.

Finally you make it into the broad, high valley of **Tarap**, in which about 1,500 *Dolpo pa* live in four villages.

The two most important villages are named **Thakya** (4,200 meters) and **Do** (4,090 meters). As a result of the climatic conditions, only a small crop of potatoes and barley is possible, which at the present time is no longer enough to meet the basic needs of life.

Most of the *Dolpo pa* are therefore forced to live as semi-nomads, and spend the long hard winters together with their herds of livestock – primarily goats,

sheep and yaks – in lower-lying areas. The salt trade with Tibet represents another important source of income.

In the Tarap Valley there are many beautiful gompas to be admired. They are partly bound to the Buddhist Nyingma tradition of the *Bön* beliefs. Observe the unusual construction of the **chortas**: a remarkable feature is the additional wooden roof between *harmika* and *bumpa*, which is found only in the Dolpo region.

Beyond the village of Do, one leaves the central area of Dolpo and arrives within two or three days by way of the wild, cavernous Tarap Valley to **Khanigaon** (2,800 meters; police check-post) or **Tarakot**, where the majority of the residents are once again Hindus. All areas east of the settlements between Thayka and Tarakot were restricted until recently. Opening them was talked about, so you will have to inquire locally as to what their status is.

From Tarakot, you can reach **Dunai** in a strenuous one-day-long hike. The town

doesn't have much to offer and is only a stop on the way to the airport of **Juphal**, which is located two and a half to three hours from Dunai.

With a total area of 3,555 square kilometers, the **Shey-Phoksumdo National Park** is the largest such nature reserve in all of Nepal. It was established in 1984, after the Nepalese government finally became aware of the unique character of both the culture and the landscape of this remote region.

There are approximately 3,000 people living in the area of the national park, of which the majority belong to ethnic groups of Tibetan ancestry. There are also a few Brahmans and Chetri. All of the residents must, of course, obey the special rules of the park. This, of course, tends to regularly give rise to tensions and even conflicts. For example, no open fires are allowed, and hunting and fishing are forbidden, as is the felling of trees.

Above: In the upper regions yaks and tzos are kept as domestic animals.

For heating and cooking only broken branches and dead trees can be used. The wood that is used to build houses even has to be paid for, and carries a high price-tag indeed: 430 rupees for every cubic meter.

Each family is only allowed to make use of their own private land and soil. This means that housing construction, agriculture and even livestock breeding are not permitted on the land of the national park. But because the property owned by the families is no longer sufficient for their living needs (due to longer life-expectancy and lower child mortality rates with the same number of births, division of the private lands through inheritance) they have tried to find other sources of livelihood. Yet, wool production, weaving work, and a larger amount of livestock breeding haven't solved the problem. So it often happens that the locals disobey the law and, for example, allow their animals to graze freely on national park land, which of course causes serious damage to the younger trees.

One of the most important functions of the park directorate is therefore to check up on the observance of the laws. Further jobs include the maintenance of the paths as well as the observation of the wildlife, including blue sheep, wolves and the snow leopard. There are long-term plans for the installation of new, wider paths, which will also be accessible to horses, and it will be possible to bring more materials into the park. The construction of a lodge is also planned which should one day serve to accomodate tourists.

With the Langtang Valley standing as a visible organizational example, the actual goal is a large increase in tourism, which is also, naturally, supported strongly by the Dolpo residents themselves. This could in the short term improve the local infrastructure and economy; but it could also open up a brand new set of ecological and social problems in the long term.

JUMLA / DOLPO

Accommodation

Neither Jumla nor the Dolpo region have made adjustments to trekking tourism. Therefore, there are lodges for an overnight stay in only a few villages. So bring along your own tenting equipment, food and other provisions.

In Dunai, the capital of the Dolpo region, there are three simple lodgings.

In Jumla, the capital of of the Kamali zone, as well as the Jumla district, there is one small lodge, as is also true of Juphal in the Dolpo area, where there is also a landing strip.

When staying overnight in the Rara or the Shey-Phoksumdo National Parks, a fee of 150 NR per person per night must be included in your calculations; this must usually be paid together with the entrance fees for the national parks.

Hospitals

Except for a small, primitively equipped hospital in Jumla, there is no medical care in the entire Jumla and Dolpo region.

Telecommunication

There is no telephone network in the entire region. There is the possibility in Jumla and Dunai of sending a telegram from the telecommunication office. However you cannot rely on the receiver actually getting it.

In case of an emergency, you are advised to use the radio phones of the following institutions: district police stations in Jumla, Gumgarhi, Hurikot, Khanigaon, Tarakot and Dunai, national park administrations, and the towers of Jumla or Juphal airports.

Porters

These can, in principle, be hired everywhere. However, keep in mind the language barrier, and the fact that the local porters are not thought of as very reliable. The daily fee in spring 1995 was about 200 NR per porter with a load of 20-30 kg.

Various

Nying ma or Bön monasteries are to be found in Naphukuna, Pungmo, Ringmo and in the high valley of Tarap. You must ask for permission if you want to see one of the monasteries from inside.

Jumla is the capital of the Kamali zone, as well as of the Jumla district. It has approximately 4,000 inhabitants and lies at 2,347 meters altitude. It is the capital of the Dolpo region. It has various administrative authorities, a hospital, a school, a telecommunication office and a landing strip.

Dunai, with about 2,500 inhabitants, is located at 2,200 meters altitude. It is the capital of the Dolpo region, with the corresponding authorities, a school and the district police office.

The only landing strip in the Dolpo region is located in Juphal, about two to three hours away from Dunai. The entrance to the main administrative office of the Shey-Phoksumdo National Park is located in Sumdua at Pugmo. The entrance fee is 250 NR per person.

The headquarters of the 106 square kilometers Rara National Park is in Hutu at the northern end of Rara Lake, the largest lake in Nepal.

Trekking Permits / Restricted Areas

Since 1991, the trekking areas of Humla, Mugu and Dolpo, which were hitherto closed to foreigners, have been opened. A trekking permit must nevertheless be applied for at a local agency. Fees can be very high (see page 243).

Inquire at the Immigration Office in Kathmandu, whether the regions Phijor, Saldan, Tinje, Chharkabot and Mukut in the Dolpo area are now accessible.

Getting There

The quickest way to Jumla over land is by public bus via Nepalganj to Surkhet (Birendranagar) – travel time of about 46 hours. From there it takes seven to eight days walking over Dailekh and Kalikot.

To Dunai, the district capital of Dolpo, the best way from Kathmandu is by bus to Pokhara, from there eight to ten days hike through the villages of Baglung, Dhorpatan (2,700 m, has a landing strip), then past Puphal Lake.

For the flight connections a twenty-seater Twin Otter aircraft is used: there is only one direct flight from Kathmandu to Jumla per week (one way costs US$ 127). The connection via Nepalganj is better, because it is flown to several times daily from Kathmadu as well as from Jumla (except in the monsoon season). A one way flight from Jumla to Nepalganj cost ca. 600 NR. Connecting flights to Kathmadu several times daily at US$ 99. Besides RNAC, Nepal Air Charter and Nepal Airways also fly from Kathmandu.

From Kathmadu to Dunai / Juphal you can only fly via Nepalganj. From Nepalganj to Juphal there are two flights weekly – 600 NR one way – from there to Kathmadu flights several times daily for US$ 99. The RNAC office is right at Juphal airport.

Worthwhile Detours

From Jumla (2,340 m) you can make a beautiful three to four day tour up to Rara Lake (3,000 m), which – at 13 square kilometers – is Nepal's largest lake, surrounded by high mountains.

1 Far Western
2 Mid Western
3 Western
4 Central
5 Eastern

CHINA

Jumla
Dolpo Mustang

Annapurna
Pokhara**Pokhara**
NEPALHelambu Solu Eastern
KathmanduValley Kath.Khumbu Nepal

Langtang

Lucknow Terai

Biratnagar

BANGL.

Patna

Allahabad Varanasi

INDIA Rajshahi

YOGIS, YAKS AND YOGHURT

HELAMBU
GOSAINKUND
LANGTANG

Helambu and Langtang are the two trekking areas located closest to the capital city. They stretch between the chain of hills which forms the northern border of the Kathmandu Valley and the main range of the Himalayas or the national frontier with Tibet.

Helambu is the name of a region which more or less corresponds to the **Malemchi Khola** river area. Langtang designates the high valley of the **Langtang Khola** river north of Helambu. The Langtang Khola joins the **Bhote Kosi** river at the village of Syanbensi and forms the **Trisuli** river. The latter is a veritable El Dorado for hard-core river rafting enthusiasts.

Helambu and Langtang are well suited for the hiker with a tight time budget because they are easily reached from the Kathmandu Valley. A choice of routes which combines both regions is certainly very rewarding, but at least 14 days of pure hiking-time must be allowed. The crossing from Helambu to Langtang – or the other way around – leads either over the **Laurebina Pass** (4,609 meters) and the lake grouping of Gosainkund, or over the difficult **Ganja La** (5,200 m). Certainly, in many respects both regions

Preceding pages: The Langtang area is famous for its colorful festivals.

stand behind the Solu Khumbu or the surroundings of Annapurna in their spectacularity. In the mountain chains of the Langtang Himal and the Jugal Himal, along the northern edge, there are no eight-thousand-meter peaks, and "only" one seven-thousand-meter peak each – the **Langtang Lirung** (7,234 meters) and the **Big White Peak** (6,979 meters). And the relatively well-known cheese factory in Langtang is hardly a major touristic attraction.

The lure of this region lies more in its diversity: The visitor can acquire a profile of the entire country from the densely populated Kathmandu Valley to the limitless solitude of the eternal snows on the mountains very near to the Tibetan border.

Such a profile encompasses the differentiated and altitude-dependent forms of vegetation as well as social and economic activities from the valley level up to the mountain slopes and high plateaus (called *lekhs* by the Nepalis). Those who already know a bit about the ethnic diversity of Nepal will ascertain that here, in an almost improbably ideal manner, the various altitude levels are inhabited by completely different ethnic groups. Let us begin in the Helambu region, the furthest western extension of the settlement area of the famous Sherpa people.

HELAMBU

The village of **Tarke Ghyang** (2,560 meters) is on a significant section of the most important route in Helambu. Tarkhe Ghyang is attractive primarily as the center of a sub-group of the Sherpas. They differ in their dialect from their famous ethnic cousins in Solo Khumbu. At one time the Rana kings took their harem-girls from the Sherpas in Helambu because the women there were renowned for their beauty. The most memorable sight is that of the town's orderly and dense rows of stone houses, whose roofs all present the same picture with white prayer banners and fine shroud of smoke emanating from countless open fires in the interiors.

Each visitor to Tarke Ghyang should enjoy *tsampa* and butter-tea at least once in the serene joy of a Sherpa residence. In the common living, sleeping and cooking room sometimes an almost pedantic cleanliness and order dominates. Also worth seeing in this village is the **Temple in Bhutanese Style** with its impressive frescos of demons in the entrance area. It originates from the early 18th century, but was given its present form after thorough renovations in 1969.

To get to Tarke Ghyang there is a whole series of route variations, with which a round trip can be put together according to available time, season of the year, individual preferences and the equipment you have with you. In addition, from the Langtang Valley you can cross into the Gosainkund region in the west and the Ganja La to the north.

As a rule, **Sundarijal** – northeast of Kathmandu – is the starting point for a trek into Helambu. The path winds its way predominantly through humid oak and rhododendron forests on up to the **Shivapuri Lekh**, which here demarcates the northern limits of the Kathmandu Valley. After about five hours this day's stage of the journey ends in **Pati Bhanj-yang** (1,767 meters). Here, on the other side of the Shivapuri Lekh, you find yourself in the middle of a densely-populated area of Tamang villages. The crops are especially broad in variety (particularly millet and fruit trees), giving the classic Nepalese terraced landscape an especially attractive appearance. On your excursion through Pati Bhanjyang you must get a glimpse on the beautiful red-brown Tamang houses with their large, shady verandas.

Behind Pati Bhanjyang the path splits, offering two very contrasting tour variations. The first and simpler path leads in an eastern direction, down into the valley of the **Malemchi Khola**. Further on it follows the eastern bank of the Malemchi upstream. Tarke Ghyang is accessible in three relatively short day-long stages, with overnight stays in **Tala Marang** and **Thimbu** (from Tala Marang a broad and by and large level trails leads down to **Panchkal** on the Kathmandu-Kodari road in about seven hours).

The trail up-river from Tala Marang proceeds initially through really low altitudes, where you might be rather overwhelmed by the heat and sun in the warmer seasons. Perhaps you can find some refreshment with a swim in the cool water of the Malemchi or in one of the truly frequent tea houses along the trail. The higher you get up into the valley, the more noticeable the changes in the settlements and the human physiognomy. In **Kiul** and **Thimbu** you will already encounter Sherpa families living alongside the Tamang.

The climb up from Thimbu to **Kakani** (also accessible by road) is attractive for its landscape, but also fatiguing. It brings you past some of the especially beautiful chortas and caityas, taking you finally into the region predominantly settled by Sherpas.

The other trail from Pati Bhanjyang into Helambu proceeds almost exactly in a northern direction onto the range of

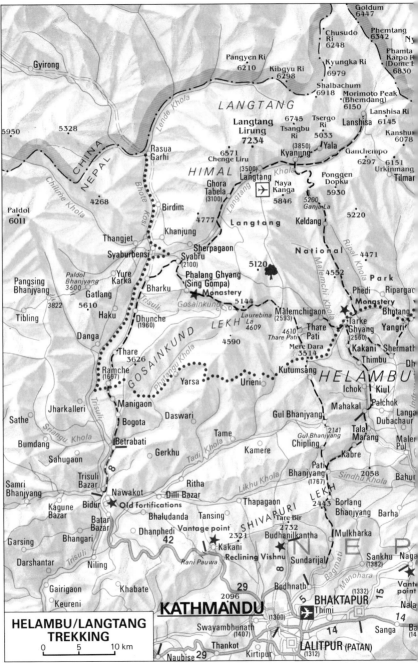

HELAMBU/LANGTANG TREKKING

0   5   10 km

Map labels:

C H I N A

Pō Chu

npo Gang
(White Pk.)
79
Zhogsum

Nyalam

66
kpa   6256
rje   Ladies
       Peak
       (Gumba   6637
       Chuli)   Phurbi
                 Chyachu

6067

Choksum

Bhote Kosi

Zhangmu
(Khasa)

ahathan
Tempathang

Nasum Khola

Kyerpa
Danda
4471   *Bhairav
        Kund*

Kodari
(1663)

Bhoti Khola

3981

Gampo-
thang

Pulping

Marming

Nampha   Ghumtang   Lartza

3465   Kalam   2742
        Sangu   Kaseri

hoche

Kipche   Ghumang   Barabise
                     (819)

557   Jalbire   Sun Kosi
       Selang   Bazar
              Lamosangu
       Binjel   Tauthali
awalpur   Chautara   2050 Perku
       Irkhu   Sildhunga
           Baliphi

Sisaghat   Tamche

pur   Simthali
Rowa Pati

Jhvani Khola
Indrawati
Arniko Highway
Sun Kosi

8   Saping   2252
Panchkal   Dolalghat   Mulharka

21   Karketar   Gotphani

Vantage point,
Bhagvati Temple   Arubothia
Dhulikhel   Kottimal
1786   2048

BAIRAVKUND

LEKH

27

15

16

---

mountain ridges which represent the watershed between the two river systems of the **Malemchi/Indrawati Khola** (in the east) and the **Tadi Khola/Trisuli Ganga** (to the west).

On this route you should allow anywhere from three to four days to get to Tarke Ghyang. Between November and January you should reckon with snow on the upper section before Thare Pati; the path is passable, however, with the help of a guide who knows the area. In good weather you have a splendid view of the mountain world. The first day of the journey leads over **Chipling** and the Tamang village of **Gul Bhanjyang** (2,141 meters) into the Sherpa settlement **Kutumsang**. Past Kutumsang there are no further permanent settlements until **Malemchigaon**. The only possible overnight accommodation consists of half derelict stables (*goth*), and with a little luck you might get a warm meal in one of these *goths* in **Thare Pati**.

Thare Pati is also the starting point for a tour in the region of the **Gosainkund Lekh** (see below). In order to negotiate the descent to Malemchigaon, you must first of all walk back along the ridge for a long while. The path downward steers you through a magical forest of rhododendrons hanging with lichens. In the Sherpa village of **Malemchigaon** (2,593 meters) the source of livelihood is once again agriculture, which is obvious at first glance. Tarke Ghyang lies on the opposite side of the valley at roughly the same altitude. In order to make it over there, however, you must cross the Malechmi Khola, which flows 700 meters below you. An alternative and infrequent used trek into Helambu is the descent to the lakes of **Panch Pokhari** at about 4,000 meters altitude, which can be reached in four days via the villages of **Shermatang**, **Yangri** and **Yarsa**. In two further, very lonely days from there you meet the Chinese Road (Kathmandu-Kodari) at **Baliphi**.

GOSAINKUND

The **Gosainkund Lekh** is a relatively easy way to pass between the upper Helambu and the Langtang Valley. It is also, however, a destination for those trekkers who want to experience the mountain world around the holy lakes of Gosainkund. Every year at the full moon between the middle of July and the middle of August tens of thousands of Hindus make a pilgrimage to these lakes in order to take a ritual bath in the cold mountain waters. According to a legend the streams feeding the lakes had their origin when the god Shiva rammed his trident into the rocks above them.

Coming from Kathmandu, the shortest access leads either via **Pati Bhanjyang** and **Kutumsang** (Helambu) or via **Dhunche** (Langtang). The trail over the Gosainkund Lekh is as follows: The base

Above: The Gosainkund Lake. Right: A young woman from Helambu.

for the crossing of the **Laurebina Pass** (4,609 meters) is **Thare Pati** (around 3,400 meters), an uninterrupted collection of half-derelict stables (*goths*), which offer a place to stay overnight in case of need. During the high trekking season several of the cabins of the Sherpas from the village located nearby are open for business. The next overnight accommodation after Thare Pati is the pilgrim shelter on the **Gosainkund Lake** (4,381 meters), but it can scarcely be reached in a single day's hike. The path proceeds behind Thare Pati initially at the same altitude past several streams that feed the Tadi Khola. In the event of bad weather, you can find shelter under several overhanging cliffs (*gopte*). The path up to the Laurebina Pass is not difficult in itself, however it rises in altitude more than 1,000 meters. You will find outstanding camp sites on the foundations of several abandoned *goths* at around 4,000 meters. After crossing over the pass there is a breathtaking view of a portion of the Gosainkund Lakes (i.e. **Surja, Gosain,**

Sarasvati, **Bharain Kund**) and of the mountain world of the Langtang and the **Ganesh Himal**. From the pilgrim huts on Gosainkund you can reach the **Sing Gompa** on the same day. This is the first permanent settlement since Malemchigaon or, respectively, Kutumsang, both of which lie a four days' journey behind you. The village of **Sing Gompa** is arranged around a monastery. The local government cheese factory offers several simple places to stay. With the descent to **Syabru** on the next day, you arrive at the connecting point with the Langtang trek. In **Dhunche** (1,960 meters), one more day's journey on, you can get on the bus to **Trisuli Bazar**.

LANGTANG

The valley of the **Langtang Khola** has been a part of the **Langtang National Park** since its inauguration in 1976; its 1,700 sqare kilometers make it the largest protected zone of the Himalaya states. The national park, with its especially varied fauna and flora, also encompasses the upper Helambu (north from Tarke Ghyang), the Gosainkund Lekh and the Jugal Himal further to the east. The destination of the majority of the treks in the Langtang Valley is the village of **Langtang** (3,500 meters) and its attending summer settlement **Kyanjing** (3,850 meters). These are located in a wide arid valley on the other side of the tree line and framed by splendid mountain scenery.

The inhabitants of the upper Langtang Valley describe themselves – as do the Sherpas – as the *Bothiya*, a group with Tibetan origins. They are, however, not difficult to tell apart from each other, both from their appearance and their way of life. The main economic pillar of the Langtang Bothiya is the keeping of yaks. The herds wander in a seasonal rhythm from the forest underneath **Ghora Tabela** all the way up into the furthest valley of the Langtang Khola, at an ear-

lier time even up into the Tibetan Highland. Therefore, located everywhere in the upper section of the valley are only seasonally occupied summer settlements. A modest amount of agriculture (around the village of Langtang) contributes to self-sufficiency, with the cultivation of potatoes, barley and buckwheat. Evidence of Tibetan Buddhist tradition is everywhere in the upper Langtang Valley. Countless mantras chiselled in stone accompany the hiker on the long mani wall between Langtang and Kyanjing. The gompa in **Kyanjing** and the chortas strewn about everywhere are also among such religious manifestations.

An attraction of a different sort is the **cheese dairy** in Kyanjing – not only because of its delicious yoghurt and the swiss cheese which you can obtain there. The dairy was constructed in the mid-1950s, a short time after the valley was visited for the first time by a foreigner (H.W. Tilman). The dairy in Kyanjing was the first of numerous mountain cheese dairies in Nepal. The initiator was a Swiss dairy specialist and developmental assistant. The primary goal of the project was to find new methods of preserving and marketing the cheese from the remote high valleys. The increasing influence of the Chinese in Tibet gradually closed access to a portion of the traditional summer pastures on the other side of the border, and in addition, one of the most important markets for the sale of clarified butter (*ghee*), into which the milk had until then been processed. The hard cheese now produced is taken by carriers in the direction of the capital city. From Kathmandu, the greater portion of this cheese is then exported to India.

For the trekker it is rewarding to spend a few days in the upper Langtang Valley. There are almost no limits to what you can discover. You'll need about five hours for the ascent to **Tsergo Ri** (5,033 meters) over the high meadow of **Yala** (eastern Kyanjing), which is known for its spectacular mountain views. If you have in mind to cross over the **Ganja La**, enjoy the outstanding view of the pass from Tsergo Ri and brace your body for the altitude adjustment. The short tour to the small summit immediately north of the lodge in Kyanjing is also well worth your while. A day-trip leads to the cabins of **Lansisa**, nestled on the edge of the **Langtang Glacier**. It is also possible to rent a horse for this excursion.

Coming out from Kathmandu you find the lively little trading center of **Trisuli Bazar**. This is one starting point for a visit to the Langtang Valley. The 73-kilometer-long connecting road between Kathmandu and Trisuli was constructed in the 1960s in connection with the erection of what was then the largest hydroelectric plant, located north of Trisuli. In the mid-1980s, the lower section of what

was originally the Langtang trek was opened up with a road to Dhunche. It leads on further over the Trisuli River to the foot of the Ganesh Himal, at an altitude of over 4,000 meters. Zinc and lead have been discovered there, which are now being extracted. The local residents cannot expect much to come from the construction of this road: It is feared that wood will be plundered from the forest-rich area, and there is an almost insoluble problem with the enormous erosion which occurs where the road has not been competently built to match to the steep terrain conditions.

Leaving Dhunche (1,960 meters) you can reach the Sherpa village of **Syabru** (2,100 meters) by way of Bharku, in about seven hours. Syabru's houses seem to hang like a chain of pearls on a mountain ridge. If you plan an excursion to the Gosainkund Lakes you must either leave the main path to Langtang between Dhunche and Bharku, or, coming out of Syabru, turn in a southerly direction towards **Sing Gompa**. On your way from Syabru in the direction of Langtang, you can make it down to the Langtang Khola in about one and a half hours. Then you follow the river through dense, humid forest for about two hours and finally cross it at a massive bridge.

On the considerably drier south bank you will reach, after about one and a half more hours, a collection of tea houses and lodges, among these the famous "Lama Lodge." From the Lama Lodge to the **Ghora Tabela** military post (3,100 meters) it is about a four-hour walk, and the upper section of the trail runs through an open larch forest in an increasingly widening valley floor. Passing by some interesting gompas, you arrive in another two hours at Langtang (3,500 meters). From there to **Kyanjing** (3,850 meters) it is still two to three hours of contemplative hiking. Altogether you should allow two and a half days for the journey from Dhunche to Kyanjiing.

Right: Everywhere throughout Langtang, chortas and prayer flags show that Buddhists live here.

The Ganja La Pass

The **Ganja La** (5,200 meters) connects Kyanjing with Tarke Ghyang in a line running almost exactly north-to-south. With the Gosainkund Lekh, it is the second crossing point between the Langtang Valley and Helambu. However the Ganja La is by far the more wearisome alternative, because of the high altitude and the difficult terrain. The name means "Pass of the Great Snows," and the Ganja La is notorious for its frequent heavy snowfalls. The pass is usable from May until the beginning of November, however, even during these times snow fields must be crossed in the upper section. One must expect snowfalls here. The path is unmarked to an extent, and during fog or snow storms one can easily get confused and lost. A guide who knows the region well is recommended! Because there are no permanent settlements to be found during the three day-long stages between Kyanjing and Tarke Ghyang, tent and other necessities must be brought along.

After you leave Kyanjing going upriver – then crossing the Langtang Khola – you still have about six hours of climbing left before reaching the top of the pass. It is recommended that you count on spending one night on the road, at the *goths* at about 4,400 meters for example. In the 400-meter altitude difference before the top of the pass you must ascend through broad snowfields; the very last section before the pass requires a light scramble on a slippery base.

The descent from Ganja La in southerly direction leads you over typical moraine fields. Crossing is particularly fatiguing when a blanket of snow covers up the gaps and holes between the individual blocks of rock. A poorly placed foot can quickly result in injury. Around four hours of hiking time are necessary to get to the first *goths*. From these it is then still a one and a half day march to Tarke Ghyang. The path leads on mainly along the east side of the main range of the mountain massifs of **Dhukpu** and **Yangri Danda**.

A Village In Nepal

In 1990, Chandra Tamang (34) was *sirdar* at a trekking agency in Kathmandu. He made his first contact with the trekking business ten years ago in Pokhara, where his father had sent him to learn the English language. His trekking career began as a kitchen assistant, then he worked as a Sherpa before he finally advanced to his present position. For the time being, Chandra is employed by his agency the whole year round. However, for his monthly salary of 800 rupees – in his home village this is just enough for the purchase of two goats – he must actually work for only five months a year. He spends the remaining time as a farmer in his home village of **Bhalche**.

Bhalche is located more than two hours on foot away from Trisuli Bazar at 2,000 meters above sea level on a slope

Above: Those who work in the trekking business rarely see their families during the trekking season.

high above the **Salankhu Khola**, a tributary of the Trisuli River. Chandra means *moon*, and the addition "Tamang" is an indication of his ethnic membership. In Bhalche all of the 5,000 inhabitants are Buddhists, but for all that, only half consider themselves to be Tamang, the remainder being Gurung. Marriages between the two groups, however, are thoroughly acceptable. Chandra's family has the good fortune of being among the richer ones in the village. They possess a stately house in Balche itself, as well as a meadow out on the lekhs for pasturage during the monsoon seasons. On the farm terraces, potatoes, maize, millet, wheat, barley, radishes and mustard are harvested. One hour away on a path up the valley there are several fields for the cultivation of rice. Several cows, water buffaloes, sheep, goats, chickens and a piece of forest complete the family estate. With all of this they can, to a great extent, provide for themselves. Only tea, sugar, soap and a few "luxury goods" are purchased from the market in Trisuli Bazar. Unlike his father, Chandra can afford to send his son (16) and his daughter (8) to school for the whole year. Of course, as a result, he must forgo their assistance with the house and field work. During Chandra's absence in the trekking season his wife employs day-workers from the poorer families for the work on the field.

In spite of the relative affluence which Chandra's family has achieved, the way of life in Bhalche has changed only a little, partly because the village is located off the beaten path of the popular trekking routes. A transistor radio is an expression of the highest luxury, and in order to find a doctor one must go on foot to Trisuli. The population expresses its enjoyment of life and intimate contact with their religion in the traditional festivals, especially the Dasain festival in October, when the herds come down from their pasture areas, and the Tamang and Gurung celebrate together.

HELAMBU / LANGTANG / GOSAINKUND

Accommodation

Those who have set off on their own with no tent will always find shelter as long as they stick to areas with human settlements. But first and foremost, keep in mind that you can simply forget about European ideas of comfort, service and the like. In the seventies, the non-organized trekkers in **Helambu** and the **Langtang Valley** spent the night in a *bhatti* (tea shop) or in a private house, always in the same room as the hosting family. Today there are lodges everywhere, especially in **Langtang**. They are mostly a room or a house. Wherever you spend the night, the host will prepare a simple hot meal for you (lodging fees at present range between 20 and 50 rupees, simple meals around 100 rupees). Attention: Beer and other bottled beverages must be carried in over long distances and are therefore expensive.

Hospital

A hospital is in **Trisul Bazar**, a pharmacy (dispensary) in **Dhunche**, however, in case of serious illness go immediately back to Kathmandu.

Altitude Adjustment

Sufficient acclimatization of the body is essential and should be observed at the passes of **Ganja La** and Laurebina (**Gosainkund**), where in a short distance extreme altitudes are achieved. Proceed with caution when trekking in the upper Langtang Valley.

Trekking Season

The best trekking times are in autumn (Ocober/November) and in spring (February-April). While you can trek the whole year round in the lower regions of **Helambu**, on the higher stretches, cold and snowstorms can be expected already in November. The blossoming of the rhododendrons in the higher regions (mainly in Malemchigaon after Thare Pati) in April and Mai is particularly beautiful. At these times in the lower-lying valleys (Helambu) it can be rather hot. The **Ganja La** is not passable until at least May. High-alpine experience desirable).

Equipment / Provisions

Crampons and rope are only recommended for the negotiation of the **Ganja La** and **Yala Peak**. There you must also take tent and provisions. This is also necessary for the excursion to **Panch Pokhari**, and highly recommended for the **Gosainkund** trek.

Guides

A locally informed and experienced local guide makes a deeper understanding of the land and the people possible. It is absolutely necessary to have a guide for crossing the **Ganja La**.

Various

The **Kyangjin Gyang Monastery** (3,000 m) is located about half a day's march up the valley from the village of **Langtang**. Nearby is a cheese dairy built in 1954 with developmental assistance from the Swiss. In **Dhunche** (Langtang region), a payment must be made at a checkpost for the entrance to the **Langtang National Park**. The path to Langtang through the **Trisuli Gorge** (later named Bhote Khosi) also marks a significant trade route which led from here to Kyirong in Tibet before the Chinese/Tibetan border was closed.

Getting There

The most important points of departure of the described treks are simple to reach from Kathmandu. The best way is to take a taxi (16 km; 1 hour) to **Sundarijal** (Helambu/Helmu trek). The trek begins west of Sundarijal at the end of the road where a water pipe comes out of the mountain.

To get to **Trisuli Bazar** (to the high alpine Langtang Valley and the holy mountain lakes of Gosainkund) you can take the public bus (73 km), which departs from the north western city-section of Paknajol (near the tourist center Thamel). A small bus brings you from there in 5-6 hours to **Dhunche**.

In **Kyanjin** in the upper Langtang Valley there is a STOL landing strip; small chartered aircrafts can land there – no official RNAC flights.

Rewarding Detours

When you have hiked around **Gosainkund Lake** and climbed past the four further lakes – Bharainkunda, Sarasvatikunda, Dudkunda and Surjakunda – to the pass (4,600 m), you have made it to the **Helambu** region (ca. seven hours from Gosainkund to Tare Pati). North of the **Kyangjin Monastery** at ca. 4,800 meters altitude (see Various) is a beautiful vantage point, the high meadow of Yala. From here you can climb the **Yala Peak** (5,500 m) or the **Tsergo Ri** (4,950 m), which is easier to ascend. Climbing irons and pick are recommended.

From **Trisuli Bazar** you can undertake an excursion to the former fortress town of **Nuwakot**. On the road from Trisuli Bazar to Kathmandu you drive over the **Kakani Pass**, where you can stay overnight in simple accomodation.

Festivals

Every year, hundreds of believers make a pilgrimage to **Gosainkund Lake** between mid-July and mid-August to pay homage to Shiva and bathe in the lake during the full moon. In addition to the Tibetan New Year – called *Lhosar* – which occurs at the end of February/beginning of March, in May/June mask-dances are performed in **Helambu**.

IN THE SHADOW
OF EVEREST

SOLU-KHUMBU
NAMCHE BAZAR
EVEREST BASE CAMP
IIINKU AND IIUNKU
ROLWALING VALLEY

SOLU-KHUMBU

It must be the dream of each and every visitor to Nepal to see Mt. Everest at least once. At 8,846 meters it is the highest mountain in the world. This experience is much more intensive when you follow the beat of your own drummer and hike up to the area on your own instead of latching onto one of the organized excursions from Kathmandu.

Because the infrastructure of the Solu and the Khumbu has been greatly improved in the last few years, it hardly poses much of a problem anymore either for the individual trekker or the travelers in organized groups. A network of so-called lodges – which closely resemble the standard lodge arrangements in the Alps – has grown up over a broad section of the Khumbu. The ever-friendly Sherpas – the original residents of the Khumbu – will provide important assistance in all your undertakings.

The Sherpas

The Sherpas actually originate from Kham in eastern Tibet. The name *shar pa* means "they who come from the East."

Preceding pages: Mount Everest (and Lhotse). Left: Chukung Ri base camp.

The first Sherpas came from Tibet about 600 years ago to settle in Khumbu. The reasons for this re-settlement are to be found as much in differences among religious conceptions in Tibet as in the violent altercations they had with the Khampas. At any rate they settled in Khumbu and lived there in semi-nomadic state as small farmers or traders. The name Khumbu goes back to *Kumbila Tetsan Gelbu*, the local patron deity, who defends the land and people from evil. The Sherpas are – as adherents of Tibetan Buddhism – a very religious people. The examples of their religiosity are everywhere: There are stupas, monasteries, gompas, mani-walls, prayer-banners, passers-by murmuring their mantras, and prayer wheels as well as the house altars which no Sherpa household is without.

Almost all of the festivals have a religious origin. One of the most significant is called *Dumje,* which takes place in June or July. This is a celebration of the birthday of the legendary master teacher and religious founder Padmasambhava, who brought Buddhism to Tibet in the eighth century and founded the Nyingmapa Order. Along with this is celebrated the anniversary of the day when Lama Sangwa Dorche, the founder of the monastery of Pangpoche, achieved enlightenment, and also the festival for the wor-

157

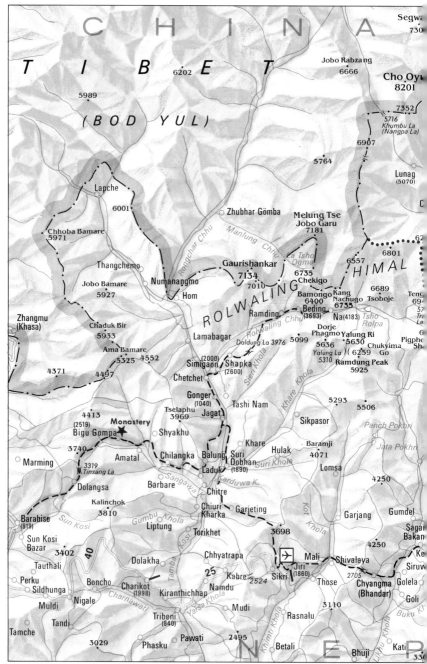

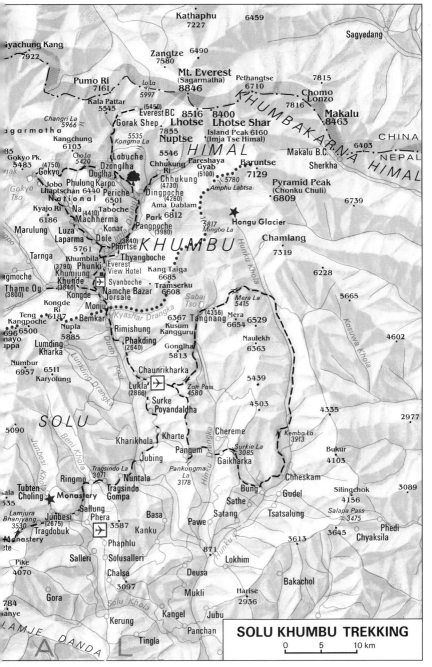

Kathaphu 7227 • 6459 • Sagyedang •

iyachung Kang • 7922 •

Zangtze • 7580 • 6490 • Mt. Everest (Sagarmatha) Pethangtse • 7815 •

Pumo Ri • 7161 • Lo La 5997 • 8846 • 6710 • Chomo Lonzo •

Kala Pattar • 5545 • (5450) Everest BC 8516 • 8400 • 7816 • Makalu • 8463 •

Changri La 5966 • Gorak Shep Lhotse Lhotse Shar • CHINA

agarmatha • Kangchung 6103 • 5535 Kongma La • 7855 Nuptse 5546 • Island Peak 6160 (Imja Tse Himal) Baruntse • Makalu B.C. • 6403 • NEPAL

85 • Gokyo Pk. 5483 • Cho La 5420 • Lobuche • HIMAL • Sherkha • Sherkha •

nak • Gokyo (4750) • Dzonglha • Chhukung Ri • Pareshaya Gyab (5100) • 7129 • Pyramid Peak (Chonku Chuli) 6809 • 6739 •

Gokyo Tso • Jobo Phulung Karpa • Dughla • Chhukung (4730) • 5780 Amphu Labtsa •

Lhaptschan 6440 • Periche (4260) Dingpoche • HIMAL

Kyajo Ri • Na (4410) Taboche • Ama Dablam • 5817 Mingbo La • Hongu Glacier • Chamlang 7319 •

Marulung • Machherma • Konar • Pangpoche (3980) 6812 •

Luza • Dole • (3840) • 6228 •

Tarnga • Laparma • Phortse • K H U M B U •

gmoche • 5761 • Khumbila • Thyangboche •

Thame Og (3800) • (3790) Khumjung • Phunki • Everest View Hotel • Kang Taiga 6685 •

Khunde (3840) • Syanboche • Tramserku 6608 • Sabai Tso •

Teng • Kongde Ri • Kongde • Namche Bazar • Jorsale • Mera La 5415 • 5665 •

Kangpoche 6187 • Monju • 6367 Tangnang (4356) Mera 6529 •

696 6500 • Nupla • Bemkar • Kusum Kangguru 6654 •

nayo ppa • 5885 • Rimishung • Gonglha 5813 • Naulekh 6363 • 4602 •

Lumding Kharka • Phakding (2640) •

Numbur 6957 • 6511 Karyolung • Chaunrikharka • 5439 •

SOLU • Lukla (2866) • Zatr Pass 4580 • 4503 • 4335 • 2977 •

5090 • Surke Poyandaldha • Chereme • Surkie La 3085 • Kemba La 3913 • Bukur 4103 •

Kharikhola • Kharte • Pangum • Gaikharka • Chheskam • 3089 •

Jubing • Pankongma La 3178 • Bung • Gudel • Silingchok 4156 •

Tragsindo La 3071 • Nuntala • Sathe • Satang • Tsatsalung • Salapa Pass 3475 •

Ringmo • Tragsindo Gompa • Basa • Pawe • Phedi Chyaksila •

Tubten Choling • Monastery • Sallung • Phera • 3587 • Kanku • 3613 • 3645 •

Lamjura Bhanjyang 3530 • Junbesi (2675) • Tragdobuk • Phaphlu • 871 • Lokhim •

Monastery ete • Salleri • Solusalleri • Deusa • Bakachol •

Pike 4070 • Chalsa • 3097 • Mukli • Harise 2936 •

Gora • Kangel • Jubu •

784 anye • Kerung • Panchan •

LAMJE DANDA • A • L • Tingla •

SOLU KHUMBU TREKKING

0   5   10 km

ship of the deity Khumbila. There are two New Year's festivals: One in January especially for the farmers, and one in February, when the farmers are already occupied with their work in the fields. The Sherpas have become famous throughout the world as the tough, perserverant and enduring carriers of loads to the highest summits in the world. However, today we can also appreciate their multi-purpose services as guides, interpreters, cooks, traders, and yak and lodge owners – almost always singing and whistling, unpretentious and helpful.

Getting there

There are two possibilities to get to the Khumbu: The more comfortable, faster, but also more expensive way is the flight from Kathmandu to **Lukla**. The 20-seater Twin Otter aircraft takes off as a rule only in good weather – first of all because they are flown by sight, and secondly, because the landing field in Lukla consists only of a bumpy grass strip, which turns into a morass when it rains.

The second possibility consists of a six-day-long march beginning in **Jiri**, which you can easily reach from Kathmandu by public bus – as long as the roads haven't been damaged as a result of the monsoons.

This tour via the **Deorali Pass – Junbesi – Tragsindo La – Nuntala** is on the one hand somewhat more fatiguing and burdensome – in that one has to climb up and down numerous chains of hills. On the other hand, it is also very alluring, because you have the chance to admire the stunning variety of the central mountain landscape. Villages of the Tamang, Chetri and Rai are interspersed with terraced fields and rainforests. Later on you arrive at the first Sherpa settlement, and the vegetation gradually becomes scantier.

Right: Yaks can be used to carry heavy loads at high altitudes.

There are lodges in each village, so that you can pretty much organize your journey according to your desires and mood.

Solu-Khumbu-Highway

Each of the some 9,000 trekkers who visit the Everest region annually must, perforce, engage in this trek twice: On the way there and on the way back. This is therefore the most heavily traveled path in the whole of Khumbu and is jokingly designated the Solu-Khumbu-Highway. So, it's also not surprising that here the most accommodation is offered and that it's hardly possible to lose your way on the well-trodden path.

Our detailed description of the hiking trails of Khumbu begins in **Lukla**. And here we encounter the first problem. Confronted by ones own piles of luggage, the trekker might start wondering: Who should carry all this stuff? Travelers with organized group-treks can only laugh at this problem, because upon arrival pack animals and Sherpas stand at the ready, so that they will have to carry only a light day-rucksack with essential utensils.

The individual lodge-to-lodge trekker, who makes ample use of the network of accommodation in order to feed himself and have overnight quarters, will carry everything himself and shoulder his 70-liter backpack among the stifled titters of smug onlookers. However, he too – either in Lukla or other larger villages – can hire a Sherpa as a carrier, who will carry his baggage for appropriate payment. Sherpas and "porters" are by no means the same, though.

A Sherpa functions today more in the sense of a guide. That means he knows the area very well and can make himself understood both with you and the local residents. A "porter" is frequently no Sherpa at all, rather a member of one of the central mountain clans – for example a Tamang, Magar, Gurung or Rai. They work solely as carriers, which means that you probably won't be able to communicate with them and that the organizational execution of your tour is for you to plan. This usually also applies in cases where you hire a Sherpa to work as a porter.

From **Lukla** (2,866 meters) the path leads first of all conveniently downwards, and after about two hours you reach **Phakding** (2,640 meters, 3 lodges). On the way you pass numerous teahouses and lodges, and the valley landscape of Khumbu – with its forests of rhododendron, fir and spruce, many shrubs and bamboos – invites you to dally for a while. Wheat, maize, barley, millet, rape seed and silver beets are primarily cultivated "down here".

On the way to the entrance of the Sagarmatha National Park – comprising a large portion of the Khumbu region – you will be confronted with the most difficult problem that exists in Nepal: The steadily progressing logging of the forest and the resulting damage by erosion. If you knew what the **Dudh Kosi Valley** still looked like just a few years ago you would be horrified at the numerous landslides, which, spreading ever further, threaten valuable farmland and interrupt traffic on important thoroughfares. A major part of this damage has been brought about by the recent dramatic increase in tourism; the roughly 3,000 inhabitants of Khumbu today provide more than 9,000 trekkers with accommodations (mostly constructed of wood, with interior furnishings also of wood) and food (cooking and heating is done with wood).

Save the Nature!

You can very easily make your contribution to the preservation of this unique landscape by following the recommendations of the *Himalaya Trust*:

1. Make no fires yourself, and don't use any wood!

2. Don't take hot showers! This service is now offered in many lodges, howeve, is costs a lot of wood. Abandon the idea – a little bit of dirt has never hurt anyone!

3. Don't order complicated meals in the lodges; if there are several people in your party, order the same dishes – this saves wood too.

4. If you have brought cooking utensils along, cook preferably with gas or camping fuel!

5. Burn your garbage, and don't bury burnable wastes!

6. You can prevent erosion damage by always keeping to the trails!

7. Try to convince other tourists and the locals to behave just as responsibly as you do yourself!

With these things in mind we arrive at the Sagarmatha National Park in Monju, and by the way, the 300 NR which each trekker has to pay as an entrance fee shouldn't bother you too much – it is not much money by western standards. In addition, this money is used by the *Himalaya Trust* – which oversees the national park – for such sensible things as the improvement of the school system, improvement of medical care, and the requirements of environmental protection. If you are traveling as a member of an organized trekking group, proof will be demanded of a sufficient amount of kerosene for cooking (per participant one liter of kerosene per day). If you don't have it, you must buy coupons for the corresponding amount (one liter 25 NR), which can be traded in at Namche Bazar.

From **Monju** to Namche Bazar takes about four hours. First you climb down to **Jorsale**, then you cross over a large suspension bridge, and afterwards you follow the river bank – always staying at the same altitude. Here you should keep in mind that the path to use after the next river crossing (smaller wooden bridge) is the one that leads straight and relatively steeply upward into the forest. Don't turn left onto the path which leads along the river, in the way that many carriers do. Of course you'll reach your goal this way

Above: Mani walls with carved mantras line the path in the Khumbu. Right: The Sherpa settlement of Namche Bazar with its typical long houses.

too, but not until you've taken a small al-pine climbing tour, and then at a later point you must cover about ten meters hand-over-hand on a fixed steel cable. The valley then becomes noticeably nar-rower, and finally you reach another bridge. After this point the path climbs 500 meters steeply up the mountain, and by this time at the latest you should fol-low an important mountain-climbers' rule since you are now located at a rela-tively high altitude for Europeans. Go slowly! Don't try to race the Sherpas – you'll lose anyway! Once you've arrived at the teahouse – the only one between Jorsale and Namche Bazar – you have made it through the worst.

Of course, the path leads still further up the mountain for about an hour, but it isn't so steep anymore. And on a clear day on the right, **Mount Everest** makes its first appearance. The Sherpas call it **Chomolungma**, because according to their beliefs Miyo Lungsangma, the mother-deity of the earth, thrones on its summit.

NAMCHE BAZAR

Today, **Namche Bazar** is the main vil-lage of the Sherpas and also the most populated village in Khumbu. The town has everything you need: A bank, a post office, and numerous lodges and shops in which you can purchase everything from souvenirs to mountain-climbing equip-ment. The handcrafted articles that are on sale everywhere, which are naturally all "old and genuine Tibetan," in reality originate for the most part from the work-shops of the Kathmandu Valley, where they are frequently cheaper to get. When buying anything check both the quality and the price carefully.

Every foreign visitor must report to the police station in Namche Bazar, where his arrival is entered into a book and his trekking permit is marked with a stamp. The police station is located about 200 meters above the path on which you en-tered the town. Here you have the oppor-tunity to combine the pleasant with the necessary, namely climbing the rest of

the way up the hill. Located at the top is the **Headquarters of the Sagarmatha National Park** with a small **museum**, and from here you have a fantastic view of the highest mountains in the world: To the north are **Nuptse** (7,855 meters), **Everest** and **Lhotse**, then further to the west **Ama Dablam** (6,812 meters), on to **Kang Taiga** (6,685 meters) and **Tramserku** (6,608 meters); to the east we see the powerful massif of the **Kyajo Ri** (6,186 meters), and finally further north the holy **Khumbila** (5,761 meters), seat of the local deity Tetsan Gelbu. Namche is the base camp for all further undertakings, because here the paths into the various valleys go their separate ways.

Walks around Namche

The half-day-long hikes to the surrounding villages are also suitable for ac-

Above: A dragon on the wall of the Chiwong Gompa monastery at Solu. Right: A lama at Thyangboche monastery in Khumbu.

climatizing yourself. There are two possibilities to reach the respective places from Namche. The longer – but more comfortable – is the path leading out of Namche on the left side of the valley, which runs on in the direction of Everest. After roughly 90 minutes you reach the **Sagnasar** "intersection," where four hiking trails meet. The path that leads up to the left takes you to **Khumjung** in only half an hour.

The shorter, faster variation leads steeply up the **Namche Gompa** to the right, over the chain of hills and on past to the **Syanboche** landing field. There the path splits, and you can hike further directly to Khunde (left), Khumjang (straight ahead) or to the **Everest View Hotel** (right). All three destinations are accessible in one-and-a-half hours' walking time.

Khunde has become well-known because of its **hospital**, the largest in the entire Khumbu region, which was furnished by the *Himalaya Trust*. There are three permanent employees: A western doctor, who works on a two-year exchange program, and two local helpers. The hospital is financed by the Trust, by charitable donations and income from the treatment of patients. If you should come to Khunde, by the way, a donation of medication is always welcome. Antibiotics and drugs for gastritis are in greatest demand.

Spread out over the year there are some 5,000 local patients, for whom the most common illnesses are infectious illnesses of the lung, dysentery, and skin and eye complaints. The preponderant majority of the foreigners who seek out the hospital annually suffer from two forms of illness: Diarrhoea and altitude sickness. A hint concerning the latter: Many lodges possess oxygen bottles, which can be used in emergencies to resuscitate those with altitude sickness.

The equipment of the hospital, including an X-ray machine, permits the treatment of all the above-mentioned illnesses – with the exception of altitude sickness

(here the only help is being transported to lower altitudes). Blood transfusions and more complicated operations cannot be performed here. For these cases the patient must be flown to Kathmandu by a helicopter which must be requested from Namche Bazar. The Khunde Hospital has two external stations, which can only offer a sort of first-aid service.

The locality of **Khumjung** (3,790 meters; two lodges) is located a bit below Khunde and, with its two-storied houses as well as its fields demarcated by a stone wall, is a typical Sherpa village. Founded roughly 500 years ago, it is the oldest Sherpa settlement and was, because of its location directly at the food of the holy Khumbila, for a long time the main village of the Khumbu.

In the houses we find granaries, stables and store rooms on the ground floor while the upper floor is used exclusively as a living area, in which during the evenings everyone huddles around the warm stove, near which they also sleep. The gigantic, polished copper kettle is the pride

of every Sherpa housewife. These often serve for the production of *chang*, the national beverage of the Sherpas, which is produced by the fermentation process of a barley or rice mash.

Two other sights also worth seeing in Khumjung are both of the chortas (Tibetan for stupa – reliquary shrines), the middle section of which, called a *bumpa* (pot) shows Tibetan architectural influence. Located directly next to these one can visit one of the **Hillary Schools**, which can be attended by students free of charge. The **Everest View Hotel** (3,850 meters) which is famous for its view, was closed for a long period. After being renovated by a Japanese contractor – who also undertook the restoration of the Syanboche airstrip – the hotel has been in service again since autumn 1989. (Price for a double room: around US$ 150).

Namche Bazar – Thame

This tour is a rewarding and light day's hike; the path is little-trodden, but offers

a wonderful view. It is also quite suitable for getting acclimatized! The path first leads left steeply upwards from the gompa in Namche, around the mountain ridge and then continues at the same level high above the gorge of **Nangpo**. After a two-hour march through spruce and rhododendron forests you arrive at **Kongde** (3,500 meters, one lodge). Some noteworthy sights here include several incense altars in front of the houses, as well as numerous *lhatos,* little cubic constructions bearing sticks hung with prayer-banners. These relics of the pre-Buddhist and animistic *Bön* beliefs are symbolic portrayals of the axis of the cosmos. The area is also renowned for its large number of begging children. Above Kongde there is a small convent of the Nyingmapa order, which one can visit – for a little obolus.

After Kongde the landscape becomes starker, with only some grass and a few

bushes like barberries and junipers. After a further two hours and the crossing of an imposing gorge you come to **Thame Og** (3,800 m, one lodge). This spread-out farming village is located on the valley floor of the Nangpo River, and particularly in the morning sunlight you have a splendid view of the northern walls of the **Kongde Ri** (6,187 meters), **Teng Kangpoche** (6,500 meters), **Panayo Tuppa** (6,696 meters) and **Pigpherago Shar** (6,718 meters). A strenuous task is the climb up the last 200 meters to the **Thame Gompa**, a monastery which seems to be glued to a rocky wall. From the stupa at the entrance gate of the monastery grounds you can catch a glimpse, far to the right in the distance, of the **Cho Oyo** (8,201 meters).

Continuing along an extensive mani-wall with mantras chiseled into it, you arrive at the residences of the monks and finally to the gompa itself. It belongs – as do almost all of the monasteries in the Khumbu – to the Nyingmapa order. A *Mani Rimdu* festival occurs here in May,

Above: A well-earned rest on the Gokyo Ri (5483 m), towering above the Gokyo Tso.

166

not quite as famous as that of the monastery of Thyangboche, but identical in content: It describes the legendary deeds of Padmasambhava in the form of *cham*-dancing (mask dancing).

Namche Bazar – Gokyo

This is a three to four-day hike along the Dudh Kosi River with beautiful views of **Cho Oyo** (8,201 meters), **Gyachung Kang** (7,952 meters) and the western **Khumbu Himal**. Starting from Namche you hike – as already described – to Sangnasar and in the same direction further on a steep path upward to the top of a pass (3,973 meters; one hour), from where you have a wondrous view of the **Phortse** (3,840 meters) opposite. The stone walls around the fields here serve not only to demarcate the private lands, but also offer an effective protection against wind erosion and landslides.

After a one-hour descent you reach **Phortse Drangka** lodge, a picturesque camp site located in a forest directly on the river bank. When you cross over the bridge, you proceed upwards to **Phortse** (half hour) and on further to **Pangpoche** (four hours). From Phortse Drangka you can hike to **Gokyo** either in two heavy days of trekking – each with six or seven hours of walking-time – or in three far more leisurely days. There are lodges in **Dole** (4,040 meters), **Luza** (4.369 meters) and **Machherma** (4,410 meters). At first the trail climbs steeply; after Dole it becomes flatter, but continues steadily up the mountain until you pass by summer pastures and finally reach **Gokyo** (4,750 meters, three lodges) with its three crystal-clear lakes.

A well-trodden path leads in three hours to **Gokyo Ri** (5,483 meters), which offers a fantastic panorama. **Cho Oyo**, **Mount Everest**, **Lhotse**, and **Makalu** (8,463 meters) are only four of the 14 eight-thousand-meter peaks which can be admired from here.

You can make it in three days to **Dughla** in the Imja Khola Valley via the **Cho La Pass** (5,420 meters) and Dzongla (4,843 meters). This tour is only suitable for mountain climbers. There are no lodges along the way. The path over the **Ngozumpa Glacier** is not easy to find and changes constantly. The descent from Cho La is very steep and can be icy during bad meteorological conditions. The reward for all this fatigue is the view of the tremendous northern precipices of the **Jobo Lhaptschan** (6,440 meters) and **Taboche** (6,367 meters), as well as the lovely **Tshola Tso Lake**.

EVEREST BASE CAMP

This is a four-to-five day hike to the foot of the highest mountain in the world. From Namche you climb first of all via Sangnasar down to **Phunki** (3,250 m), where you cross over the Imja Khola River. After the bridge you run into a series of water-powered prayer wheels as well as two lodges.

Starting here, the path leads steeply upwards to **Thyangboche**, which you reach after three hours of hard work. In 1989, the monastery burnt down completely, but rebuilding has already started. However, the unique situation of Thyangboche (3,890 meters, 3 lodges, 1 store) allows you to soon forget the fatigue, since the north faces of Tramserku and Kang Taiga seem almost close enough to touch, and the views of Everest, Lhotse and Ama Dablam in the light of the evening sun are unforgettable experiences. Hiking on further from Thyangboche you arrive at **Pangpoche** (3,980 meters, 2 lodges), after about one-and-a-half hours' walking-time and crossing over the Imja Khola. Shortly before the village, the path divides – the lower leads past Pangpoche directly to **Periche** (two hours); the upper brings you to the actual village. There's a monastery here, too, which is cared for by one of the Thyang-

boche monks. It was founded approximately 300 years ago by Lama Sangwa Dorje and shelters the ominous **Yeti Scalp** and **Yeti Hand** up on the second floor. A Sherpa legend tells how, when Sangwa Dorje had retreated to a cave in order to meditate, he was visited by a Yeti, who brought him food and water. After the Yeti died, Sangwa Dorje had his hand and scalp preserved in the monastery. Whether or not you believe this is left to you, but if you want, you can view both relics for a small bakshish. The *Dumje* festival also goes back to Sangwa Dorje, who celebrated it for the first time in this monastery.

If you want to insert a little alpine intermezzo into your tour, you can climb up to the **Taboche Meadow** (4,380 meters, no lodge) in about an hour on a steep path. If the weather conditions are

Above: High in the mountains – Thyangboche monastery which burned down in 1989. Right: An extraordinary relic: The scalp and hand of the legendary yeti.

good, you can ascend a 5,305-meter high sub-peak of Taboche. First you climb the crest, which is opposite the meadow, and then it is an easy climb over the ridge (three to four hours walking time). From the summit you have an outstanding view of the surrounding snow-covered peaks.

Phortse is accessible from Pangpoche by way of a little-traveled high altitude trail in around three and a half hours. The trip is recommended not only for the great view of the mountains Tramserku, Kang Taiga and Thyangboche, but also because of the fauna on this side of the valley: There are still a lot of pheasants and ghorals, which you might have a chance to spot.

Once you have reached **Periche** (4243 meters, 2 lodges), whose hospital is almost as well-equipped as the one in Khunde, it's not much farther to **Lobuche** (4,930 meters, 3 lodges). In the course of your four-hour hike you will notice a long series of little stupas. These were erected for the many Sherpas who lost their lives during expeditions to Mt.

Everest. In the meantime, you may also have noticed that the landscape has altered considerably. Coniferous and rhododendron forests now lie far below, and the miniature gentian and edelweiss are a pleasant sight in this otherwise monotonous grassy desolation. On the isolated fields the only crop that can still be cultivated is potatoes, the main source of food for the Sherpas.

The final – and at over 5,000 meters the highest – lodge is located another two hours' distance from Lobuche in **Gorak Shep**. This is the starting point for two undertakings which are among the most rewarding that can be found in Khumbu: The trail to the **Everest Base Camp** leads upward on the right side of the Khumbu Glacier, passing by ice caves and accompanied by the continuous rolling thunder of avalanches which come echoing over from the north face of Nuptse. Ice-climbing equipment is not a necessity, because there are no steep passages to overcome and the glacier in this area is covered almost everywhere with stone rubble.

Once you have reached the **Everest Base Camp** (5,540 meters) after a three-hour hike, you might be disappointed at first, because the camp itself consists of little more than a large accumulation and arrangement of rocks; however, the moment you shift your gaze upward you will be stunned by the gigantic masses of ice which slide down from the **Khumbu Ice Fall** at an extremely slow rate. You will hardly be able to imagine how mere humans have ever been able to make their way through it. If you are lucky, you might observe a few mountain climbers performing their dangerous exercises. Please note that the climb to the summit of Mt. Everest has virtually been booked out for several years to come.

In good weather, the ascent of **Kala Pattar** (5,545 meters) – starting from Gorak Shep – is only a question of your condition. You can climb up to the summit on the well-trodden path in about three hours. This vantage point offers the best view of Everest and Nuptse that you could possibly wish for.

Namche Bazar – Chhukung Meadow and Island Peak

This is a three- to four-day hiking expedition into eastern Khumbu, with splendid views to Lhotse, Lhotse Shar (8,400 meters), Baruntse (7,129 meters) and Makalu. The greater part of this trek follows a course similar to the trail to Kala Pattar, except that in Periche you don't turn to the north, but in an easy half-day's hike pass through **Dingpoche** (4,260 meters, lodge) to the **Chhukung Meadow** (4,730 meters, lodge).

The **Chhukung Ri** (5,546 meters) rises up immediately north of the Chhukung Meadow. This roughly four-hour ascent is technically easy, because the path leads partly over moraine rubble. Looking out from its summit you get a wonderful view of the south wall of Lhotse and Lhotse Shar as well as over to Island Peak, Makalu and Baruntse.

Above: The wonderful Khumbu Ice Fall; seen from the Everest Base Camp.

Island Peak (6,160 meters): This tour, which can be accomplished in two days, can only be recommended for experienced mountain climbers, who must take along ice-climbing equipment. In order to ascend Island Peak a climbing permit (1995: US$ 400) is mandatory. From the Chhukung Meadow, the road goes over **Pareshaya Gyab** (5,100 m); after which you continue left, climbing up the rib that stretches down to the south from the summit massif. At an altitude of about 5,500 meters you will find a protected camp-site (walking time four to five hours).

The next day begins before sunrise; you climb through the last stretch of craggy rock and arrive to a trough at 6,000 meters' altitude after conquering a steep glacial cliff. This is crossed by simply making a detour around a crevasse. After overcoming one final steep section you come to the summit ridge (five hours' climb) with a tremendous view of Makalu, the south face of Lhotse and the icebergs of the Imja Basin. The later descent to the Chhukung Meadow is still possible on the same day.

A march lasting two to three days over the steep and difficult **Amphu Labtsa** Glacier and through the **Amphu Labtsa Pass** (5,780 meters) brings you to the lakes of **Panch Pokhari** and down into the **Hunku Valley**. This should only be attempted by experienced mountain climbers with ice equipment.

HINKU AND HUNKU VALLEYS

This region is reserved for those trekkers who are not dependent on the lodges. The high-altitude areas of both of these valleys serve only as yak pasturage during the summer months; for the remainder of the year they are unoccupied. On the one hand this means that here you are completely on your own. However, this also implies the great privilege of experiencing largely untouched and unadulterated nature.

You'll need six days to travel from Lukla over the snow-covered **Mera La** (5,415 meters) into the **Hunku Valley**. First off you go in a southeasterly direction into the **Surke Drangka Valley**, and then – climbing ever more steeply – up to the 4,580-meter altitude **Zatr Pass**.

After crossing over two further ridgebacks you climb down again to a ghostly, lichen-covered rhododendron forest and proceed into the **Hinku Valley**. Going upstream, you follow the **Hinku River** almost to its source, then, however, turning east at the **Tangnang Meadow** (4,356 meters) and arriving after a steep ascent behind **Khare** (5,099 meters) in the glacier region of the **Mera**.

This 6,654-meter-high mountain – which may still be climbed with a normal climbing permit (1995, US$ 400) – is technically very simple, and its summit can be reached in seven hours from **Mera La**. The descent down into the Hunku Valley takes only one more day. However, those who wish to gain access to the lakes of **Panch Pokhari** from this side must pack up their belongings for another three days in order to climb the thousand meters that still separate them from the 5,400-meter-high lakes.

Of course if you decide to turn downriver, you can take a gigantic loop – taking an extra seven to eight days – over the passes **Kemba La** (3,913 meters) and **Surkie La** (3,085 meters) proceeding on simpler trails back again into the **Dudh Kosi Valley** and so make it back to **Lukla**.

ROLWALING

West of the Khumbu, directly on the Tibetan frontier, there is a wild, lonely high valley, the **Rolwaling Valley**, which is called simply "the grave" by the indigenous Sherpas on account of its location down between steep ice-covered peaks. Many mysterious stories have been passed on about this valley, through which the forefathers of the present-day Sherpas once came. It is here that the notorious and celebrated Yeti is supposed to make his home. Entire research expeditions have, so far unsuccessfully, attempted to find him.

There are three factors which have helped to preserve this splendid valley from the ravaging onslaught of tourists. First of all it is relatively arduous to get there, secondly there are neither lodgings nor food to buy, and thirdly you need a special permit to be allowed to hike into the Rolwaling Valley.

You must purchase – pro-forma – a climbing permit for the **Ramdung Peak** (5,925 meters, cost as of 1995: US$ 400) regardless of whether or not you want to climb the mountain. Those who aren't scared away by these inconveniences will be richly rewarded for their efforts. Alone the approaches to the **Rolwaling Valley** are worth the investment: The path leads you through a wonderfully variegated landscape, – on one hand

through Tamang and Chetri villages with their typical terraced fields, on the other through dense, gloomy primeval forests and over broad ridgebacks with wonderful views.

Two variations are possible: The first is a four-day hike from **Jiri** (1,860 meters; reachable with the bus) over the **Chordung Ridge** (3,698 meters), **Suri** (1,890 meters) and **Gonger** (1,040 meters); the other is a six-day hike starting from **Barabisi** (819 meters; public bus) via **Tinsang La** (3,319 meters), **Bigu Gompa** (2,519 meters), **Chilangka** and **Gonger**.

You finally set foot into the Rolwaling Valley after the village of **Simigaon** (2,000 meters) located high above the Bhote Kosi. Above the **Shapka Meadow** (2,600 meters) the path divides. Taking the road to the right is recommended, for while it is certainly more arduous, it is also decidedly the more rewarding. After

Above: Walking through virgin snow on the journey to Rolwaling over Yalung La.

172

a four-hour ascent you reach the **Daldung La** (3,976 meters) which has a fantastic view of the 7,134-meter-high **Gaurishankar** opposite.

According to old Sherpa mythology, this is the seat of the goddess Tashi Tserringma, who is the guarantor of a long life. Gaurishankar is also holy for the Hindus: Shankar, the name of the northern peak, is a designation for Shiva in their everyday spoken language. The southern summit, Gauri (literally: "the white") is a synonym for the feminine manifestation of the god.

From Daldung La there is a four-to-five-hour climb down on a really adventurous path through dense rain forest to the **Rowaling River**, which you then cross. There you meet up again with the other path, which rewards with a beautiful landscape, but doesn't snake down to Simigaon quite as spectacularly.

After about two and a half hours' walking time up-river you reach the Sherpa village of **Beding** (3,693 meters) – the only noteworthy settlement in the Rolwaling Valley. If it should happen that the monk belonging to the **Gompa** is in the village, you can ask him to show you around the gompa. 150 meters higher a rocky hermitage is visible, where Padmasambhava is supposed to have meditated some 1,200 years ago.

The last human lodgings of the valley is in **Na**, which is located about three hours' distance from Beding. From here, you have an absolutely overwhelming view of the mountain-giants **Chekigo** (6,735 meters), **Bamongo** (6,400 meters), **Kang Nachugo** (6,735 meters), and above all, **Tsoboje** (6,689 meters).

Over the **Yalung La** (5,310 meters) you reach the Khare Kola Valley and the Bhote Kosi in two and a half days.

Over the **Trashi Labtsa** (5,755 meters) you come into the Khumbu in four days. This is a difficult and fatiguing tour, which requires ice-climbing equipment.

SOLU-KHUMBU
Accommodation

This trek is among the most popular in Nepal. There-fore, there are plenty of lodges and hotels along the usual routes. Costs for an overnight stay (bringing along a sleeping bag is recommended) in the dormitory: 10-20 NR. The larger and more comfortable lodges offer double rooms (very simple, thin partition walls): 50-100 NR. Those wishing to make the trek to **Rolwaling** should bring along tenting equipment and provisions. If you use camp-sites that are located on private land, normally there is a fee of about 20 NR per tent. Prices for meals are about the same everywhere: Soups 10-15 NR, omelettes 20-30 NR, cakes and muesli 20-30 NR. The following applies for all bottled drinks: the further the distance from Kathmandu, the more expensive they are. Beers cost 100-200 NR, Sodas 40-60 NR, while in contrast *rakshi* and *chang* (indigenous alcoholic beverages) cost only about 10 NR.

Hospitals

In **Khunde** and **Periche** there are hospitals with foreign physicians. Treatment costs: 150 NR per treatment plus medications. For in-patient treatments: 150-200 NR per night. The hospital in Khunde (3,481 m) was founded by the *Himalaya Trust*, which was brought into existence by Sir Edmund Hillary. In addition, there are small hospitals in **Jiri** and **Paphlu**. There are first-aid stations located in **Bong**, **Chaunrikharka**, **Monjo**, **Gomila**, **Namche Bazar**, **Thame**, **Phortse**, and **Deboche**.

Radiotelephones

Since there is no telephone network here, you can only contact the outer world through radiotelephones. Installations for this purpose exist only at the tower in **Lukla** and at the police station and national park headquarters in **Namche Bazar**.

Postal Service / Bank

There are a post office and bank in **Namche Bazar**. Opening times of the bank: 10.30 am-2 pm (closed Saturdays). The post office is open 10 am-4 pm (closed Saturdays).

Porters

Porters can be hired directly on location. Two basic payment practices have developed: Either you pay your helper a lump sum and the latter takes care of his own accomodations and board, or you pay for his services separately and cover the extra for the room and board wherever you are.

For a Sherpa-guide you can calculate approximately 110-150 NR per day (without lodging or board). A porter receives about 80-100 NR per day. Those who have booked their tours through an agency in Kathmandu pay about US$ 35-40 per day. It has been determined that in altitudes up to 6,000 meters no

load above 20 kg can be carried. Over 6,000 meters only loads up to 17 kg are permitted.

Various

After the monastery **Thyangboche** (Tengpoche) burned down completely in January 1989 there are only two remaining monastery grounds in Khumbu that are particularly worth seeing: **Thame** and **Pangboche** (allegedly the oldest monastery; with Yeti relics!) At this time a reconstruction of the burned-out Tengpoche Monastery is being attempted with the support of the King Mahendra Trust. In October/November there are mask dances in the Tengpoche Monastery; in May at the Thame monastery.

Each Saturday, a large market takes place in **Namche Bazar**. Since 1983 Namche has had electricity produced by a small hydroelectric power plant.

The **National Park Museum** and the central administration of the **Sagarmatha National Park** are located here. In the park everyone must bring along his own fuels; at the entrance to the park, kerosene is available. In the park grounds no wood can be cut down, gathered or purchased from the local people (this also applies to the other national parks). The famous Sherpa artist Kappa Pasang is usually in **Khumjung**.

There are aircraft landing fields in **Jiri**, **Phaplu**, **Lukla** and **Shyangboche**.

There is an office of the RNAC located in **Lukla** (open from 10 am to 4 pm daily except Saturdays). Attention: Flights depend on the weather, and frequently don't take place for days, which pushes the prices up. In Lukla you can stock up on staples as well as luxury goods like chocolate, canned fruit, batteries.

Getting There

You can reach the Solo Khumbu region in a six-day march beginning in **Jiri**, which can be reached by public bus or taxi from Kathmandu, as long as the roads aren't too damaged by the monsoons. This tour – via Deorali Pass, Bhandar, Kenja, Lamjura Pass, Junbesi, Tragsindo La and Nuntala – is certainly very strenuous, but it's also very stimulating. On the drive to Jiri, your trekking permits will be checked. You can fly in by aircraft to four landing strips: **Jiri** (1,900 m), **Phaphlu** (2,700 m), roughly 10 km south of Ringmo – from here you can get to Namche Bazar in four days; **Lukla** (2,800 m) is the only landing strip that is normally flown to daily (cost of flight ca. US$ 85 one-way); recently, you can also fly with Charter Nepal Airways (Tel: 410091, Kathmandu). From here you can get to the Tengpoche Monastery in two or three days; **Shyangboche** (Syampoche, 3,700 m), previously only charter flights to Hotel Everest View, but this might have changed. Inquire!

NEPAL'S FAR EAST

KANCHENJUNGA
MAKALU

KANCHENJUNGA-TREK

For some time now the remote East and the Kanchenjunga, which is the second-highest mountain in Nepal and the third-highest in the world, has also been opened up to group travelers, and to some extent to individual tourists as well. One can still discover a piece of the original Nepal here, without the excessive proliferation of pie shops, restaurants and lodges which transforms many a trekking experience in the heavily-traveled regions more into a trip to the coffee-shop instead of a real encounter with the country and its people.

For this hiking trip too, the traveler must bring along all the necessary provisions and equipment. Particularly for larger groups, it is sensible to have engaged the entire entourage you will need in Kathmandu, since here in East Nepal you cannot count on being able to find carriers and other assistants. There is nothing at all to be bought along the way in the few pasture huts and little hamlets, and even in the larger villages the stores are for the most part not prepared for larger groups. The point of departure for this tour is **Taplejung**, situated in the set-

tlement area of the Limbus. It is a small village nestled in the hill region with a landing strip located about 500 meters higher at **Suketar**, which is flown to by the Royal Nepalese Airline, departing usually from Biratnagar. Waiting for the aircraft at the landing strip are not only local people, but also a checkpost for the tourists. The other way to get to the region is to take a public bus to **Dhankula**, but you will be traveling in the company of many friendly Nepalese, chickens, goats and other domestic animals, crammed into an antique bus.

The trail leads over terraced fields onto a mountain saddle lying at an altitude of 2,550 meters, after which you leave the valley of the **Tamur Khola** in order to climb down to the small town of **Lal Khar** (2,200 meters) and two further small hamlets. The crossing of the **Phao Khola** is on a suspension bridge. You can spend the night in **Kunjur**. Following further along the mountain chain – up for a while, down for a while – you cross the **Khaksena Khola** on another suspension bridge, pass by the little villages of **Funfun** and **Anpang** and, finally, to pitch camp again in the village of **Mamakhe**.

The next day's stage leads further northeastwards in the direction of Sikkim and the Kanchenjunga, on which the small hamlet **Yamphudin** (1,670 meters)

Preceding pages: A view of the Yalung Glacier from Kanchenjunga base camp.

presents a good opportunity to set up camp. After a steep ascent to a mountain saddle (2,440 meters), the trail again leads downwards and crosses over the **Omje Khola** (2,230 meters). The valley of the Omje Khola is sparsely populated, and its steep flanks and its vegetation of hemlock firs, oaks and rhododendrons are impressive.

The path now climbs steeply again to the top of the **Deorali Danda** (3,300 meters), which provides a wonderful view over the mountain world of the Kanchenjunga with its tremendous glaciers. After one more day's hike you can figure on setting up your next camp in the little village of **Tseram** (3,770 meters).

Going past the meadow of **Lapsang** you hike on to the meadows of **Ramze** and **Oktang** along the moraine of the huge **Yalung Glacier**, while the spectacular summits of the **Ratong** (6,678 meters), **Kabru** (7,338 meters) and the entire chain of the **Kanch** peaks – the highest of which reaches a proud 8,586 meters – are always before your eyes. At **Oktang** the trail ends, and any further trek is only possible directly over the glacier – in other words, passable only for expeditions.

The Kanchenjunga was conquered for the first time on May 25 and 26, 1955, by a British expedition under the leadership of G. Band, N. Hardie and S. Streather. The actual **Kanch Basecamp** is located further up on one of the **Tso Glaciers**.

For those who would like further variation and enjoy beautiful views of **Makalu** (8,463 meters) and the **Chamlang** (7,319 meters), a return path is recommended through the Tibetan settlement of **Ghunsa**. This can be reached in two days starting from the Ramze Meadow over **Tseram** and several passes that lie over 4,000 meters – among them the Tamo La. This trail represents an interesting change of landscape in comparison to the approach already described, and provides splendid views on some bizarre

black rock formations. It also gives a final glimpse of **Khumbarkarna** (7,710 meters), which in mountain-climber's literature is often referred to as **Jannu**. The first checkpost along the trail awaits you beyond Taplejung in Ghunsa.

The path follows the Ghunsa Khola steeply up and down and soon reaches the settlement of **Phalay**, which is inhabited by Tibetans from the area of Mustang. Outward from the valley the path continues on to **Ghaia Bari**. This is close to the source of the **Tamur**, which later joins the **Arun** to form the **Sapti Khosi**. Following the Tamur leads to the original departure point of **Taplejung**. For those who want to hike further, there is the path over **Dhoban** and **Nundaki** which slithers all the way to **Chainpur**, and the nearby village of **Tumlingtar**.

Chainpur is located at a height of 1,600 meters and extends along the path over the ridgeback. It is one of those small, friendly little towns that possess their own unique charm. One is impressed by the neat houses with their beautiful wooden balconies and the often blindingly white color of their façades. This is actually a settlement area of the Rai, but in Chainpur, Newar traders and craftsmen have also settled, and nowadays they have considerable impact on the character of the village.

Chainpur is well known for its metal working and brass casting, which has been used primarily to make utility articles like lamps and vessels. Even to this day, copper kettles and pots belong to the traditional dowries at weddings. The mines are gradually being exhausted, however, the flood of cheap Indian mass production goods is presenting the toughest competition to the traditional crafts.

The locality of **Tumlingtar** (3,900 meters) – to which the Royal Nepalese Airline also flies – is the point of departure for two additional trekking tours. In a march lasting ten days one hikes the path already described to **Taplejung**, and then descends towards **Thapapani Danda** (1,378 meters) and **Phidim** in the Mechi precinct. After passing over **Suke-pokhari** (2,850 meters), the highest point in this journey, one finally arrives at the rather tropical **Ilam** (1,200 meters).

During many trekking tours you have to contend with some very cold and in-auspicious weather, but here, because of the lower altitude, it is the heat that you will have to tolerate. The return trip to Kathmandu can be made either by bus via Birtamod, Hetauda and Mugling – this variant requires two days travel time – or by bus to Birathnagar from where there are airplanes.

MAKALU BASE CAMP

Starting out from Tumlingtar you reach the **Makalu Base Camp** (5,000 m) by making a rewarding seven-day-long tour. Since you will find yourself, from Tashigaon onwards, in an uninhabited region for ten days, this tour requires elaborate preparations. From Tumlingtar, the trail leads over a mountain ridge up to the district center **Khandbari** and further to Arunthan. Continuing ever further north, the path goes high along the ridgeback above the Arun and on the Munche and Num. At this point it turns in a northwesterly direction, proceeding to the last inhabited place of **Tashigaon** at an altitude of some 2,200 meters.

From the base camp there are fantastic views of the summits of Mount Everest, Lhotse and the Makalu. A return path variant via the base of Baruntse, Sherpani Col (6,110 m), and the passes West Col (6,135 m) and Amphu Lapbtsa (5,780 m), can only be undertaken by genuine expeditions.

The **Arun** has its source in the regions of the Makalu and the Lumbusamba Himal. It is possible to go on a three to four day Arun river-rafting from **Tumlingtar**, which must be organized from Kathmandu.

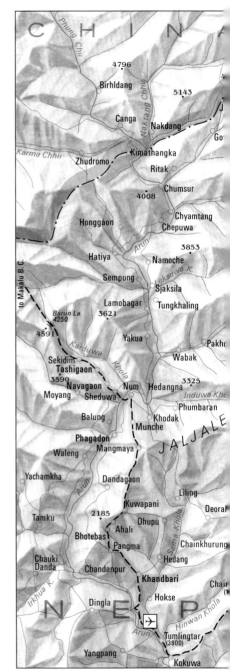

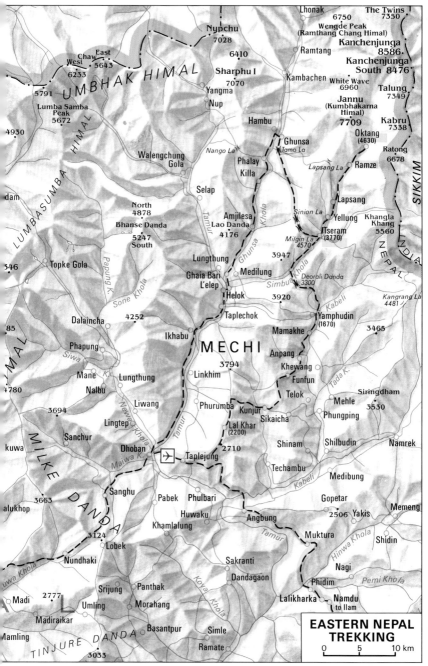

Lhonak
The Twins 7350
Nupchu 7028
6750
Wengde Peak
(Ramthang Chang Himal)
Ramtang
Kanchenjunga 8586
Chaw East
West 5643
6233
6410
Sharphu I 7070
Kambachen
White Wave 6960
Kanchenjunga South 8476
UMBHAK HIMAL
5791
Yangma
Nup
Talung 7349
Lumba Samba Peak 5672
Hambu
Jannu (Kumbhakarna Himal) 7709
Kabru 7338
4930
Ghunsa
Tomo La
Oktang (4630)
Ratong 6678
Walengchung Gola
Nango La
Phalay Killa
Lapsang La
Ramze
LUMBASUMBA HIMAL
Selap
Tamur
Lapsang
SIKKIM
dam
North 4878
Amjilesa
Lao Danda 4176
Sinion La
Yellung
Khangla Khang 5560
Bhanse Danda
5247 South
Milgin La 4570
Tseram (3770)
346
Topke Gola
Papung K.
Lungthung
3947
Deorali Danda 3300
NEPAL INDIA
Sone Khola
Ghaia Bari
L'elep
Medilung
Simbua Khola
Kangrang La 4481
85
4252
Helok
3920
Kabeli
Dalaincha
Taplechok
Yamphudin (1670)
3465
Phapung
Ikhabu
MECHI
Mamakhe
Siwa
Mane
Lungthung
3794
Anpang
Khewang
Nalbu
Linkhim
Funfun
Siringdham 3530
4780
3694
Liwang
Telok
Mehle
MILKE
Lingtep
Phurumba
Kunjur
Sikaicha
Phungping
Sanchur
Lal Khar (2200)
Shinam
Shilbudin
Namrek
kuwa
Dhoban
Taplejung
2710
Techambu
Newa Khola
Tamur
Maiwa K.
Kabeli
Sanghu
Pabek
Phulbari
Medibung
3663
Huwaku
Angbung
Gopetar
Memeng
alukhop
DANDA
Khamlalung
2506 Yakis
3124
Lobek
Tamur
Muktura
Shidin
Nundhaki
Hinwa Khola
uwa Khola
Sakranti
Nagi
Srijung
Panthak
Dandagaon
Phidim
Pemi Khola
Madi
2777
Umling
Morahang
Koya Khola
Lalikharka
Namdu (to Ilam)
Madiraikar
Basantpur
Simle
Mamling
TINJURE DANDA
3033
Ramate

EASTERN NEPAL TREKKING

0   5   10 km

179

1 Far Western
2 Mid Western
3 Western
4 Central
5 Eastern

THE TERAI

LUMBINI

CHITWAN

JANAKPUR

THE TERAI

Bordered to the south by the Ganges plain and in the north by the towering foothills of the Himalayan Range, the **Terai** is the most important economic and industrial region in Nepal. This subtropical plain in southern Nepal is a narrow strip stretching from west to east with a maximum width of 40 kilometers, at between 60 and 600 meters above sea-level. The Terai makes up 23 percent of the total land area of Nepal, and approximately 44 percent of the Nepalese population lives here.

Characteristic for this subtropical zone is its moist, warm climate with temperatures of over 40 degrees C in June/July and a precipitation level of over 2,000 millimeters during the monsoon season, which sets in during June. From the beginning of April up until that time a withering heat dominates, with temperatures of over 50 degrees C.

About half of the Nepalese population here is linguistically and ethnically influenced by neighboring India in particular. Among the oldest ethnic groups who live here are the Tharu, numbering roughly half a million. They live pre-

Left: A dangerous meeting with a rhinoceros in the tall elephant grass.

dominantly in the villages which are strewn around the western and central Terai, today making their living from agriculture. Up until now their cultural origins have remained unclear. One of the remarkable cultural features are their roomy houses, built of clay and decorated with fish patterns and other frequently abstract animal motifs. The Tharu still worship their own gods and spirits for the most part; however, here and there a few Hinduist deities can also be found in their villages.

The Tharu are the only ethnic group who had probably already settled here in Chitwan during the 12th century. Up until a short while ago they still lived from hunting, gathering and fishing in small groups. With the exception of the grains that grow wild, which they harvested, they were hardly familiar with genuine agriculture. Scarcely anyone else ventured into this region because there were no roads; in addition, almost the whole valley consisted of swampy primeval forest full of malaria-carrying mosquitos and wild animals.

In search for new farmland and better living conditions, about 10,000 families annually have been moving out of the mountainous regions into the Terai for some time now, where land shortages are becoming a constantly growing problem.

181

In comparison to the high mountain regions – where around 25 people per square kilometer live – in the Terai there is now an average of 200 people per square kilometer. The numbers are increasing because the border with India is open for Nepalese and Indians. It is assumed that the uncontrolled immigration wave has given three to five million Indians the opportunity to settle in the whole of Nepal as greengrocers and factory workers. They are known for being particularly wily businessmen. Especially notorious are the Indian Marwari, a trader group which, it is said, participates in two-thirds of the trading businesses, and has enormous influence over Nepalese economic policies. Together with roughly 10 percent of the larger Nepalese landowners they are supposed to own some 50 percent of the arable land.

Above: A Tharu crosses the Narayani river on the back of a water buffalo. Right: A fisherman at work. Far right: A ceremonially decorated elephant.

The population increase is leading to more and more tension, especially in the important industrial and trade centers in the Terai. However, in the country too, overpopulation is putting pressures on the availability of the highly fertile land. Roughly two thirds of the country's agricultural production comes from the region of the Terai. Rice, maize, wheat, beans, lentils, jute, sugar cane, and more recently even coffee are being cultivated here. In several areas the farmers even produce up to three harvests annually, because sediments important for the soil are deposited onto the flat plains, dissolved and carried by the torrential rivers plummeting from the Himalayas. But the swollen rivers also create flooding, destroying crops, washing away huts, and inundating entire villages.

LUMBINI
Buddha's Birthplace

Those travelers who enter Nepal from India through the small city of **Bhairawa**

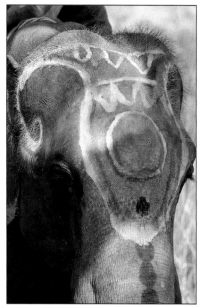

in the southwest should not fail to visit **Lumbini**, 20 kilometers away from there. Buses make the trip regularly, but you can also make an agreement to take a taxi there. As the birthplace of Siddharta Gautama – also named Buddha Shakyamuni, the Enlightened One, the historical Buddha – Lumbini has become a famous place of pilgrimage for Buddhists from the entire world.

Like so many of the royal sons of his time, Siddharta lived surrounded in luxury at his father's court. At the age of 29, during four trips to the city, he was confronted for the first time with human misery. The sight of an old man, of a sick person and a dead body taught him the perishability of all material. His encounter with a monk kindled in him the desire to work toward eliminating misery. He secretly left his home, wife and child. After years of asceticism in Bodh Gaya near Benares, and with the help of various meditation exercises, he achieved the enlightenment that made him Buddha, the Awoken One. He answered the question about the reason for the entanglement of living beings in the cycle of existence in the first of his Sarnath sermons, known as "The Four Noble Truths." They form the very heart of his teachings. Some of the most important postulates that have been handed down to this day are the ideas that, 1) Everything in the world is transitory and filled with pain, 2) The misery of existence is caused by lust and ignorance, 3) Freedom from this cycle is only possible through quenching the "thirst," that is the will to live, for which Buddha suggested an eight part road to salvation involving schooling in morals, meditation, wisdom and insight. Release – i.e. enlightenment – is synonymous with the extinguishing of existence, the complete freeing from this world, the achieving of Nirvana. Before reaching this point, man must go through an endless cycle of different existences, including some painful states.

Hinayana, or Buddhism of the "small vehicle," grew from this original Buddhism around the 4th and 5th centuries

B.C., and later split further into Thera-vada Buddhism among others. By the end of the first century A.D., however, conflicting views of the teachings led to a schism climaxing in Mahayana Budd-hism, the Buddhism of the "great ve-hicle." The idol of this tendency is the figure of the Bodhisattva ("whose being is enlightenment"), who had already earned the necessary requirements to become Buddha and achieve Nirvana, but who deliberately avoided the final step in order to help other beings on their way to enlightenment. The special mani-festation of Mahayana Buddhism known as Vajrayna Buddhism, with its exercise of magic and secret teachings, is still alive and well in Nepal today.

In 1895, a German archeologist first discovered the now famous stone col-umns of the Indian Emperor Ashoka,

Above: A Magar girl adorned with red flowers washes the dishes. Right: A Budd-hist monastery in Lumbini, the birthplace of Buddha.

who had them erected around 250 B.C. in honor of Buddha and as a monument to his visit here. The inscription on the col-umns describes the place of Buddha's birth in the **Kapilavastu Plain**, the capi-tal of which – during Buddha's lifetime – was probably **Tilaurkot**, 27 kilometers away. King Suddhodhana, ruler of Kapi-lavastu, was the father of Siddharta Gau-tama. Descriptions of this place were made by Chinese monks from the 5th and 7th centuries A.D.; in the 13th century Malla rulers from West Nepal made jour-neys to this place of pilgrimage. Since the 13th century, the increasing influence of the islamic Moguls caused this once so sought-out pilgrimage destination to be forgotten.

Lumbini stepped again into the lime-light in 1967, as the then General Secre-tary of the United Nations, U Thant – himself a pious Buddhist –, visited this village. At his initiative, an international program of support for the re-building and expansion of this pilgrimage destina-tion was designed and executed. With

Mecca and Jerusalem as the centers of Islam and Christianity as examples, Lumbini was – according to U Thant's plan – to receive a similar position of value for the Buddhists of the entire world. The original plan was impressive: It included representative monasteries for all the different orientations, national or religious, of Buddhism, an archeological museum with finds from excavations, a library and an information center as well as a large garden crossed with canals, in which it was envisaged that monasteries and pilgrim lodgings would be erected so that a quiet and contemplative atmosphere could be provided.

But those who look for these things in Lumbini will be disappointed. Besides the **Ashoka Columns**, several votive stupas and the stone foundation of the ruins of a monastery, today there is only a lamaist monastery in Lumbini with a larger-than-life sized portrait of Buddha Shakyamuni in its interior, and a monastery with a marble statue of the Enlightened One donated by Burma.

The **Maya Devi Shrine** located nearby was named after Siddhartha Gautama's mother. Its most important item on display is a stone relief with a representation of the birth of the Enlightened One – which according to the legends is supposed to have occurred here.

According to another legend, on the way from Kapilavastu to the house of his parents Queen Maya Devi is supposed to have settled under a shorea tree in the palace gardens of Lumbini in order to give birth to a son. Located south of the shrine is the **Pushkarni Pond**, where Buddha took his first purifying bath.

CHITWAN

The **Chitwan** region demonstrates just how different the regions of the Terai can be. Towering to the north is the 3,000-m-high Mahabharata Range, in the south the Siwalik Hills (150-500 meters high), also called the Churia Range, separate the valley from the flat plain of the exterior Terai. Here the subtropical jungle is broken up by broad grasslands and impenetrable swampland. In earlier times, when the logging of the forests had not yet begun, this region in the interior of the Terai was an impenetrable jungle populated by wild animals and contaminated with malaria, where only the Thurus could live, for they were supposed to be resistant to this illness.

On the other hand, the Chitwan Valley was a splendid hunting grounds for the Nepalese and Indian Rajas, who enjoyed organizing large hunting expeditions for tigers and other wild animals for their European guests. Hundreds of elephants were employed for such safaris. However, today the existence of many species of animals is endangered.

Since the Nepalese Government started carrying out its large campaign against malaria contamination, in cooperation with the World Health Organization, roads have been constructed and the attempt has been made to gain more farmland for the increasing population by drying out swamplands. This has brought with it the logging of the shorea forests, which has sorely restricted the living area of wild animals. For example, today in Chitwan there are no longer any wild elephants. This was the reason why in 1973 it was decided to found the **Chitwan National Park**. The success is encouraging. The number of animals is increasing – as is the number of visitors, which now has become almost a matter of concern. The park is considered one of the most interesting and beautiful in all of Asia.

As a result of the extension of the road network (Kathmandu-Muglin-Narayangadh) and its connection with the East-West Highway, Chitwan is becoming an important intersection for Nepalese transportation. Within the shortest time new schools and hospitals were built in the neighboring cities of **Narayangadh** and **Bharatpur**, and in the meantime in **Hetauda**, 50 kilometers away, a considerable small industry has been developed.

JANAKPUR
Sita's Birthplace

Not far away from **Biratnagar**, the largest city in the Terai with around 131,000 inhabitants (128 km from Kathmandu), **Janakpur** is in the southeast of the plain. To experience some local color, you can take a chance with the bus that shuttles from Kathmandu.

In mythical times this is supposed to have been the location of the capital of the old Mithila Kingdom, the king of which was the holy Janak, the father of Sita. The place played a significant role in one of the two great Indian epics, the *Ramayana*, as the birthplace of Sita, later the wife of Ram, the hero of the epic named after him. Ram as well as Sita are worshipped as incarnations of the god Vishnu and his spouse Lakshmi.

Each year on his birthday in April, Ram is worshipped as rescuer, emancipator and protector by the hundreds of pilgrims who stream into Janakpur to **Ram Mandir**, the temple dedicated to him. In 1927, the building was renovated by the Rana-Premier Chandra Shumsher. The golden roof also originates from that time. Sita's birthday – *Janaki Nawami* – is celebrated in May, just as elaborately, at the **Janaki Temple** dedicated to her. It is a destination for Hindu pilgrims from throughout the Asian subcontinent.

The enormous grounds were constructed by the Maharani of Tikamagadh (India) and completed in 1907 after 12 years of building, in the style of the Mogul-Rajasthani architecture. The temple is the main attraction in Janakpur.

The most significant festival in Janakpur is the *Vivaha Panchami* in November/December – commemorating the anniversary of the marriage of Sita and Rama. Thousands of pilgrims from Nepal and India come here at this time. A traditional marriage procession and ceremony then takes place. The festival is celebrated every year with great enthusiasm.

NARAYANGHAD

MODERATE: **Narayani Safari** with pool and tennis court in Bharatpur in the neighborhood of the landing strip; reservations through Hotel Narayani in Patan, Tel: 521442.

CHITWAN

LUXURY: Tiger Tops Jungle Lodge, in the park, single room US\$ 425. Tiger Tops Tharu Safari Resort, reservation in Kathmandu, Durbar Marg, Tel: 415659.

MODERATE: **Gaida Wildlife,** Tel: 220940. **Chitwan Jungle Lodge**, Tel: 228918. **Machan Wildlife Resort**, Tel: 225001. **Temple Tiger**, Tel: 221585. **Island Resort**, Tel: 226022.

BUDGET: in Sauraha at the entrance to the National Park.

BHAIRAWA

BUDGET: **Shambala Guest House**, **Pashupati Lodge**, **Lumbini**, **Himalaya Inn**, **Kailash.**

LUMBINI

BUDGET: **Lumbini Guest House.**

JANAKPUR

BUDGET: **Wellcome, Janakpur** and **Rainbow.**

BIRGANJ

BUDGET: **Diyalo**, **Sagar Lodge** and **Koseli.**

HETAUDA

BUDGET: **Avocado.**

Miscellaneous

Elephant rides in the National Park, camera safaris for rhinos.

Elephant Polo: In the first half of December each year in Chitwan / Meghaula a "World Championship" elephant race is carried out.

Bhairawa / Sonauli is located on the Nepalese/Indian border and is one of the most popular points of travel both in and out. Starting from here you can drive over Tansen to Pokhara or get to Kathmandu via Chitwan/Narayanghad (either over Muglin or over the old road in Hetauda). At the Napalese border there is a tourist office.

Birganj is another popular point of travel into and out of Nepal. At the Nepalese customs there is a branch of the Nepal Rastrya Bank. Note: Those leaving from India must set their watches ahead fifteen minutes. There is a tourist office opposite Birganj bus terminal.

Traffic Connections
NARAYANGHAD / CHITWAN PARK

BUS / CAR: Narayanghad can be reached from Kathmandu by bus and taxi. The trip takes ca. five hours by bus. If you want to take the bus to Chitwan, take the one in the direction of Hetauda/Birganj and get out at Tadi Bazar behind Narayanghad. From there on foot or by ox-cart it takes 8 km in an hour or so to Sauraha. On the way you must wade through the Buri Rapti River, if no jeep, ox-cart or boat is crossing over. From Kathmandu you can join an organized tour including hotel reservations in Chitwan.

BOAT: You can book a day-long river trip in a rubber raft from Muglin to Chitwan Park or Narayanghat during which you will be received at some safari camps. These tours are to be booked in Kathmandu.

AIR: There is a landing strip in Narayanghad/Bharatpur. Three flights per day to Kathmandu (Royal Nepal, Everest Air, Nepal Airways). One way flight costs US\$ 50. In addition, in the area of Narayanghad is the Meghauli landing field. The Tiger Tops Jungle Lodge is 8 km away.

BHAIRAWA / LUMBINI

BUS: From the central bus station in Bhairahawa you can ride to Pokhara by public bus via Tansen (184 km); the fastest connection to Kathmandu from Bhairahawa goes through Narayanghad and Muglin (ca. 10-12 hours, 292 km.). Those wanting to go to Chitwan Park can get out in Tadi Bazar before Narayanghad. Night buses also travel this route.

FLIGHT: There is a landing strip for domestic flights in Bhairahawa. There is a daily direct flight to Kathmandu, US\$ 72 one-way; flights once a week to Pokhara.

BUS / CAR: Regular bus connections from Bhairawa to Lumbini (22 km). The bus ride takes about one hour. It's faster by taxi – you have to haggle about the fair.

BIRGANJ

BUS: Buses to Birganj start out from the central bus station in Kathmandu. There are also night buses. From Birganj, busses drive through Muglin to Kathmandu (272 km). You can also use the old road behind Hetauda through Daman – it is shorter, but time consuming because it is windy.

FLIGHT: There is a landing strip with direct flights to Kathmandu in Birganj/Simra (US\$ 44 one-way). Note: in the monsoon season the strip is often under water and therefore unusable.

JANAKPUR

BUS: Daily bus connections to and from Kathmandu – nights also. The journey lasts about twelve hours. The buses run partly via Birganj.

FLIGHT: The RNAC offers regular flights from Kathmandu to Janakpur.

THE HIDDEN KINGDOM

TREKKING IN MUSTANG

On a high plateau north of the mountain giants of Annapurna and Dhaulagiri, between Nepal and Tibet, lies the little former kingdom of Mustang. It is surrounded by a ca. 6,000-meter-high chain of mountains. Until May 1992 this "forbidden" kingdom was practically inaccessible. With few exceptions, foreigners were not allowed to enter it.

Legend and myth enshrouds the history of Mustang, which is also called Kingdom of Lo. Only one day's ride from the Tibetan border, and at 3,790 meters, is the old fortified capital of Lo Manthang with its medieval royal palace and significant fifteenth century Buddhist monasteries. The about 10,000 Lopa people living in Mustang belong ethnically and culturally within the Tibetan sphere. They are Bhotiyas – the Nepalese name for the Buddhist inhabitants of the Himalayas who speak Tibetan. This fact is reflected in their way of life and their clothing, their writings and festivals. Their religious ideas in particular follow Vajrayana-Buddhism. Various teachings exist within the Vajrayana. In Mustang the so-called Ngor-Sakya school has a special tradition.

Preceding pages: Typical gate – chörten in Tsarang. Left: In Kagbeni begins the Tibetan cultural sphere.

In Lo one will often see ghost-traps at the entrances of houses. They offer protection against demons. These traps, consisting mainly of juniper branches and animal horns, are reminders of the animistic *bön* religion, which is much older than Buddhism itself. This bön tradition is most probably the source of the strong shamanistic elements found in Tibetan Buddhism today. One will also see water-driven prayer mills.

The trails to the capital lead along bizarre rock formations of sandstone, granite or limestone, along steep clay-cones and slopes out of which the wind has eroded the most fantastic shapes. The Saligram stones which are considered holy, originate in the up to 200-million-year-old slate sedimentation of the Jurassic and Cretaceous periods. They are petrified ammonites and one can often find them along the rivers. It is believed that they bring luck. One can discover ancient caves high up above the valleys in the steep rock massifs. Some of them are inhabited to this day, for example in Garphu and Nyiphu. Spelaeologists have discovered in Mustang traces of the oldest human settlements in the Himalayas.

Mustang is as dry as a desert and often very windy. The climate is mainly Tibetan continental with short, hot summers and temperatures that can reach 30 °C.

Winters are long and severe, and the thermometer will often drop to minus 15 °C. Up to a height of 4,000 meters-plus, the countryside is characterized by alpine steppes with poor vegetation.

Those who can watch snow leopards or blue sheep (baral), which are extremely rare, can consider themselves very lucky. The Tibetan antelope and the Kashmiri deer are probably now extinct, and one will only seldom see argali sheep or the Kyang, a kind of wild donkey. Marmots and calling hares on the other hand are to be found more frequently, as are golden eagles. Himalayan and bearded vultures circle overhead. Especially impressive is the migration in October of the Demoiselle cranes. Arriving from Central Asia, they fly in their thousands high over Mustang heading south, to Gujarat in India.

Above: Winnowing Lopa women at the barley- and buckwheat harvest near Thingkar. Right: Jigme Palbar Tandal, the king of Mustang

The river known in the south of the Mustang district as Kali Gandaki is called Mustang Khola in the north, beginning from the settlement of Kagbeni. It cuts its way through the whole area in a deep gorge. Its sources are said to be in the Tibetan border area on Mount Dongmar (6,480 meters), the seat of the Mustang royal family's patron god.

The Mustang Khola is fed by many tributaries, which have compact villages along their banks, built mostly of beaten clay, and also scattered settlements, which are like little oases in this arid, desert landscape. Accordingly the area of the region under cultivation is quite small and requires irrigation. Barley and buckwheat are the main crops.

October is harvest time and it is one of the most beautiful experiences to go into the fields on a sunny working day when the poplar leaves are slowly turning yellow. One can see how the cereal is threshed with a flail to the rhythm of harvest songs, while horses tread in a circle over the sheaves, and women winnow the grains in flat baskets. One can hear their songs long into the night.

Besides Tibetan poplars and willow trees along the irrigation canals, one will find in Mustang mainly juniper bushes and trees. Their branches are burned in the Buddhist monasteries in order to drive away evil influences. There is also the occasional Himalayan pine and mountain cypress. Bigger tree concentrations are scarce. They can be found for example in the area of Gyakhar and Samar, where one can see mule caravans departing with transports of wood for other areas. Villages benefit from a specific timber allowance, otherwise dried animal dung is generally used for heating purposes.

Many Lopa people migrate during the cold season to the south and trade in textile goods and herbs.

The Upper Mustang Conservation and Development Project (UMCDP), a worthy initiative, takes care of the "controlled tourism" of this region. It organizes afforestation projects with willows and poplars, lays out herb gardens, builds bridges and tracks, irrigation canals and small hydro-electric plants, encourages the use of solar energy, supports the construction of a monks' school in Lo Mantang and the restoration of the area's monasteries.

Trekking in Mustang

Two thousand trekkers are allowed each year into Mustang, but one's visit must be organized as an expensive package tour by a Nepalese agency (addresses p. 101), and one must be accompanied by a liaison officer. There are other expensive charges to be paid: US$ 700 for the first ten days (every subsequent day US$ 70), US$ 15 for a nature conservation fee, plus US$ 5 per week for the trekking permit. One has to provide for one's own tents, provisions and kerosene. One can hire mules in Jomosom and Kagbeni.

One has to retain the group's trash, and deposit it on the way out in Kagbeni, at the UMDCP post.

There are several routes to the capital of Lo. They are generally strenuous, with passes at about 4,000 meters high, but not as difficult as for example a trekking through Dolpo.

It is advisable to plan at least 14 days for the trek. One can fly with several airlines from Kathmandu and Pokhara to Jomosom. There, at the north end of the airport facing the Om-Lodge, a checkpost inspects your trekking permits.

The trek begins in Jomsom (2,743 meters), leading either on a high path or along the Kali Gandaki river bed to **Kagbeni** (2,810 meters), ca. three hours away. If you have time, at the half-way point you should make a detour to **Lupra** (2,950 meters), which you can reach from Jomosom in two hours. Here is one of the few Bön gompas in Mustang, founded as long ago as 1160. From Lupra one can return either along the Panda river to the starting point of the detour in

193

the Gandaki Valley, or take the trail via Muktinath, Dzong (Tshong) and Tetang to Tshuksang, where one hits again the main route.

In Kagbeni one has to register again with the UMCDP bureau, because it is here that the restricted area of Upper Mustang begins. This picturesque old fortress town has nice Tibetan style lodges and an old Sakyapa gompa. There is also a kerosene depot and a tree nursery of the UMCDP.

From Kagbeni one can make an excursion to **Tingri** on the other side of the Kali Gandaki, about one hour away. It has an interesting Nyingmapa monastery, occupied earlier by nuns, and today quite dilapidated. For the quite long and steep, but nevertheless worthwhile way up from Kagbeni to **Mukinath** (3,800 meters), one needs about six hours.

But the usual route to Lo Manthang leads from Kagbeni to **Tshuksang** (2,920

Above: The Amchi-Lama of Lo is an expert in the Tibetan art of healing.

meters) in five to six hours. It is advisable to rest for lunch in **Tanbe** (2,930 meters). One can reach Tshuksang from there in two hours. From here one can make trips to **Tetang** and to the Nyingmapa monastery **gompa Khang** (the key to be picked up in Tshuksang).

The UMCDP has built a medical station in Tshuksang. Above it, in a steep rock face, there is a rock gompa that can be visited. In Tshuksang one has to decide whether to take the west route over Tshele, Samar (3,560 meters), Gelung (3,500 meters) and Gemi (3,540 meters) to Tsarang (3,530 meters), or the east route to Lo Manthang. Less experienced trekkers are advised to take the west route because of the easier climb over Samar.

On the east route one reaches the capital Lo Manthang from Tshuksang (2,920 meters) via Pee, Tangye, Luri Gompa and Dri. It is a long walk to the secluded camp of **Pee** (3,950 meters). For eight to nine hours one climbs through an indescribable rock landscape. Pee is a small settlement, only a few goatherds live here in their tents and share the small water source that also has to be used by the trekkers. At this altitude, it gets dark early and the wind can cut through you.

The trip on the next day takes ca. four hours. From Pee one crosses the **Narsing La** Pass (4,110 meters) and from there one descends 800 meters into **Tangye**. The image of the village is characterized by a big group of chorten, symbolizing one of the eight important stations in Buddha's life. The stripes in which they are painted show that they belong to the Ngor-Sakya school.

From Tangye (3,310 meters), one can reach via the Mustang Pass (5,450 meters) the Damodar Himal with the sacred **Damodar lakes**, and then via Nar and Phu one can descend into the Marsyandi Valley.

About six hours from Tangye on the road to the capital is the little village of **Dri** (3,340 meters), fit for an overnight stay. On the way there, one can only cross the river bed of the Tangye and the Mustang Khola during the low-water season. At other times of the year, one should take the high path.

From Dri one can make a day-trip to Luri Gompa (3,370 meters) of about eleven hours' duration. After crossing the Ghechang Khola, there follows a steep climb up to 3,550 meters. Then, following the road to Yara, one passes rock cones with ancient caves. After a total of ca. six hours one can see the jewel of **Luri gompa**, a rock temple high above the valley, which can be reached after a short, steep climb. You absolutely must hire in advance a guide with a key for this hermitage.

It is mainly the marvellous 14th century wallpaintings that prompt our admiration here. They are in a room of four by four meters, that almost fills a chorten. The gompa belongs to the Drukpa Kagyüpa school and is probably the only place in Mustang to be dated earlier than the monasteries in Lo Manthang itself. The way back to Dri leads through the villages of Ghara and Yara.

One should plan six to seven hours from Dri to **Lo Manthang** (3,790 meters). The day begins with a difficult climb over rubble and scree. One feels one has been transported into a moon landscape. The path leads above 4,000 meters and the view on arrival is breathtaking. One can see the fortified capital of Lo Manthang in the plain, the mountains surrounding it and the border with Tibet. It is advisable to rest in Lo Manthang for two to three days.

The town has an almost fully medieval appearance. Traditionally, it is said to have been founded by King Amepal in the fifteenth century A.D. He invited the lama Künga Zangpo, a member of the Ngor-Sakyapa school, to come from Tibet to Lo. There, Künga Zangpo built two monasteries, **Jampa Lhakang** and **Thubchen Lhakang**, which charm their

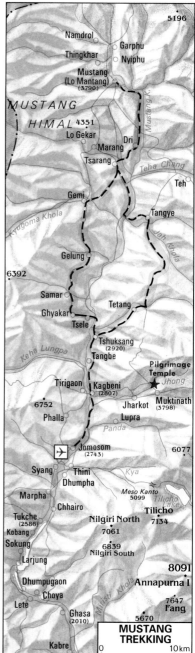

visitors to this day with their wonderful paintings and carvings. Unfortunately, these buildings are badly in need of restoration. The 44 mandalas on the first floor of the Jampa Lhakang are of artistic value.

High walls surround the town's maze of narrow streets, roofed passages and houses tangled up with each other. The town's ca. 145 multi-floored buildings have cattle on the ground floor, food and merchandise on the floor above and the living quarters on the top floor. Bundles of firewood are traditionally stored on the roofs.

There are now even some souvenir shops in Lo Manthang offering goods imported from Tibet and India. Though with the help of UMCDP, local suppliers have again resumed constructing ghost-traps and making other artefacts for sale to tourists.

In the four-floor **raja palace** in the town centre, which can be visited, lives the 25th King of Lo, Jigme Palbar Tandul (Bista). His rani, the queen, comes from Shigatse.

No one but the king is allowed to ride through the gates of the town on horseback. The palace and the town walls were probably built in the 15th century. The **Chöde Lhakang** (new monastery) was built later to the north of the town walls. It is the only town monastery still active in Manthang. Under the abbot Tashi Tenzing, about 40 monks live here, adhering to the Sakya tradition. In a small modern building near the main temple one is allowed to take photographs after gaining permission.

One should leave at least two days for trips in the area. One can make a day trip to the **Namgyal** monastery, about one hour from Lo. In the Namgyal gompa, at 4,000 meters and with excellent views,

Right: Great piles of firewood on the roofs are regarded as symbols of wealth in Tshuksang (Altitude 2920 meters).

many monks follow the Vajrayana ritual. One can continue the trip via Phuwa up to the summer residence of the raja in **Thingkhar**.

The day trip to **Garphu** and the gompa in **Nyiphu** can be mastered only on Mustang ponies (ca. 500 rupies per day). You will still find a few inhabited caves. There, parallel with the Mustang river, runs the old Tibetan trade route, "for centuries used by pilgrims and apostles, robbers and conquerors", as the Italian explorer of Mustang, Giuseppe Tucci, wrote after his journey in 1952.

About four kilometers west of Lo is the **Samdruling gompa**, belonging, like Luri, to the Kagyüpa school.

Leaving the medieval Lo Manthang with a heavy heart, one should not fail to make a detour to the **Lo Gekar gompa** (3,870 meters), even though this is not on the direct route to Tsarang (3,530 meters). This trip takes eight hours and leads over three passes higher in parts than 4,000 meters. Lo Gekar (Kar Gompa) is a Nyingmapa settlement. It is said that the founder of Buddhism in Tibet, Padmasambhava, hid so-called treasure texts at various places in Tibet as well as here in the 8th century.

From Lo Gekar one continues to walk for two hours to Tsarang, passing the picturesque settlement of **Marang**. Those with time to spare can take a high path to **Tangmar**, and pass its red rocks and caves.

Tsarang has one of the most impressive monastic complexes in Mustang. It was built in the 16th century and is under the care of Sakya monks. A visit to the old, uninhabited royal palace of Tsarang is worthwhile for the splendid decoration of the small palace temple. The walk from Tsarang to **Gemi** takes only about three hours. When leaving Tsarang, one walks past the big gate chörten typical of Mustang, ascends a pass of 3,820 meters and descends to Gemi (3,450 meters). This is the third

biggest settlement of the region. Not far away from the entrance to Gemi one can admire the 300-meter-long *mani* wall, the longest of its kind in Mustang. It consists of thousands of stones encarved with the holy mantra *om mani padme hum*, donated by pious Buddhist pilgrims and traders.

Until the American-Chinese rapprochement of the early 1970s there was a camp of the Tibetan exile-Khampas here supported by the CIA. Following Tibet's 1959 annexation the CIA had organized from Mustang the resistance against the Chinese occupation of Tibet.

The next day-trip leads from Gemi to **Gelung** (3,500 meters) in about four hours. After a climb of 400 meters to the Nyi La Pass (3,950 meters) one descends to Gelung, where one should not miss the **Tashi Chöling monastery**, a Ngor Sakya gompa. Women are not allowed to visit the temple of the patron god.

The next day one walks from Gelung to Samar in about four hours. If you have time you should chose the longer route

via the rock hermitage **Rangchyung Chörten** (3,450 meters). Lying in the middle of a deep gorge and of very solitary aspect, this cave complex is one of the most holy places in Mustang, similar to Lo Gekar, because tradition has it that Padmasambhava also spent some time here. Pilgrims are always arriving at this spot, and it is considered to be a "place of power". From here one has to climb a steep 350 meters (to 3,780 meters) to continue along a gorgeous high path to **Samar** (3,560 meters). There one can now find a small lodge thanks to the training of small hotel managers organized by members of the Upper Mustang Conservation and Development Project (UMCDP).

From Samar the road continues into the valley, passes the settlements of **Gyakhar** and **Tshele**, where the region of the Thakali language begins, reaching **Tshuksang** and then **Tangbe** (2,930 meters). From here one can reach the starting point of Jomosom (2,743 meters) via Kagbeni in a day.

NATIONAL PARKS

If the measure of economic well-being was a country's natural endowment, then Nepal would certainly be one of the richest lands in the world. Within scarcely 200 kilometers this kingdom of interior Central Asia presents a truly unique ecological spectrum, beginning with an altitude of less than 100 meters above sealevel and rising up to the highest point on earth at 8,846 meters.

Inside the 147,000 square kilometers of the country there are four distinct biotic provinces. Almost 23 percent of the area of Nepal consists of the hot and humid Terai lowland, a continuation of the fertile subtropical Ganges Plain of India. The "Midlands," a central region of rugged mountains and terraced farmland, takes up almost 44 percent of the country. The remainder is dominated by the Himalayan Mountains with their extensive uninhabitable zone of eternal snow and ice, and with the Trans-Himalaya Region, which, with its treeless steppes, has the semiarid character of Tibet.

These extremes are endowed with a wealth of fauna and flora which is beyond comparison in the entire region. Geography has made of Nepal a crossover zone between both of the most extreme ecological spheres in the world – between the paleoarctic region in the north and the oriental provinces of South Nepal. These regions offer a natural laboratory for zoological, geographical and ecological investigation.

In the steaming, hot and wet jungles and the grasslands of the Terai alone there are over 100 kinds of mammal – from prehistoric pachyderms such as the

Preceding pages: An early-morning elephant ride in Chitwan National Park.

Indian rhinoceros and elephant, to large predatory cats like leopards and tigers. The cold temperate zones of the highland and the mountains of the north shelter one of the rarest types of wildcats in the world – the snow leopard – and various kinds of wild sheep and mountain goats.

Nepal is a paradise for bird lovers. Over 800 bird species have been observed here – more than half of all the recognized species in South Asia. While South Nepal offers refuge to a series of coastal birds like herons, seagulls, terns, ducks and moor hens, the oak and rhododendron forests of the Mahabharata Mountains, the advance ranks of the Himalayas, are home to at least a dozen kinds of pheasant with iridescent plumage. Nepal also offers a broad array of butterfly varieties. Up until now, over 600 varieties have already been registered; and among them are several of the rarest species on the planet.

Unfortunately, only little is known about the country's vegetable kingdom. One analysis of Nepal's flora shows that so far 5,000 kinds of flowering plants and 540 types of ferns have been isolated, of which 250 are indigenous varieties of angiosperms. The combined number of varieties is two-and-a-half times larger than the known count for Great Britain, a country a fair deal larger than Nepal. Among the flowering plants of Nepal there are 30 types of rhododendron alone, one of which is the national plant. The country has a wealth of rare and endangered varieties of orchid, many kinds of medical herbs and wild ornamental plants – the ancestors of a number of garden flowers that decorate many a western living-room today.

As opposed to many of its fellow developing nations, Nepal has at its disposal an excess of water resources: Meltwater fed rivers, lakes, streams and other bodies of water with a great wealth of life forms; for example, the *tomahseer* – one of the most coveted freshwater fish

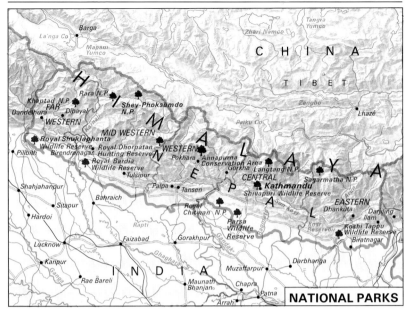

NATIONAL PARKS

among Asian anglers. Other types of aquatic animal include the rare Ganges dolphin, now threatened with extinction and two kinds of crocodile – the swamp crocodile and the Ganges gavial. Besides this "megafauna" there are also smaller kinds of animals in great numbers to be found in Nepal, among them various snakes, some poisonous or dangerous, others perfectly harmless, lizards, turtles and other reptiles.

Nature Conservation in Nepal

The animal world of Nepal has in fact always attracted the attention of adventurers and explorers. At one time Nepal was also popular as the Shah and Rana rulers' hunting grounds for the great beasts.

With the collapse of the Rana regime in 1951 and the political instability of the 1950s, there followed a heavy destruction of the forests and wildlife, with significant losses. Thanks to the far- sightedness and intervention of the then King

Mahendra in the mid-1960s was protection guaranteed against the encroaching clear-cut deforestation and the pressures for agricultural land.

Mahendra's son, the present King Birendra Bir Bikram Shah Dev, has led this initiative. Since then, nature protection has become an integral part of the socio-economic development planning of Nepal. At present, there are 13 national protected areas, which comprise more than 9 percent of the total land area – one of the highest percentages in all of Asia. The National Park and Nature Protection Decree of 1973 placed 26 mammals, nine species of bird and three reptiles under comprehensive protection, so that their hunting and commercial exploitation are responsibly prohibited.

You can get the best insight into the fauna and flora of Nepal through a description of the national parks and wildlife reservations, which have been purposely distributed about the country so that they provide an exemplary representation of the kingdom's eco-system.

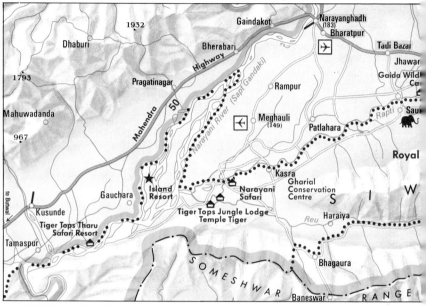

CHITWAN NATIONAL PARK

The Royal Chitwan National Park (RCNP), the first in Nepal, was established in 1973, 100 years after the dedication of Yellowstone National Park in the USA, which was the first national park in the world. The RCNP is located in the inner Terai, covering an area of 93,200 hectares, and extends through a river valley which includes the flood plains of the **Rapti**, **Reu** and **Narayani Rivers**. Its altitude reaches from 150 up to 815 meters at the **Churia**, a chain of hills that divides the park into two major watershed regions. The climate is subtropical with maximum temperatures up to 38 degrees C in May and June, with the lowest values (5 degrees C) in December and January. The average annual precipitation stands at about 2400 millimeters; the wettest months are from June until November, during which some 90 percent of the monsoon rains fall.

The flora and fauna of the Chitwan are among the most abundant in Asia. In ad-dition, this is the territory of the last surviving examples of the Asiatic rhinoceros in Nepal which has been almost completely eradicated because of the alleged aphrodisiacal properties of its horn.

The vegetation is dominated by shorea forests, which cover 70 percent of the area's surface. The remainder is a mosaic of bottomland forests, tall grasslands, lakes, swamps, and other bodies of water. There are pure shorea woodlands in the lowlands at **Kasra** – the headquarters of the park. In the remaining area these are mixed with other types of trees and bushes. Fir trees appear in the Churia Chain and often stand mixed with shorea trees. The grassland and the lowland forests are in a constant state of change as a result of frequent overflooding and fires. Khair acacias and the *sissoo Dalbergia* predominate in the flood plains of the lower rivers and on the islands of the Narayani River. Otherwise in the lowland forests, the kapok tree and the vehellar dominate the tree species. More than ten kinds of tall, dense grass cover the

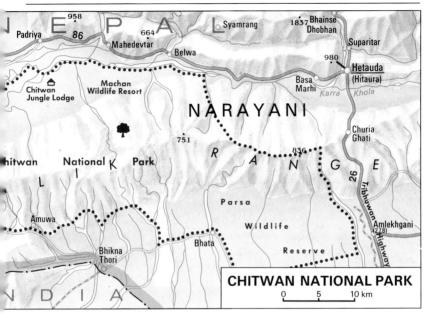

CHITWAN NATIONAL PARK

0   5   10 km

forest clearings and glades; these are collectively designated as elephant grass.

In addition to the approximately 300-350 rhinoceroses, the Chitwan National Park is rich in other types of large animals. Among the predators there are some 60-70 tigers, the biggest hunters of the park, which have been the subject of intensive study over the last 15 years. This research project, which is collectively supported by the Royal Government of Nepal, the King Mahendra Trust for Natural Conservation, the Smithsonian Institution and the World Wildlife Fund, is the only one of its kind in Asia. The methods of investigation are a combination of traditional hunting techniques of the indigenous peoples and modern scientific research techniques with a western stamp on them. Large mammals such as tigers and rhinoceroses are anaesthetized with chemical drugs. The sleeping animal is then fitted with a specially designed neck-band carrying a radio transmitter before it reawakens and is set free again. These free-running animals are then followed with radio apparatus from the backs of tame elephants.

Other common predators from the cat family are the leopard, the swamp lynx, and the Bengali cat. In the scattered territory of the park – alongside jackals, foxes and wild dogs (dholes) – there are also smaller predatory animals represented such as civet cats, martens, mongooses and otters. One can also observe the sloth bear from the omnivore family here as he seeks through the forest floor after termites, while two types of apes – the rhesus monkey and the langur – swing from limb to limb in the tree-tops. Wild boars and deer including the sambar, chital or axis deer and the muntjac are the most frequently seen hoofed animals in the park.

Visitors who come to Chitwan during the dry season (between the end of February and May) are often rewarded for this by getting a chance to see gaur – the largest asiatic species of wild cow – as they move from the Churia Hills to the floodplain lowlands and grasslands.

With the recorded number of over 450 species, the park is famous for its profusion of birds; several types such as the bankiva hen and the peacock are to be found here all year-round. Others, such as the demoiselle crane, change their locations inside the park, still others, like the Indian goose and the rust duck spend only their winters in the park.

Visitor Information: In 1984, the Royal Chitwan National Park was declared a World Heritage Site by UNESCO – an agency of the United Nations – because of the abundant variety of its animal world. Located 90 kilometers southwest of Kathmandu, it is the most popular tourist destination in the Terai. There are flight connections to **Meghauli** and **Bharatpur**. You can reach the park by automobile on the Tribhuvan Rajpath Highway – by turning west from He-

Above: Unfortunately, there are now only 60 - 70 tigers left in the Chitwan National Park. Right: Unluckily, the Ganges gavial is rarely seen in the wilderness nowadays.

tauda, or by turning south in the direction of Narayangadh from the road between Pokhara and Kathmandu at **Mugling**. From **Narayangadh** you drive eastward to **Tadi Bazar,** from where it is still 6 kilometers to **Saura,** one of the entrances to the park.

There is a well-developed network of overnight lodgings, from unassuming "low-budget" accommodations up to the super-deluxe category, which vary in price between less than US$ 15 per day for an accommodation outside the park, to more than US$ 190 for a resort hotel within the park limits. The most popular way to see the park's wildlife is with a safari through the jungle, riding on the back of an elephant. Round trips and bookings for a visit into Chitwan can be arranged in Kathmandu. Tiger Top's Jungle Lodge, Gaida Wildlife Camp, Chitwan Jungle Lodge, Machan Wildlife Resort, Narayan Safari, Temple Tiger and Island Resort have received concessions from the government enabling them to maintain tourist establishments

inside the park. These companies have their own elephants and are recommended because they work under the supervision of the state. Other accommodation outside of the park is dependent on the state-owned elephants in Saura – which are only available to tourists when they are not required for state purposes. They are given out only in the morning and evening hours according to the "first come, first served" principle. Altogether, they are not available very frequently – as a rule only between January and March. Several private hotels in Saura have their own elephants, which are not allowed to enter the park, bringing their guests instead to the **Tikoli Forest**, a forest that has already suffered heavy destruction. The visitor centers in Saura and the Gharial Conservation Center offer opportunities to learn about the flora and fauna inside the park boundaries.

Seeing the park on foot cannot be recommended, since several people are gored or killed by rhinoceroses every year. The best opportunity to observe wildlife close up – in safety – is by taking a ride on an elephant with the professional guidance of a member of the park's personnel. One further available form of observation is a river cruise on the **Rapti** with a dugout boat, which costs 100 rupees for a 45-minute group trip. Dugouts are, however, known for their tendency to capsize occasionally, therefore you should take precautionary measures for your cameras and binoculars.

SAGARMATHA NATIONAL PARK

"As the highest point on the surface of the earth, Sagarmatha and its surroundings are of the greatest significance not only for Nepal, but for the whole world." With these words Nepal's Prince Gyanendra announced the establishment of the highest national park of the world, as he spoke before the Third International Congress of the World Wildlife Fund.

The park encompasses an area of 1,243 square kilometers in the upper watershed region of the Dudh-Kosi River and is located northeast of Kathmandu in the Solu Khumbu District. The territory is characterized by a dramatic landscape, since the park includes many of the highest mountains in the world. Seven of its summits are higher than 7,000 meters, among them that of Sagarmatha or Mount Everest (8,846 meters), and geologists contend that their altitude is increasing, as their folding continues further. The climate is cool and moist in summer, in winter cold and dry. 80 percent of the rain falls during the monsoon months (June-September), giving out an average of less than 1,000 millimeters annually.

The park is extended over six zones of vegetation. The lower sub-alpine area between 3,000 and 3,600 meters altitude has forest consisting of spruce, Scot's pine and juniper. The upper sub-alpine zone above 3,600 meters consists of birch and rhododendron forests. Scrub brush with dwarf rhododendron are found in the lower alpine zone above the tree-line (3,800-4,000 meters) together with several flowering herbs such as the lily and the primrose. The density of the brush decreases with the temperature. Above 5,000 meters the snow-rhododendron is the only representative of its species, together with alpine plants such as the buckthorn, horse-tail or shave grass, and the blue Himalayan poppy. Above this zone the vegetation is confined to species of lichen, moss, dwarf and reed grasses and finally discontinues altogether at the permanent snowline, which is around 5,750 meters.

As a result of a combination of geological and geohistorical factors there are only a few types of mammals in the Sagarmatha National Park in comparison to the Terai region. In spite of this, from the goat-antelope family there are the serau, the goral and the Himalayan thar; from the deer family there are the musk-deer or moschus and the muntjak. The smaller mammals that appear in the park include the calling hare or pika, the Tibetan mountain-shrew, the Tibetan woolly hare, the Siberian fire-weasel, the masked palm civet-cat, and the marmot.

The bird community is estimated to include about 120 species. Among the more remarkable are the Himalayan pheasant and the blood pheasant. The Himalayan griffon-vulture and the bearded vulture have been seen at altitudes of 7,600 meters, and mountain-climbing expeditions have reported that they have encountered mountain crows at up to 8,200 meters. Among the 30 types of butterfly which occur in the park, there is the silver mountain butterfly.

The Sagarmatha National Park has great cultural significance. It is also the home of the famous Sherpas, and was therefore one of the first locations placed on the list of World Heritage Sites by the United Nations. The existence of the legendary creature of the snows, the Yeti – a kind of Nepalese Big Foot – probably did not play a major role in the decision.

Visitor Information: The best time to visit Sagarmatha is between October and May, except in the months of December and February, during which daytime temperatures usually stay well below the freezing point and the region also records heavy snowfall, which makes hiking difficult if not impossible. The park has over 6,000 visitors per year, so that along the main trekking route a number of lodgings have been established, among them the Everest View Hotel in Shyangboche. Carriers can be hired in Lukla for a fee to be bargained, and meals are served in many of the little teahouses along the path up to the Everest Base Camp.

LANGTANG NATIONAL PARK

The Langtang National Park, which has also existed since 1973, is located in the central Himalaya region of Nepal, 32

Right: Rapacious vultures in upper Langtang feast on scraps.

kilometers north of Kathmandu. It encompasses a land area of 171,000 hectares, representing the main watershed areas of the Trisuli and Bhote Kosi Rivers. The altitude reaches from 790 meters at the Bhote Kosi up to 7,234 meters on the summit of the Langtang Lirung. The northern limits of the park are defined by the international Nepal-China (Tibet) border; the Gosainkund Lake and the Dorje Lakpe range divide the park into eastern and western flanks.

One of the most outstanding characteristics of the park is the great variety of its vegetation types. Located in the altitudes below 1,000 meters, there are tropical species like the shorea tree. The Indian castanopsis and the Scots pine are to be found in the sub-tropical sector between 1,000 and 2,000 meters. The vegetation in the montana zone between 2,000 and 3,000 meters consists of oak and Himalayan hemlock, especially in the wetter areas. In the sub-alpine zone coniferous trees predominate; in the more arid areas are the larch and the Scots pine,

while rhododendrons are to be found everywhere. The occurence of larches is of particular interest because of the unusual distribution of its species in the Langtang.

The vegetation in the Langtang is especially varied because of the immense differences in altitude as well as micro-climatic conditions. Found among the smaller mammals in the park are the small panda bear, the calling-hare or pika, the showy marmot, and several varieties of shrew and wolf. One of the hoofed animals that can be seen on the slopes of the Langtang Valley is the Himalayan thar, which has a population of about 200 animals. Other larger mammals which are distributed through the park are the goral, the serau, wild boars, muntjaks and the musk-deer. The ape species are represented by the rhesus monkey and the langur, while the Himalayan black bear is the only representative of his species.

The Trisuli and Bhote Kosi Valley system is an important route for migratory birds, which fly back and forth between

the Indian Plain and Tibet in autumn and springtime. More than 180 types of birds have already been registered in this region, among which are such rare species as the long-billed ibis, the white-crowned redtail, the scaly woodpecker, and the golden-tailed honey guide. The pheasant, partridge, eagle, vulture and hawk species are the same as have been described for the Sagarmatha National Park.

The park also offers sites of cultural interest, for example Helambu or the holy lakes of Panch Pokhari and Gosainkund. The latter attracts tens of thousands of Buddhist and Hindu pilgrims annually, especially during the *Janai Purne* festivals in summer.

Visitor Information: Traveling to this park is very much easier than getting to the other national parks in the Himalayas. From Kathmandu you can ride either by

Above: A lively stream in the Annapurna Conservation Area. Right: At high altitudes lichen thrives on the few scramny trees.

taxi or by bus to **Dhunche**, where the park's headquarters are located. As an alternative you can take the public bus to **Sundarijal** and hike in through Helambu. To get to the remote areas in the eastern sector you start out on foot from **Chautara** or **Tatopani**, both of which can be reached from Kathmandu by bus.

SHEY-PHOKSUMDO NATIONAL PARK

Shey-Phoksumdo is the largest national park in Nepal (355,500 hectares) and was established in 1984. The greater part of it is located to the north of the Himalayan Main Range on the Trans-Himalayan Plateau in the Dolpo district.

Of particular interest in this park are the **Kanjiroba Himal** and **Phoksumdo Lake**, Nepal's second-largest lake, which lies at an altitude of 3,660 meters. The landscape in the heart of the park resembles the cold arctic desert typical of the Tibetan Highland, where annual precipitation is under 500 millimeters.

The vegetation of the trans-Himalayan region consists of sparse bush with juniper, caragana, lonicera and other plants that are adapted to the cold northern conditions of the semi-arid climate. On the river terraces there are also isolated occurences of poplar and walnut.

Several of the Himalayan mammals which have already been described for Langtang and Sagarmatha are also found here. The park is also famous for the rare snow-leopard and the pamir sheep – called the *nayan*. Additionally, several of the endangered animal species of Tibet, such as the wild yak, are found here.

According to unsubstantiated local assertions, the chiru and the Tibetan wild ass occasionally cross over the border from Tibet. The 55 varieties of bird living in the park include particular trans-Himalayan species such as the Tibetan lark, the mountain linnet, and the Adams snowfinch.

Shey Gompa is a monastery from the 11th century which has great religious significance for the Buddhist pilgrims of the surrounding area. A herd of half-tame blue sheep are kept there, which are carefully taken care of by the monks and can be examined close up.

Visitor Information: Large sections of the park may not be entered by foreigners, however, one can obtain a trekking permit for the ascent of **Ringmo**, which is on the south west side of the lake. If you don't want to travel on foot from Jumla, then the best way to arrive at the park is by aircraft. There is a regular flight from the Royal Nepalese Airline between Nepalganj and Juphal, which is two hours' distance from the seat of the Dunai district administration.

Leaving from there you reach **Sundawa** – where the park headquarters are located – in a two-day-long hike. From there it is still one-and-a-half days further to Ringmo.

The best visiting time is between April and June – the months with the mildest climate. There are, however, no services for tourists, so that visitors are, unfortunately, completely on their own.

RARA NATIONAL PARK

The Rara National Park, established in 1976, is in the **Mugu District** in West Nepal, 24 kilometers north of **Jumla** in the region of the Karnali River. It encompasses an area of 10,600 hectares, of which 1,020 are lake surface.

The Rara Lake is the most beautiful part of the landscape as well as the largest lake in Nepal, and lies at an altitude of 2,990 meters. The lake basin forms the northern half of the park area; the **Chuchamara Dara** stands – in the shape of a horse-shoe – at the lake's edge and rises up to the highest point in the park with 4,038 meters. The lake is 167 meters deep, and is thus the deepest in the whole region. Rainfall during the monsoon season (May-August) amounts to some 400 millimeters, while in winter (November-March) you may easily have to contend with a blanket of snow more than a meter thick.

The lake is surrounded primarily by spruces, which are mixed in several places with oak, rhododendron, juniper and also Scots pine. The northern slopes of the Chuchumara Mountain have spruce and birch above 3,350 meters.

Almost all of the Himalayan animals which have already been described are also found in this park, such as the small panda, the Himalayan black bear, the wild boar, the musk-deer and other hoofed animals.

There are more than 60 species of birds; permanently settled game birds, most of the pheasant and partridge varieties as well as migratory waterfowl are important representatives of the park's bird world. To name a few among the former: The stone hen, the Himalayan royal hen and pheasant types such as the red-back pheasant, the Valaisian pheas-

Right: A leopard in the Chitwan National Park has his daily wash.

ant and koklas pheasant; among the latter the mallard duck, teal or greenwing duck, the great crested grebe and the coot. Otters are frequently seen in the water, and the marinka is a common fish in the lake.

Visitor Information: There are two ways to get to Rara. The first is by air from Kathmandu to Jumla, followed by a two-and-a-half day hike. The other requires a week-long foot march after arriving at **Surketh** by aircraft or by bus. The best times for a visit are from October to December or between March and May.

Along the narrow hiking path to **Bhulbhule** in the neighborhood of the park border there are several teahouses which also offer some food. By the park headquarters in Rara there is also a guesthouse which visitors may use with the permission of the park administration – they must, however, bring along their own sleeping bag and food.

ANNAPURNA CONSERVATION AREA

The Annapurna Conservation Area (ACA) is in the central Himalayas north of Pokhara. It covers an area of 2,600 square kilometers, which is extended over five districts of the Gandaki and Dhaulagiri zones. The area is famous for its high mountains – just within its bounds there are seven peaks measuring over 7,000 meters. It is also known for its deep valleys, which contrast with the immense mountains. North Mustang, which was recently opened to the public, was integrated within the Annapurna reservation in Summer 1992.

The landscape of the region changes with the altitude, which ranges from 1,311 meters in Tatopani to 8,091 meters on the summit of Annapurna I. Accordingly, the climatic conditions here are enormously differentiated. The southern slopes of Annapurna receive among the highest annual amounts of precipitation,

with over 3,000 millimeters, whereas the northern area in the rain shadow of the Trans-Himalaya sector registers the lowest precipitation levels in the country (under 300 millimeters).

As a result of the huge differences in climatic conditions and altitude, the breadth of biological variation in the animal and plant world is particularly high. During the trek lasting a few days you cross bamboo forests from the subtropical world of Pokhara before entering the magical glacial paradise of the Annapurna Base Camp. In the lowest places one finds subtropical communities; schimas, the indian castanopsis, alders, and Scots pines stand on the dry slopes. In the temperate forest zones at the higher altitudes oaks and rhododendrons are distributed, while bamboos are growing in the wettest regions – for example in the Modi Khola Valley.

Higher up on the drier mountain slopes the bamboos are replaced by coniferous trees – Scots or pitch pines, spruces and hemlock firs. Above these regions sub-alpine communities are located, including birches and junipers, while yet further up in the alpine zone species of rhododendron bushes grow.

In the conservation area there are more than 400 species of birds, among them the only indigenous or exclusively Nepalese variety – the harrow thrush. The Kali-Gandaki Valley also represents an important stretch for more than 40 migratory birds, among them the demoiselle crane. Almost all the species of pheasant, predatory bird and small animal species that are found in other sections of the Himalayas occur here. The snow leopard, the small panda, the Himalayan musk deer, the muntjak and four varieties of sheep and goat-antelope species are found in this region as well.

The Annapurna Conservation Area Project (ACAP) is Nepal's most recent initiative for the protection of this unique region. With a less restrictive and more flexible style of management than is usual in the national parks and reservations, the indigenous populations in the

conservation area are permitted to continue their traditional lifestyles and subsistence agriculture. These ways of life are integrated into the greater framework of a plan for a healthy management of resources and economic development.

The ecological and cultural disposition of this region is influenced by a series of factors: Too rapid population growth, badly devised agricultural development, and the immediate effects resulting from trekking tourism.

As a response to these negative influences, the **King Mahendra Trust for Nature Conservation (KMTNC)** has developed a new approach in which nature conservation is combined with consideration of human requirements and local development.

These conservation measures began in 1986, and the ACA is the most recent of Nepal's protected regions. The program

Above: Unpious Rhesus monkeys at Svayambhunath. Right: Rhododendrons in Nepal flower in March-April.

is multi-dimensional and attemps to find a middle way between the requirements of the indigenous peoples and those of nature.

Nature conservation on a small scale and the application of alternative energy sources ought to keep the environmental consequences of the visiting tourists as slight as possible, while simultaneously guaranteeing a sustaining future for both the land and people.

With 30,000 visitors annually, the ACA is far and away the most popular trekking destination in Nepal, partly because it is at only a few days' walk.

Visitor Information: The Annapurna Conservation Area is best reached by taking a bus or aircraft to Pokhara. From there, continuing from the end of the road, after a two-day-long hike to **Gandruk**, you arrive at the ACA headquarters. In addition to the information posts in **Chomrong** and **Gorepani,** the ACA maintains a small museum and visitor center on the Prithvi Narayan Campus in Pokhara.

Except during the monsoon season (June to September) one can visit the ACA almost the whole year round. Tourists must pay 200 rupees per visit for an ACAP user's-fee, which is charged in addition to the trekking fees. The user's fee serves to support various ACAP projects. Establishing kerosene depots is considered as important here as educating the owners of the lodges in various modern methods of nature conservation. The problems caused by excess refuse is particularly accute in those areas visited by mass tourism.

THE KING MAHENDRA TRUST FOR NATURE CONSERVATION

The King Mahendra Trust was called into existence in 1982. The Trust is an autonomous, non-governmental organization for the common good, which was established under the general leadership of King Birendra Bir Birkam Shah Dev. It is directed by a committee, the members of which consist of prominent Nepalese from both the public and private sectors, as well as foreign members of international repute.

The committee chairman is His Royal Highness Prince Gyanendra Bir Bikram Shah Dev – Nepal's foremost defender of nature. The Trust has branch offices in the whole world – Canada, France, Germany, Japan, England and the United States. These well-known international establishments support the Trust in their respective countries and deliver essential financial and technical resources to the Foundation.

Considered superficially, the combination of the goals of conservation and economic development could be seen as self-contradictory. The Trust, however, does not share this viewpoint.

In consideration of the constantly recurring damage by flooding and landslides, and in the face of the fact that the country is almost completely dependent on its own resources, the Trust emphasizes that effective conservation of nature brings with it an appropriate approach to development and building of the economy. Therefore, the Trust pursues the goal of "natural conservation for development toward self-preservation" and plans its measures accordingly.

The Trust is engaged in two main working areas: The first as coordinator and mediator, the other as the executive judge of model projects which should put together a reasonable utilization of natural resources with the economic and social development of the population of Nepal.

A great portion of the time of the employees of the Trust in Kathmandu is applied to their tasks as coordinators and mediators. For example, interested parties must be brought together to promote projects and development activities which they wish to have supported by the

Trust. The Royal Government of Nepal also receives technical advice and suggestions concerning environmental and development policies. The Trust also lends its support to the Department of National Parks and Wildlife Conservation. Close connections are also maintained with foreign assistance organizations which are active in the area of environmental protection in Nepal, among others, the World Wildlife Fund.

Over the last five years, the Trust has been responsible for the management of over 20 different projects. For some of these the main concern was the improvement of basic data, in other cases environmental management, nature conservation research or development.

The Trust is an institution for the common good and receives no regular governmental budget appropriations. Therefore it must devote a great deal of time to procuring necessary means. For this purpose the Trust has an ambitious program with which it mobilizes support both domestically and in foreign countries.

213

SYMBOLS

When you land at Kathmandu's Tribhuvan Airport, the Nepalese usually greet you with a *namaste* or *namaskar*, which is a demonstration of respect and deference. With this he places his hands together at chest height, while bowing slightly forward. The deeper this bow is, the more respect, love, honor and reverence is being demonstrated towards one's counterpart.

The national hymn of Nepal is a song in praise of the king, who is also considered to be a reincarnation of the god Vishnu. All three branches of authority – legislative, executive and judiciary – rest in his hands.

Nepal's national coat-of-arms consists of a variety of symbols. Under the crown of the king are two red national banners with the obligatory crossed *khukris*, the

Above: Preparations for the Indrajatra festival.

Himalayan mountains flanked by the sun and moon, a facsimile of the Pashupatinath temple, the holy Bagmati River with the holy cow – highly worshipped by the Hindus – and a danphey pheasant, the country's national bird. This *danphey chari*, as the Nepalese call it, is the Himalayan pheasant, *lapophorus impejanous;* as with all members of the species, it is the male that is the most striking, with his beautiful colors and long tail.

Also on the coat-of-arms is Nepal's national flower, the red rhododendron, flanked by two soldiers: One Gurkha marksman armed with a *khukri*, and one warrior equipped with a *khukri*, bow and arrows. Finally, on the coat of arms is written in Sanskrit that "mother and motherland (are) greater than the heavens."

In Nepal's flag there are illustrations of the sun and the moon, which are seen by the Hindus as being symbols of the Hindu deities Surya and Chandra. The origin of this symbolism is to be found in the India's Vedic period, since the

Aryans principally worshipped nature-deities. The red rhododendron, which is called *laliguras* in Nepal, was chosen as Nepal's national flower. It grows in the Himalayas at altitudes above 2,000 meters in real rhododendron forests.

Simrik is the Nepalese name for carmine red, the national color. For example, the statues of the ape-god Hanuman are generally painted with a mixture of red pigment mixed with mustard-seed oil, and then covered with a red cloth.

Red is also the color of the point-shaped *tika* that one sees on the foreheads of the Nepalese. This consists of a mixture of powdered cinnobar, rice flower and yoghurt. The *tika* is applied by a brahman or elder as a blessing of the gods; it is received after a visit to a temple or after a *puja*. On certain high festival days women wear red saris, especially the Tij-festival and on the day of their marriage. Also, Nepal's living goddess Kumari – an incarnation of the goddess Taleju – wears red.

The word *Om* and the *swastika* – or sun-cross – are among the symbols of religious belief in everyday life. *Om* has its origin in Sanskrit, and is considered a holy syllable, and as such is frequently used at the opening of religious ceremonies and at the beginning of works of literature. In the private realm, this symbol is frequently found on visiting cards and letter-heads. One also finds *Om* applied to the doors of houses, and various equipment and machines. The swastika was originally a symbol for fire. They are thought of as lucky symbols, and are to be seen on temples, stupas, pagodas, and house doors. This sign is supposed to bring prosperity and success, since it is a symbolic representation of the concept of life as a constant process of coming into being.

On the doors in Kathmandu and on the stupas of Svayambunath and Bodnath one will notice the all-seeing Eyes of the original Buddha, which look upon the people with compassion and sympathy. Between the eyes there appears – as a sign of enlightenment – the mystical third eye, as it is erroneously characterized. This is really a tuft of Buddha's hair, the so-called *urna.* Appearing where the nose would be is the Nepalese number 1, a symbol for unity.

The streets of the Kathmandu Valley are full of holy cows – notorious for their calmness and nonchalance. The Hindus believe that the five products of the cow – milk, sour milk, butter, urine and dung – have purifying properties. Besides this, the cow is Nepal's national animal, called *gaitrimata* (mother-cow). Once a year in the Kathmandu Valley, the Gaijatra festival – which extends over eight days – takes place in honor of the holy cow and to commemorate the dead.

The national weapon of Nepal and, respectively, the Gurkha soldiers is the *khukri*, a curved knife. No household in Nepal lacks one, where it is used to chop wood, meat and vegetables. The good luck of the Gurkha batallions is, logically, thought to depend on the aptitude of the Gurkha in the employment of his *khukri*. The crossed *khukri* on the national coat-of-arms are the symbol of the protective force of Nepal's Ghurka army. The knife's sheath is made of simple wood which has been embellished with leather or ornamented with silver and turquoise stones. There are also two smaller knives kept in the sheath of the *khukri*; these are called the *kardo* and the *chamak.* The kardo is sharpened and is used for cutting; in contrast the chamak is blunt and is used to sharpen the *khukri* and – together with a flint-stone – to kindle fires.

Yeti, the snow-man, has also become a national symbol of Nepal. In the face of numerous yeti-quests – or even hunting expeditions – the Nepalese government was forced to set down laws forbidding its killing and declaring this creature to be the property of the people.

GURKHAS

Gunfire flashed through the darkness. As soldier Lal Bahadur Thapa tried to make his way through the lane he jumped a watch-post equipped with machine guns and slit the throats of two enemy soldiers with his *khukri*. Creeping stealthily he climbed the hill; on the way, two more men fell victim to his small, crooked knife. A short time later, Gurkha Lal Bahadur was awarded the Victoria Cross, England's highest decoration, for his bravery in North Africa during the Second World War in a battle where the British attacked fortified German and Italian positions roughly 200 miles south of Tunis.

In 1982, the British Gurkhas again did justice to their reputation; the BBC reported: "As the Gurkhas advanced on Argentinian positions, the enemy troops dropped their guns and abondoned their mortars and machine guns." The only Gurkha killed in the Falklands War was Buddha Prasad Limbu, who lost his life as he searched for Argentinian mines. Many Falkland civilians paid him their last respects.

"Ayo Gurkhali" goes the fear-inspiring battle cry of the agile Gurkhas, who enjoy an almost legendary reputation because of the skill they demonstrate in the jungle. This shrill cry has frequently created fear and panic in the enemy lines. The Japanese as well as Rommel's Africa Corps were beset by fear and horror in this manner. When the Gurkhas pull their *kukhris*, Mahakal's nectar (that means blood) must flow.

Who are the Gurkhas? For the history of Nepal and the Gurkha troops, the Gurkha principality located west of the Kathmandu Valley – founded by the Shah Dynasty – is of particular significance. In the 15th century, the Rajputs

Right: Relief on the Sahid Dheka in Kathmandu showing a Gurkha parade.

from the Indian Rajasthan retreated from the Islamic Mogul rulers to western Nepal and, in addition, constructed a strong fortress there, from which sprang the present-day town of Gurkha. Around the middle of the 18th century, the ruler of the Gurkhas, Prithvi Narayan Shah, felt himself powerful enough to attack the Kathmandu Valley and respectively the Malla Kings who governed there. The Valley was ultimately conquered in 1768. The conqueror named himself the King of Nepal and introduced a period of Nepalese expansion. This was first put to a halt by the British general Ochterlony in 1816. The British-Nepalese Treaty of Sugauli was signed on March 4th, 1816, and Nepal had to surrender the provinces of Kumaon and Gharwal to England. Also in the treaty, the right of the English to conscript Nepalese for the British colonial wars was introduced.

Today, the holy Castle of Gorakhnath watches over the city of Gurkha, to which the Gurkhas owe their name. The expression Gurkha (or Gorkha) has its origins in the Sanskrit words *go* which in translation means *cow*, and *rakh (raksha)* which means *protector*. An allusion is thus made to Hindu tradition as "protector of the cows." However, not all of the Gurkha soldiers are Hindus. The majority belongs much more to the various ethnic groups of the central Hill Region and the high valleys of the Himalayas. The Gurkhas are not, as is frequently incorrectly assumed, an ethnic group of homogenous origins; they come primarily from the Gurung and Magar in West Nepal as well as from the Kirati groups – the Rai and the Limbu in the East of the country. Today, Tamang and Thakali are also numbered among them.

Presently in the Royal Nepalese Army, the largest group among the Gurkha troops is formed by the members of the Hindu caste of Chetris. The first two Gurkha battalions were formed in 1763. In 1768, they fought against the British.

One of these two battalions was put into action against the Tibetans, the other in the British-Nepalese War of 1814.

Nepal earns 30 million dollars a year through the Gurkhas. Besides tourism, they represent one of the most important sources of foreign exchange.

After India became independent of the rule of the British, the Gurkha regiments were divided between the two nations. They still take their oaths to the British monarch and, furthermore, march in procession before Buckingham Palace as honor guards for the Queen. British Gurkhas have served in Malaysia, Indonesia (Borneo), Hong Kong, Brunei and Cyprus.

The Gurkhas have better chances than other Nepalese on the marriage market, especially the British Gurkhas, since their wives and children have the opportunity to travel abroad (London, Brunei, Singapore and Hong Kong) which is a real dream for the majority of the 22 million Nepalese. The Gurkhas live very spartanly and bring the money or gold they have earned home with them. Many young boys among the Gurkhas are called Bir or Bahadur, which means "the courageous"; courage is highly regarded in the world of Nepalese men. Better to die with courage than to live as a coward, it is said.

Since India took over the role of the policeman of South Asia, the Indian Gurkhas have been put into action against enemies of India, which was best illustrated by the examples of Sri Lanka and the Maldives. In harmony with King Birendra's idea of declaring Nepal as a peace-zone, Gurkhas have been sent into action in the Sinai Desert and Lebanon on behalf of the United Nations.

But the Gurkhas are not free of national pride. The Gurkhaland movement in the Darjeeling district (India) was crushed in 1988 after 28 months of militant agitation, and the problem of the Gurkhas – from Nepal and India – is still not solved; there are many Gurkhalis of Nepalese origin who live in India or work in the Indian armed forces.

DANCES AND FESTIVALS

The Nepalese both love and dread the festivals, which fill their calendar. Of course they cost money, and one often develops a bit of an upset stomach after the inevitable festival banquets and accompanying revelries, which require mountains of meat and rivers of rice-beer and spirits. The Newar in the Kathmandu Valley have carried both celebration and festival banquetry to the greatest of extremes. According to one saying, mountain-dwellers ruin themselves with their display of status symbols, and the Newar in the valley ruin themselves with their feasts. However, the health and financial ruin is compensated for by the happiness gained by celebrating with all one's friends and relatives, as well as having been closer to the gods. For part of every festival is a worshipping of the gods – called a *puja* – in the process of which the god or goddess is venerated and receives offerings – sacred water, flowers, coins, grains of rice, burning wicks and incense, red paint powder, fruits or vegetables; frequently liquor and animal sacrifices as well. In return, the believer receives *prasad* (blessing in material form); a blossom, a paint-mark on his forehead, or a little bit of the food that was offered to the gods. Included in some festivals is the so-called *jatra*, a procession in which a god is either carried about in a chest or pushed in a festival chariot. The procession follows a pre-determined route through the city or village as the god receives offerings and gives blessings.

The numerous private festivals – with their protracted preparations and seemingly uneventful conclusions – require of the occidental guest exceptional patience and the ability to remain seated, as well as a robust digestive system. If you do not possess these prerequisites, then acceptance of an invitation to a Nepalese wedding celebration – by all means with expression of polite regret – should be

Above: At the New Year's festival in Thimi.
Right: Newar classical dancer.

218

avoided. In contrast, the action-packed and exciting town rituals are among the most colorful and impressive experiences of a trip to Nepal.

New Year Festival

The most spectacular of all Newar festivals is the New Year festival in **Bhaktapur**. It begins two days before the Newari New Year on the ninth of April and ends ten days later. In the weeks beforehand, carpenters assemble both of the festival carts for the gods Bhairava and Bhadrakali on Taumadi Place. On the afternoon of the ninth of April Bhairava takes his place in his wagon, and as soon as the priests give the sign, the chariot procession begins. At this time, old rivalries break out between the upper and lower sections of the city, often leading to dangerous brick-throwing fights. The wagons, which weigh tons, are pulled by hundreds of strong men with heavy ropes about 20 meters in length, fastened to either side. Because of the aggression which suddenly flares up, it is advisable to observe this contest from a safe distance – for example, from the stone platform on the southern edge of the square. In any case, one should not join in the rope-pull. Each year there are serious accidents in which people are run over or hit with bricks.

Three days later, on the evening before the New Year, the activities of the multitude are concentrated on Yoshimkhel Place, which is on the Hanumante River. A huge tree trunk is erected as a symbol of creation and reproduction. With this act the New Year begins. During this night Bhakapur is filled with music. In the early morning of New Year's Day the entire population, festively dressed, sets off to the river, takes a ritual bath, and worships the gods Bhairava and Bhadrakali, who have in the meantime been bethroned in open buildings in the area of the tree. The vigor and

liveliness of this New Year's morning, peopled with the freshly-bathed festival throng, is an unforgettable experience. Each family carries a sacrificial rooster to the wagon of Bhairava, on a pole of which is bound Betal, a spirit of chaos, who receives the roosters' blood. In the evening, after the family feasts, the throngs assemble again at the Yoshimkhel Place in order to bring the tree trunk crashing down; a rather dusty event – and not without its dangers.

Several years ago the trunk broke off four meters above the ground and crashed down on the crowd of people who were fortunately rescued. The erection of the pole signals the beginning of numerous processions in different parts of the city, in which the local gods, accompanied by groups of musicians, are carried in chests through their area of influence and receive sacrificial offerings.

On the morning of the second day of the New Year, a visit to the neighboring village of **Thimi** is very rewarding. Early, around 6.30 am, all the local gods are gathered at the Bal Kumari pagoda, and the shrine is encircled with hundreds of torch-carriers and drummers. The air is full of orange palm powder, with which everybody dusts each other. This festival is already over at around two hours later. You have to get up very early and bring along a dust-brush for your camera. The powder comes out of your clothing easily, without requiring more than a beating and washing.

However, you can save yourself the bother if you are going to participate in the impressive procession of the Tantric mother-goddesses Mahakali and Maha-lakshmi, which happens in the afternoon of the same day. During this procession, another paint powder, this time blood-red, is thrown about. After separately cir-cling the Bhoulachan quarter in the north-east section of Bhaktapur, the cha-riots – with both of the goddesses in them – are thrashed against each other many times with great force, making a sym-bolic show of the reproductive act. The chariot carriers take about 50 meters of running space, and then rush towards each other, crashing together and falling on top of one-another under the weight of the bucking and rearing chariots. Almost all of them are drunk on rice-beer and liq-uor. Here the ecstasy of the drummers and dancers reaches its climax.

On the fourth day of the New Year, all of the music groups drum their way along the procession route through **Bhaktapur**, seeking the gods. Following behind the musicians are the women in festive, dark-red saris carrying sacrificial offerings. All the gods are on display to receive the offerings and dispense their blessings for the New Year. This is the day of the never-ending Newar feastings and revel-ries. Comparable chariot festivals also occur in Kathmandu and Patan.

Right: The bars in front of the so-called White Bhairava are removed during the In-drajatra festival.

A Merry Death Festival

Particularly in **Bhaktapur**, the *gai-jatra* or dance festival for the dead – is very impressive. It happens as the rainy season fades away, namely on the day after the full moon. Families which have suffered a death in the previous year build a symbolic cow out of bamboo sticks and cloth, with horns of straw. On this is hung a photograph of the deceased. The holy animal is supposed to direct his soul on the right path. The desire for life of those left behind forges ahead with music, dancing and masquerade.

On this day, hundreds of cows are par-aded through Bhaktapur's procession route. One typical dance shows Newar farm women, firing up their men with home-distilled liquor. Others mask them-selves as gods and goddesses. However, it is always the young men who take the female roles. Newar women never make public appearances with music and dance. They also very rarely sing in groups during the rice-planting season. If a man turns up, the song is immediately broken off with embarrassed giggling. In contrast, among the Nepalese mountain-folk the women sing very confidently, in rivalry with the men. In the week follow-ing the *gaijatra*, the numerous dance and theater groups move around from one place to another, where an appreciative audience then immediately gathers. Here one might have the good luck to experi-ence one of the great Bhaila-pyaka or Devi-pyaka mask dances, which are often presented in a badly garbled and distorted form in the larger hotels. The Radha-Krishna dance with flute accom-paniment, in which farm boys personify the legendary Indian lovers, is enchant-ingly lovely.

On the day after the *gaijatra*, the popu-lation of **Patan** celebrates the monumen-tal *matyapuja*, in the course of which of-ferings of light are placed at some 300 lo-cations in the Buddhist areas. One can

experience the ancient music of Buddhism at its best either here or on the Hill of **Svayambhunath**. During the Buddhist procession-month Gumla (August/September), musical groups from Kathmandu proceed every morning before sunrise to Svayambhunath, where they play – as a signal to the gods that they wish to gather merit for their favorable reincarnation. In the Tibetan cloister on the Svayambhu Mountain one can eavesdrop on Tibetan ritual music during the entire year. Guests are allowed to enter and go through the temple up to the door of the monks' prayer-room and, from there, be present at the services.

Further festivals include the *indrajatra* in **Kathmandu** and the autumn festival *dasain* in all three Newar cities, during which the virgin goddesses appear, and the tantric mother-goddess is worshipped. Particularly, Durga's victory over the demon Mahishasura is celebrated over the entire country, with countless animal sacrifices. The highpoint of *dasain* occurs on the ninth day, on which all work tools and equipment, including cars, are sprayed with sacrificial blood.

The musical traditions in Nepal are as manifold as the different ethnic groups in the country. The most complex musical culture in the whole Himalaya region is that of the Newar in the Kathmandu Valley, which over the past 2,000 years has been influenced again and again by Indian traditions – without having lost its own individual character. Music and dance are always drawn from ritual and vary according to the locality. The people of the hills particularly enjoy group-singing in pentatonic melodies and the playing of the *madal* drum. The Gaine minstrels with their *sarangi* fiddles originally served the function now occupied by the media. Today they entertain tourists. The media broadcast almost exclusively modern pop-songs with the single theme "love, love, love," and, for the educated listeners, classical music from the Indian tradition, which has been practiced in Nepal for about 250 years.

ART THEFT

No one has ever counted all of the temples, shrines, and statues of the Kathmandu Valley. That would be a futile exercise. In nearly every courtyard and in many squares one finds an idol, an inscription, or the sculpture of some ruler or rich donator. Many of these art objects are centuries old, and some are of incalculable value.

For years now, organized theft, particularly of statues, has been increasing. Sometimes a small, supposedly inconspicuous statuette is missing, and sometimes you even hear about the (unsuccessful) attempt to steal the large golden statue of King Bhupatindra Malla on the palace square of Bhaktapur with a mobile crane. Occasionally the statue is "beheaded" or valuable pieces are broken

Above: Newar wood carving has earned a world wide reputation. Right: New copies of old pictures – take care when buying a thangka.

off. Old manuscripts are also painted over – mostly with erotic pictures – in order to ease their transport across borderlines and later sale.

The stolen objects are purchased by tourists and collectors, but also – through middlemen – by western museums. The culprits, however, are rarely discovered. There has been talk of drug dealers or influential politicians who have statues sawn to pieces, in order to get them out of the country by diplomatic post.

It has also been said that western art historians and other scientists are participating in this unparalleled and outrageous theft of the treasures of Nepal (and Tibet). Photographing, measuring and drawing bronzes or temples appears suspicious to many Nepalese.

The scientists' situation is paradoxical even without such an accusation: The more widely they make the history and the value of a statue known, the more likely it becomes that a theft will occur, and the more lucrative the business becomes.

How can the Kathmandu Valley – this living museum – be protected? By having watchmen patrol through the cities? By cementing all of the figures in or chaining them tight? By having the statues put in museums and damning them to business hours? All these proposals are being seriously considered by politicians and developmental assistance volunteers.

The law of the Nepalese government which requires sealed export authorizations from the Department of Archeology for older works of art has hardly brought any significant change. The customs officials are too corruptible and the civil servants too inexperienced to be able to judge whether a statue is more than one hundred years old, and therefore excluded from export.

As long as the statues are still gods, the best protection is undoubtedly contact with, and a bit of respectful fear of them. Wherever they are worshipped day after day, they are looked after much better than paid museum attendants are capable of doing. The power of the god (statues),

which can bring about disaster, sickness, and even death, still prevents the majority of the population from daring to make the quick and relatively easy deal.

On the streets one hears time and time again the story of a man who attempted to steal a statue, but who was found dead the very next day, whereas the god was recovered safe and sound. If only the buyers could hear (and believe) this!

One should really be careful when being offered a "genuine antique," thangkha or a statue on Durbar Square. No matter how aged and smoky they look, the real old pieces are no longer sold on the street. This does not mean that newer art works are necessarily third-rate. They are, after all, the product of an old tradition of handicrafts, and furthermore, buying such souvenirs directly from the artist or his agent is also a direct form of development aid. Some of the more beautiful and delicately painted thankhas require months of painstaking work. The statues are usually made individually of wax before being cast in metal.

NEPALESE CUISINE

Only after a better acquaintance with the country does the foreign visitor realize that Nepalese cooking does not consist solely of *daal bhat* – lentil soup with boiled rice – which is often portrayed as the national dish of Nepal.

Normally a Nepali eats *daal bhat* twice a day – in the morning after the first fieldwork, or before he goes to the office around 10 am, as well as in the evening after sunset.

Nepalis still usually eat with the right hand; the left is considered unclean. Included in the basic foods eaten daily, besides a large portion of lentils, are the steamed seasonal vegetables – called *tarkaari*. These can also include potato, which is classified as a vegetable in Nepal. An especially delicious accent is lent to the dish by a bit of *achar* – a sort of chutney or paste made of pickled, sharply spiced fruit or vegetables. Instead of rice, flat breads – *chapati* or *puri* – made of various kinds of flour are often used.

Normally, meat is offered only on special occasions. No main meal can be served without a glass of water. Very spicy dishes are often complemented with yoghurt. The spices – called *masala* in Nepal – which no vegetable or meat dish lack – include cumin, coriander, turmeric, fenugreek, chillis and pepper.

The choice of ingredients in a meal depends on location. In the flat Terai in the South, with its warm, humid climate, some of the foods eaten before work are: *chana churia* – chickpeas in curry sauce with mashed rice; or for instance the delicious freshly-prepared *puri julebi*. Puri is a flat bread which is fried in oil, which is eaten with fresh-fried, sweetened *julebi* pastry and curried vegetables. In addition, there is the obligatory milk-tea,

Right: No Nepalese meal is complete without ground chilli.

sometimes refined with the addition of spices like cardamom, cloves and cinnamon. So as not to go to work on a completely empty stomach, *halawa* and *swari* are eaten. Halawa is a sweetened pastry made of rice flour or semolina with melted butter, sometimes enriched with nuts, while swari is a thin flat-bread which is fried in butter.

In the Terai, the first main meal of the day is served, at the earliest, around twelve o'clock noon. This consists mostly of *daal bhat,* sometimes served with vegetables and achar, but rarely with meat or fish. In fact, the Hindus, who live primarily in the India-influenced Terai, rarely eat meat; the especially strict believers among them, none at all. They live as vegetarians. But the situation is quite different in the Terai and the central highlands, in contrast to the population of the high valleys, who eat animal products as a result of the limited land for farming.

Generally, a light snack is taken in the afternoons, for example some *gundruk bhatmas,* which are roasted soybeans with vegetables which have been pickled and later dried in the sun; or *pakoras*, which are fried balls of cheese and vegetables. Equally tasty are fried potatoes, fried egg, roasted bits of meat, or peanuts and roasted corn.

In the high mountains, where no rice and wheat grow, the locals love *dhedo*, which is barley or buckwheat flour boiled together with liquid and fat; this is eaten with sauce or vegetables – similar to polenta. Another commonly served and well-liked dish is *daal bhat,* however, here the rice is often substituted by corn, barley or millet, while for the *daal* the widest variety of lentils and types of beans are employed.

The Tibetan-influenced ethnic groups – for example the Sherpas or Manangis – especially enjoy *tsampa*, roasted barley flour mixed with liquid and fat, which can also be eaten blended with the notoriously well-known "salty butter-tea." Be-

cause most of the people in the high mountains are Buddhists, they are also allowed to eat yak meat. The milk of the yak-cow, fresh yoghurt and dried yak-cheese are considered to be particular delicacies. Steamed *momos*, which resemble ravioli, can be filled with meat or vegetables. They are especially well-liked among the Bhotyas – a Tibetan-influenced group – but the Newar enjoy them too. When fried they are called *ko-thay*.

The highly distilled fruit brandies, produced either from apples, apricots, or even pears, also came from the high mountain valleys. Here the brandy from Marpha in northwestern Nepal attained considerable renown, and now fetches high prices in Kathmandu. Of course, the Terai has its own specialties to offer in this regard. Here there are anise liqueurs and *todi* – a milky beverage with about 5 percent alcohol content, which is produced from a type of palm-tree. *Chang*, a drink resembling beer, is produced from rice, corn or wheat; it has become popular throughout the country. This is also true of *rakshi*, a spirit made from the same grains. The Newar are particularly expert at the brewing of these beverages. The Tibetans have made *tongwa* well-known; it consists of fermented millet over which hot water is poured.

Brahmans and – for the most part – the Chetris do not eat what is cooked by other castes. Alcohol, chicken, garlic, onions, tomatoes and chillis are considered by orthodox Hindus to be stimulants to the body and the senses; these are therefore avoided. They also refer to the alcohol-drinking population groups disparagingly as Matwali, who stand far beneath them in the caste hierarchy.

And finally, here is a vital piece of advice: Should you be invited into a private home in Nepal or to some party, please keep in mind that the main course is traditionally served toward the end of the visit. Before the host offers tasty little morsels such as fried liver, *sel roti,* a deep-fried rice-meal pastry, roasted chick peas and, of course, alcohol.

225

THE NEPALESE AND TIBETAN CALENDARS

If you want to become conversant with the Nepalese and Tibetan calendars, you must be able to keep straight the differing counting methods of the calendars as well as the different epochs. The calendar divides the year into months either within the lunar or the solar system. The epochs count the years of a chronology from a fixed point in the past. At present in Nepal, various calendars are in use. The most important of these are the *Vikram Samvat* (reference year 56/57 B.C.) which is the official calendar, *Nepal Samvat* (reference year A.D. 870/880), which is used by the Newar population, and the Christian calendar. Of these only the Nepal Samvat calendar is of local origin; the Vikram Samvat and the less frequently used *Shaka Samvat* (reference year A.D. 78/79) have been taken over

Above: Small butter lamps burn in front of the gods in Buddhist monasteries.

from Indian tradition. In none of the three calendars, however, has the historical significance of the reference year been unequivocally clarified. The Tibetans count in 60-year cycles. According to this system, we find ourselves in the 17th cycle at the moment. The exact determination of the year can be done in two ways: Either within a cycle *(Rabjung)* or outside of it, based then on the year during which the *Kalacakra* system was introduced (A.D. 1027). This system has its origins in Tantric philosophy; its name translates as the "Wheel of Time."

The Elements

Furthermore, the Tibetan years are designated by the five elements iron, water, wood, fire and earth, which apply respectively for two years in a row – a feminine and a masculine year; these elements are linked with twelve animals: monkey, rooster, dog, pig, mouse, bull, tiger, hare, dragon, snake, horse and sheep. The Tibetan calendar is coordinated with moon cycles, whereas the Vikram Samvat can use counting methods based on the moon and the sun as well. The lunar calendar is based on a year consisting of twelve 30-day months, in which each month is divided into two periods – those of the increasing and decreasing moon or the decreasing and increasing moon; this is determined according to whether the moon phase of the corresponding year cycle ends with the full moon or the new moon.

At any rate, twelve genuine lunar months result, whereby at the end there are about six days missing from the expected 360, so that those who know their way around this whole production must be prepared to undertake a few adjustments. As a result, a lunar-day (named *Tithi* from Hindu tradition) rarely lasts simply from the time of one sunrise to the next, and a few days are entirely obliterated – or even, if necessary, repeated.

Moreover, it is necessary to insert six additional months into the year every 19 years in order to bring the lunar year back into agreement with the solar year. There are various traditional systems for getting around these difficulties. In Nepal, there is an official committee which is entrusted with the task of producing a new Vikram Samvat lunar calendar each year, which is named *Pancanga* or *Patro.*

Among the Tibetans, there are from time to time differing versions of the same calendar (from Dharamsala, Bhutan etc.) which are produced by various personalities. These people take a variety of factors into consideration in their determination of the calendar and the decision of which days should be repeated or eliminated, in particular the combination of certain lucky or unlucky elements with individual days.

Days of Sun

The solar year here also has twelve months of differing length. In the Vikram Samvat calendar they vary between 29 and 32 solar days. According to this system, the new months begin around the middle of the month in western calendars. According to the Vikram Samvat system, which is used in Nepal, the year begins with the month *Baishakh* (mid-April to mid-May). The following months are named *Jesth, Ashadh, Shravan, Bhadra, Ashvin, Kartik, Mangsir, Push, Magh, Phalgun* and *Caitra.* These designations are also applied in colloquial speech to the lunar months.

Nepal Samvat is purely lunar calendar, which has its own Newari names for the months. It begins with the day of the new moon in the month *Kartik* (October-November).

The Tibetans count their months without giving them special names, unless they are associated with a particular festival. The first month of the year, during which the new year festivities are held, begins with a full moon which as a rule is in February – however, sometimes also in March.

Among the Hindus as well as the Tibetans the days of the week – as also found in western tradition – are named after the sun, moon and five planets. In Nepalese these are: *Aitabar* (Sunday), *Sombar, Mangalbar, Budhabar, Bihibar, Sukrabar,* and *Sanibar.*

Calendar Comparison Table

Chr. Reck.	Vikram Samvat	Tibetan Year
1990	2047/48	Iron-Horse
1991	2048/49	Iron-Sheep
1992	2049/50	Water-Monkey
1993	2050/51	Water-Hen
1994	2051/52	Wood-Dog
1995	2052/53	Wood-Pig
1996	2053/54	Fire-Mouse
1997	2054/55	Fire-Ox
1998	2055/56	Earth-Tiger
1999	2056/57	Earth-Hare

WOMEN IN NEPAL

The laughter-lines around the almond eyes of an elderly Tibetan woman; the closely-cropped scalp of a Brahman widow; the tatooed thigh of a married Tharu woman; the black skirt with unmistakable red stripes of a Jhapu farm woman; the holes in the ears of the unmarried girls, which at their weddings are to be filled with the most ostentatious jewelry possible – considering the ethnic diversity of the Nepalese population there is neither a typical face of "the" Nepalese woman, nor a typical silhouette, nor a typical style. There are considerable differences between north and south: The women of the Terai are scarcely distinguishable from their Indian neighbors, whereas the characteristic mongoloid traits of the womens' faces increase the closer they live to Tibet. Differences in the appearance of the women depending on where they live can be perceived when one knows about the cultural peculiarities; thus, for example, the Newar women as a rule wear no nose-ring. Even the Nepalese have to ask strangers about their ethnic membership.

The familial relationships – which have long-term impact upon the life of a woman – vary to a considerable degree from ethnic group to ethnic group; accordingly, the relationship of the woman to the members of the family with whom she forms a household after her marriage takes different forms. Roughly half of the women in Nepal, especially Hindu women, enter into marriages arranged by their relatives. Among the entire population of Nepal monogamous marriages predominate – the more so since this is also legally prescribed – and which, for the Hindu woman at least in theory, is indissoluble. Among many ethnic groups and also among the Indo-Nepalese popu-

Right: Ear- and nose-rings – Tamang women love to show off their gold jewelry.

lation polygamy is practiced: Primarily then when a couple has no offspring, the husband enters into a second and occasionally even a third marriage, frequently marrying the younger sister of his wife. Among several groups of Tibetan origin, in contrast, fraternal polyandry is possible: Brothers may marry one woman in common – a form of marriage that is closely connected to economic necessities. Marriage is a great dividing line in the life of a woman, because almost all women move from the household of their parents to the house of the husband, and live there with his blood relatives. Among many ethnic groups there is a popular custom that a daughter marries the son of her father's sister, so that after the wedding the bride comes into the household of the paternal sister, where she is already comfortable and knows her way around. The Hindu women of higher castes, on the other hand, most of the time marry into households where they have no relatives. Correspondingly, they have a great fear of moving from the house of their parents – where they are treated with love – to that of the husband, where they are mostly unknown, and their parents-in-law, who usually are very strict and mistrustful towards them, at least during the beginning period – and frequently up to the birth of the first child. The contact with their parents continues during this time. Particularly on ritual occasions the daughters seek out their parents, and are then confronted by the situation of how very much their roles have changed from daughters and sisters to wives and daughters-in-law.

The Man's Role

With the exception of a very narrow class of the well-to-do, the Nepalese women have a very significant economic contribution to perform in the household. On average, the working hours are estimated to be eleven per day (3.5 working

hours more than those of the men), and the demands vary with the season. The women of all groups are primarily occupied with the household (this includes the provision of water, food and fuels). However, in addition their labor is needed in other economic realms; the majority of them must also work in the fields. The members of the ethnic groups find supplementary income selling their own products in the local markets, and hire themselves out as seasonal workers far outside their villages, in order to manage a small reataurant or tea shop, for example. They are often affectionately addressed by the population as "Didi" (older sister) or "Bahini" (youger sister).

Married Life

Naturally, the cultural norms vary here in relation to women – between the much freer and more tolerant Tibetans and the far more restricted freedom of movement for women in Hindu customs. The gender-specific division can be observed not only in the area of work, but also in everyday social intercourse with relatives and acquaintances. The majority of Hindu women only converse with male members of their group behind closed doors, and in the process must observe a series of rules: They may not touch the older brother of their husband or pronounce the name of their husband and must cover their face vis à vis their fathers-in-law. The social behavior of women in the Tibetan areas of influence is much freer in relation to men, demonstrated in the first place by the fact that they can sometimes leave their villages. Nevertheless, there are also limits set on their freedoms, and their economic independence is relative. Although they have their own income at their disposal, they are at any rate clearly disadvantaged compared to the men – as are Hindu women, when it comes to the rules of inheritance. And, even as free as some Nepalese women may appear in daily life, they are still practically excluded from political positions and influence.

SHAMANISM

In a darkened, gloomy room in a Gurung house the family sits together at night watching the gesticulations of Lal Bahadur, the local shaman, who has come to a decision. Beforehand there had been a detailed questioning concerning the circumstances surrounding the illness of the eldest daughter in the house, as well as an examination of her by means of eye and pulse diagnosis. The procedure also includes a repeated questioning of the rice oracle, which isn't always definitive in cases concerning the effects of spirit beings or witches. But he could also find nothing in the gleam of the oil-lamp's flame, which was consulted. Lal Bahadur discloses his diagnosis to the family: No indication of the existence of evil spirits or a witch in the house. It must be something else – perhaps the Medicine Lama or the hospital can help.

Above: A shaman ceremony. Right: Figures made of dough to drive away evil spirits.

Change of scene: In the emergency room of the Kanti Childrens' Hospital in Kathmandu a flurry of activity dominates – like any morning there. The waiting times are considerable. Ram Prasad has been traveling on foot from the mountains for three days with his little daughter, whom he has carried in unconscious. The little one has had fever and a heavy case of diarrhoea for days. Her skin is wrinkled, her face is sunken, and her feverish eyes seem lost in their sockets. It was possible to help her at the last minute, though, with antibiotics and a salt infusion.

In Nepal, both types of medicine exist side by side – western trained allopathic doctors, Ayurvedic doctors, Lama healers and shamans, known here as *Jhakris.* The traditional healers frequently originate from the lower strata of society – i.e. castes, and increase their social status through their occupation as a shaman. A thorough knowledge of the physiology of the worlds of gods and spirits is essential, since illness is seen mainly as an impairment of the harmony between the human world and the world of gods and spirits, and there are enough evil powers like human witches *(bokshi)*, black magicians, spirit witches and evil ghosts around to disturb this sensitive balance. After determining the diagnosis, the "healing" then takes place in the form of sacrificial offerings, among them rice, animals, fabric etc. This is supposed to appease the aggressor and strengthen the protective powers. If the sacrificial offerings are insufficient, the members of the household gather together with friends and acquaintances and get merry on beer and rakshi. In the presence of previously prepared dough figures of the possible causers of the illness (witches, gods, spirits of the dead) the shaman goes into a trance and speaks, stuttering and trembling as a tool of the god who has entered him. The words indicate the diagnosis and the description of the therapy.

By nature, there are limits set on the success of the spirit and natural healers' therapies, which most recognize very well, then recommending other treatment approaches. However, the insufficiency of the public health system is clear.

At this point at the latest, all of the obvious wants of public welfare will become apparent. Average medical care for the population at large is poor at best, especially out in the province and in the mountains. Child mortality rates during the first 5 years is close to 50 percent, and the overall life expectancy is below 50 years, with women even worse off than men. Infant mortality is the highest of all Asian nations. The extent of epidemics and malnutrition is among the highest in all the developing nations. There are far too few hospitals – a total of 96 –, and these are usually in regions that are difficult to reach and are by and large poorly equipped. During the past few years, about 800 health posts have been set up to give nurses and hastily trained health workers the opportunity to give the most

basic form of health care. These people not only heal, but also occupy themselves with the hygienic conditions, nutritional problems and birth control.

In spite of progress in the last few years there are still considerable problems with the public health system, which gave rise to the development of new strategies. One approach which isn't to be underestimated is the effort from the public sector to draw the religious and ritual healers into preventative medicine and health maintenance, since they still enjoy the confidence of the population and are distributed in large numbers especially through the rural areas. Workshops are held with the traditional healers in which problems of overpopulation, hygiene and basic medical care are discussed. The healers then take this information back to the regions. The involvement of the healers in the public health system represents a sensible integration of traditional healing measures, and thus helps in the dissemination of preventative health maintenance and therapy.

NEPAL'S HIGHEST PEAKS

The Nepalese see the seats of the gods as being in the Himalayan summits; and thus in their point of view one shouldn't desecrate these divine thrones with mountain climbing, but instead offer worship and love to them. This feeling is also expressed in the names of the individual mountain giants. For example, the "Gaurishankar" is the personification of the goddess Parvati and her consort Shiva, while the "Ganesh Himal" carries the name of the son of these two deities; "Annapurna" is the goddess of abundance. Especially ascetic monks and yogis retreat to the mountainous isolation of the Himalayas in order to meditate under the protection of the gods.

The 2,400-kilometer-long Himalaya Range with its tectonic giants is the geo-historical result of a collision of the In-

Above: A view of Everest from the Kala Patar. Right: The eastern flank of Dhau-lagiri.

dian land mass with the Asiatic one. The Indian subcontinent is thought to be moving to the north five centimeters annually, in the direction of Central Asia. Because of the tectonic circumstances of the young region, earthquakes recur constantly – most recently at the end of August 1988. Kathmandu was totally devastated by an earthquake in 1934.

The highest summits of the Himalayas are to be found on the northern border of Nepal, dominated by Mount Everest, with some ten icy peaks, each of which exceeds 8,000 meters in altitude. In addition, 40 seven-thousand-meter peaks tower above the world here. Of the 14 mountains over 8,000 meters in height in the world, eight are located either entirely or partly in Nepal.

Starting out from Tibet, the English undertook the first attempt to ascend Mount Everest already in 1922. In the process, seven Sherpas lost their lives in avalanches. Summit XV of these mountain giants was named by the British in 1865 after the then-leader of the "Geological Survey of India," Sir George Everest. It was only later discovered that the Tibetans and Nepalese had their own names for the highest mountain in the world: The Nepalese call it "King of the Heavens," *Sagarmatha*, and the Tibetans see in it *Chomolungma*, who rides on a snow lion over the sea of clouds.

The first successful ascent of Mt. Everest, on May 29th, 1953 by the New Zealander Edmund Hillary and the Nepalese Sherpa Tenzing Norgay, was a worldwide sensation. But, from the Nepalese side alone, ten expeditions up Mount Everest have been abortive – not to mention the many frozen, fallen and injured people which such undertakings have claimed. The most modern means of assistance offer little protection from avalanches, falling rocks and ice, sudden changes in the weather and altitude sickness. Since then, more than a 100 mountain climbers have ascended Mt. Everest. According to the statistics, for every two successful climbers of Everest there is one death. Despite considerable currency revenues for the Nepalese government from trekking and climbing expeditions, there is still no social security for the Sherpas and carriers.

Unfortunately, the expeditions and agencies frequently fail to equip their Nepalese guides and especially the carriers appropriately; thus, success doesn't depend on their persistance, knowledge and willingness alone.

Although all of the eight-thousanders in Nepal and Pakistan (Karakorum Range) had already been climbed between 1950 and 1960, there are still some 250 unclimbed peaks over 6,000 meters with varying degrees of difficulty. Among the most beautiful summits in Nepal are the **Pumori** (7,161 meters) in the northeastern part of the country closely neighboring Mt. Everest, and the much-described **Ama Dablam** (6,812 meters), on the foot of which lays the famous Buddhist Thyangboche Monastery

– which unfortunately burned down in 1989. In northwestern Nepal, **Macchapuchare** rises up over the Phewa Lake near Pokhara. A British expedition team gave up shortly before arriving at the top, apparently because they didn't want to offend the religious feelings of the local population. There are also still a few mountain summits, which – as seats of highly worshipped gods – are taboo for mountain climbers: Until today the Nepalese government hasn't opened them for ascent.

Eight-thousanders from West to East

Dhaulagiri, 8,167 m, May 13th, 1960
Annapurna I, 8,091 m, June 3rd, 1950
Manaslu, 8,163 m, 9th/10th/11th May, 1956
Cho Oyu, 8,201 m, 19th Oct., 1954
Mt. Everest, 8,846 m, May 29th, 1953
Lhotse, 8,516 m, May 18th, 1956
Makalu, 8,463 m, May 15th/16th/17th, 1955
Kanchenjunga, 8,586 m, May 26th, 1955

NEPAL
– A DEVELOPING COUNTRY

At the beginning of the fifties, Nepal was not only self-sufficient in food production – the central region (the population of which then comprised three-quarters of the entire population) even produced a small surplus of basic food staples as well as certain goods intended only for the market (for example milk products, livestock, spices and vegetable oil). These surplus products were brought by the farmers by foot and on their own backs to buyers on the Indian border to the South and the Tibetans in the North. Since that time the economic situation of the rural population has deteriorated drastically: On average, the farmers are now only producing basic staple foods for around eight months a year. In order not to starve during the remaining four months they are forced to seek employment as menial laborers in the cities, in the Terai or in India, to earn the necessary cash to procure the food they need. Many farmers in the central regions see no other alternative than to migrate to the Terai (a fertile flatland) or to leave the country altogether. By the beginning of the next century, the Terai will be completely overpopulated. Considered as a whole, Nepal has become a grain deficit-land, and the deficit will increase further by the year 2000 – to almost 2 million tons annually.

Ecological Causes

This unhappy development has its origins in inappropriate developmental assistance and in ecological conditions: The population explosion with the corresponding increase in livestock has led to the cultivation of marginal soils at great altitudes, on slopes that were once forested, and in places which are too steep. Too intensive cultivation in unsuitable locations – without taking simultaneous measures for the preservation of the soil fertility – have the effect of leaching out the soil.

The usable land per capita has decreased from 1/3 hectare in 1970 to only 1/5 hectare in 1986. The yield per hectare for maize decreased from 1,970 kg to 1,330 kg between 1970 and 1980; for millet from 1,210 kg to 990 kg. The per capita grain production sank from 177 kg to 161 kg in the central region between 1967 and 1979 and even in the Terai from 504 kg to 433 kg (according to the FAO the gross per capita grain production must reach 230 kg in order to insure a minimal level of nourishment).

The reduction of the forests to less than the half of what they were in 1950 is a result of livestock foraging and increased cutting of the forests by the more than doubled population – it has increased from 8 million in 1950 to 22 million (and growing) now.

Thus, in the year 1982/83, 160,000 hectares of forest were cut down, while during the same period only about 3,000 hectares were reforested. The annual wood consumption amounted to around 10 million tons in the year 1982 (primarily used as fuel wood for cooking), while the natural forest regrowth is estimated at only about 2.5 million tons. The regrowth deficit of 7.5 million tons in 1980 has considerably increased since then.

Further ecological consequences include the increasing erosion of soils, the exhaustion of numerous wells as a result of the more rapid water run-off, and the increased threat of flooding in the lower courses of the rivers. As a result of the general deterioration of the economic situation in the central regions, the migration out of the rural areas (seasonal and long-term) had increased from 3.6% to 12% of the population in the year 1981.

Right: A walk along the Bagmati River reveals many environmental problems.

Questionable Development Policies

In all of the government's previous five-year-plans, neglect has been shown toward the development of appropriate environmental measures for agriculture and forestry, preferring instead to focus their attention on road construction. Thus, until 1974 the budget for road construction laid claim to over 40% of the entire budget for development. During the same time agriculture and forestry were treated in a perfunctory manner, and up to 1980 received no more than 20-25% of the budget allocations. The developmental assistance from international organizations also demonstrated the same disproportion up to 1980.

For the farmer, the implementation of ecological measures is very time consuming. His efforts are not rewarded and he won't invest if he can't expect to get a fair price for the products of his land, relative to the amount of work he has put in. No large development project financed by foreign contribution is known to the author which has consciously combined increases in productivity at attractive prices for the farmers with comprehensive ecological measures. Instead the large aid organizations have been flooding the country with their grain surpluses – which are being used in Food-for-Work programs. In such projects the farmers are paid for their work with imported foodstuffs. The long-term effects of such projects are questionable, frequently even destructive. The impoverishment of the farmers is not reduced, since no income is made; no development process is advanced in the sense of self-reliance.

Instead of this, the farmers neglect their agricultural work and become dependent on outside help. Added to this, they must take a portion of the food they receive to sell at the local market, in order to get cash to buy urgent necessities – resulting in a depression of the local market prices. It becomes less and less worthwhile for the farmers to secure their sustainance through work in the fields – a real vicious circle.

235

- Afghanistan
- Australia
- Bangkok
- Burma
- Caribbean Islands 1 /
  Bermuda, Bahamas,
  Greater Antilles
- Caribbean Islands 2 /
  Lesser Antilles
- Central America
- China 1 /
  North-Eastern China
- China 2 /
  Northern China
- China 3 /
  Central China
- China 4 /
  Southern China
- Crete
- Egypt
- Hawaiian Islands
- Hawaiian Islands 1 / Kauai

Nelles Maps

- Hawaiian Islands 2 /
  Honolulu, Oahu
- Hawaiian Islands 3 /
  Maui, Molokai, Lanai
- Hawaiian Islands 4 / Hawaii
- Himalaya
- Hong Kong
- Indian Subcontinent
- India 1 / Northern India
- India 2 / Western India
- India 3 / Eastern India
- India 4 / Southern India
- India 5 / North-Eastern India
- Indonesia
- Indonesia 1 / Sumatra
- Indonesia 2 /
  Java + Nusa Tenggara
- Indonesia 3 / Bali
- Indonesia 4 / Kalimantan

- Indonesia 5 / Java + Bali
- Indonesia 6 / Sulawesi
- Indonesia 7 /
  Irian Jaya + Maluku
- Jakarta
- Japan
- Kenya
- Korea
- Malaysia
- West Malaysia
- Manila
- Mexico
- Nepal
- New Zealand
- Pakistan
- Philippines
- Singapore
- South East Asia
- Sri Lanka
- Taiwan
- Thailand
- Vietnam, Laos, Cambodia

TABLE OF CONTENTS

PREPARATIONS

Climate / Travel Times

The best time to travel in Nepal starts at the beginning of October and lasts until the end of April. May is relatively hazy and very hot. The monsoon season lasts from the beginning of June to the end of September. In this season it is very warm, however, the climate is comfortably tempered by the corresponding pouring rain. You should remember that in the area surrounding Pokhara the rainstorms can sometimes last for days on end. Less pleasant during this period is the proliferation of leeches that tend to squeeze their way through the finest tears and loop-holes of shoes and clothing. During the autumn – from September to the end of November – in the central hill regions it is delightfully warm and also very comfortable in the evenings, but in winter this region can be perceptibly cool. In the high-altitude tourist destinations weather conditions are often raw. The Terai is therefore very suitable for a stay, whereas in summer it is the other way around – almost intolerably hot. You get the clearest views from October to December, after which this period of beautiful weather is interrupted by a few days of persistent rainfalls. During the monsoon, the peaks are frequently shrouded in thick volutes of mist for days an end. The best time to go trekking is during the months of October, November, March and April. From March on, you can see the natural environment in its full splendor. In the Kathmandu Valley in summer it can heat up to 37 degrees C; at times in the Terai to over 40 degrees. The winter in Kathmandu brings night temperatures of below freezing, while during the days the temperature can jump to 10 degrees in the shortest time. The humidity in Kathmandu during the monsoon season is very high, and in the Terai the preceeding months of May and April seem all the more dry.

Clothing

Your route and the time of your travel are decisive in the question of clothing. You should alway be prepared for a sudden change in the weather, even in summer. Therefore, you should take a sweater in summer as well. In winter a light and warm sweater/jacket is recommended. In the mountains, at any rate, you need warm wool or down clothing. You are better off forgetting about clothes made out of synthetics. In the mountains hiking shoes are always recommended. By the way, cotton clothing and sweaters as well as down jackets can be obtained in Nepal, or you can hire them in special shops. The best places with the greatest selection of new and used expedition and mountaneering equipment you can find in the Tibetan shops of Thamel in Kathmandu.

Entry Regulations / Visas

Foreign tourists can stay in Nepal altogether for five months per year. Since 1995, at the border the visa is somewhat cheaper than at embassies, and considerably less costly than at consulates (bring 2 passport photographs!). But sojourn in Nepal may not exceed 150 days per calendar year. Tourists can get a 15- or 30-day visa at the border or the airport for a fee of US$ 5, resp. US$ 25. You can get a transit visa limited to 48 hours only at the airport if you present a ticket for a connecting flight – fee: US$ 5. A double-entry visa (up to 30 days) costs US$ 40, and a multiple-entry visa (up to 60 days) will cost US$ 60. In order to extend the visa for a month at a later date (fee: US$ 1 per day), you will have to show a bank statement proving you have changed at least US$ 20 or a convertible currency equivalent a day for that month. The same applies to an extension for a third month. The extended visa will cost US$ 5 per week for the first month and US$ 10 per week for the third month (payable in NR).

The Immigration office (Tel: 412337) is in the tourist quarter Thamel in Kathmandu opposite the SAARC office in Tridevi Marg. The office is open Sunday – Thursday from 10 am to 5 pm (mid-November to mid-February until 4 pm). On Fridays it closes at 3 pm. Visas and trekking permits are handled daily from 10.30 am to 1 pm (in the winter months until 12.3 pm) and Fridays tuntil 12 noon.

You can also apply for or have your visa extended in Pokhara. Here the Immigration Office is located between the airport and the Phewa (Fewa) Lake. Unlike in Kathmandu, a visa can only be extended here for six weeks within the context of a three-month stay.

Beware: In order to extend your visa you will need an application form and a photo. You will also have to present a bank statement made out for that purpose. The bank statement should include all accompanying family members. If you overstay your welcome of 90 or 120 days without a valid visa, you will have to pay in addition to the visa fees, a fine of 200 percent of that fee!

Currency / Money Exchange / Bills

The Nepalese national currency is the rupee (NR). In mid-1995, the US dollar stood at 49,50 NR, 1 DM = 33 NR; and 100 Indian rupees were worth about 165 NR. Of course, these figures depend on the swings of the market. The NR is subdivided into 100 paisas. Coins of 5, 10, 25, 50 paisas and one rupee as well as bills in values of 1, 2, 5, 10, 20, 50, 200, 500, and 1,000 rupees are in circulation. Nepalese money can be taken neither in nor out of the country.

Money Exchange: Money should only be exchanged at banks or authorized agencies. Officially, only these places are permitted to handle foreign currency. Recognized credit cards and travelers' checks are accepted at many hotels, restaurants and shops. The use of Eurochecks can be problematic. The proce-dure is very costly and time consuming. Travelers checks in rupees do not exist.

Currency Regulations: Foreign currencies – with the exception of the Indian rupee – are under government control. The introduction of foreign currencies is not forbidden, however inquiries will be made on your entry concerning how much you are bringing with you. Indian and Nepalese rupees can not be brought into Nepal.

If you want to exchange back into the currency that you have already exchanged you must present the corresponding bank statement, but you still get only 15 percent of the value of your money back. You should definitely hold onto your bank statements, because these are important, for example, for extending of your visa. Until recently, foreigners have basically had to pay for their accomodation in foreign currency. However, simple, smaller lodges accept Nepalese money, even in the trekking areas.

Health Precautions

There are no longer obligatory vaccinations for Nepal. However, it it advisable to get immunized aginst cholera, typhus, tetanus, and hepatitis. In any case, seek the advice of your doctor/health service. Travelers in the Terai should under certain circumstances take a prophylaxis against malaria. In your travel apothecary you should definitely pack the following medications: Malaria tablets if required, drugs against nausea and diarrhoea, antibiotics, insect repellents (lotions), sun protectants (especially in the high-altitude areas), antiseptics, bandages and mineral tablets. Please note that many medications in Nepal are quite inexpensive but be careful: The expiration date is often some time in the distant past. Also, medications requiring prescriptions in the west are frequently available over the counter. Micropure or chlorine tablets suitable for the disinfection of water should be brought; they need at least an hour to be effective. If you don't take these tablets with you, make sure that you boil any water for food or drinking for at least 20 minutes. It is now common that the water offered in most hotels, and restaurants has already been boiled and filtered. If you're not sure, you should either buy mineral water or tea as a substitute. Absolutely avoid consuming salad, peeled fruits and ice-cream. Foods which are freshly cooked are safer.

Departure

It is recommended that you re-confirm any flight reservations one or two days before departure. This is especially necessary with the domestic Royal Nepalese Airlines because short-notice changes are frequently undertaken and, in general, the flights are overbooked. Also inquire repeatedly about the exact departure times! The passenger clearances at the Tribhuvan International Airport take a long time. For this reason one should be at the airport at least two hours before departure. Airport fee: 700 rupees.

Nepal in Statistics

Total area: 147,181 square kilometers; population (1995): 22 million, (population growth: 2.7 % annually); 5 regions, 14 zones, 75 districts; capital: Kathmandu (ca. 420,000 inhabitants).

Religion: Hindus 86.2 percent, Buddhists 7.8 percent, Moslems ca. 3.8 percent, Christians under 1 percent. Many Hindus are also simultaneously adherents to Buddhist conceptions.

TRAVEL ROUTES TO NEPAL

By aircraft: Ten international airlines operate over 70 weekly flights to the Nepalese capital Kathmandu. You can fly via Bangkok with Royal Nepal and Thai Airways; via Bombay with Royal Nepal; via Calcutta with Royal Nepal and Indian Airlines; via Dhaka with Bangladesh Biman and Singapore Airlines. via Delhi

with Royal Nepal, Druk Air/Bhutan and Indian Airlines; via Frankfurt with Lufthansa and Royal Nepal; via London and Dubai with Royal Nepal; via Hong Kong with Royal Nepal and Dragon Air/Hong Kong; via Karachi with Pakistan International Airlines and Lufthansa; via Lhasa with China Southwest Airlines; via Moscow with Aeroflot; via Paro with Druk Air/Bhutan; via Patna with Indian Airlines; via Singapore with Royal Nepal and Singapore Airlines and via Varanasi with Indian Airlines. Royal Nepal Airlines also offers charter flights abroad. The addresses of the airline companies are listed under ADDRESSES.

By car: Travellers by car can enter Nepal from India via the following crossings: Bhairawa/Pupandeki (in the west), Nepalganj/Banke (in the west), Gorakhpur/Sunauli (in the west), Danghadi/Kailal (far west), Mahendranagar/Kanchapur (far west), Raxaul/Birgunj (middle), Siliguri/Kakarbhita (in the east); and over the Tibetan border at Kodari.

All vehicles require an international *carnet de passage*. Nepal is accessible by car, bus or train from all major towns in India. The Kodari/Kasal border road from Tibet is often closed during the monsoon due to landslides.

TRAVELING WITHIN NEPAL

Railroad

The only short connection for public transport exists in Janakpur in South Nepal. The old locomotive might be of interest to railway buffs.

Airlines

The domestic service of the Royal Nepal Airlines has regular flights to all the important settlements in Nepal. Moreover, there are additional flights to several famous tourist spots, for example to Lumbini (after Bhairawa) –Buddha's place of birth; to the Chitwan National Park (after Bharatpur and Meghauli) as

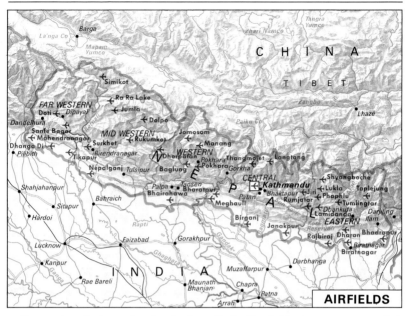

AIRFIELDS

well as various further national parks in Nepal.

The times of domestic flights are changed often and without warning ahead. For flights to Lukla, Pokhara and Bharatpur/Narayanghad, it is best to inquire at the Domestic Services of Royal Nepal Airlines/Tourist Sales Office, Kantipath, Tel: 226574/220757. Other flights are handled by Domestic Services of the RNAC in Thapathali, Tel: 223453/224497. Two charter companies also provide domestic flights: Nepal Airways, Tel: 410091/410134 (destinations: Biratnagar, Lukla, Pokhara, Nepalganj, Jomosom) and Nepal Air Charter, Tel: 229412/222290 (destinations: Biratnagar/Narayanghad, Nepalganj, Jomosom. Necon Air, Tel: 214159 (Pokhara, Chitwan, Lumbini). Everest Air, Tel: 111190 (Mountain Flight). Helicopter: Dynasty Aviation, Tel: 225602. Nepal Airways, Tel: 411610. Himalayan Helicopters, Tel: 217236.

Information about domestic flights is announced every evening at 9.15 over Radio Nepal. Foreigners must pay their flights in dollars. All year round there are several daily mountain flights with various Nepalese airlines over the Himalayan Range, including Mount Everest. The flight lasts an hour and costs around US$ 100 plus airport tax, handling and transfer fees, depending on the agency. Furthermore, the Nepalese airlines offer charter flights on demand.

Local Transportation

Buses and cars are the most important means of transportation.

Buses: The majority of buses within Kathmandu are completely overflowing with passengers and are therefore scarcely suitable for tourists. Small buses to Kirtipur (university), Patan, Bhaktapur and Dakshinkali start from around the Ratna Park and at the Bagh Basar. In 1994 a big new bus terminal for overland buses was inaugurated. It is on the Ring Road in the northern part of Kathmandu. A trip to Pokhara costs somewhere between 100 and 200 rupees.

Taxis: Besides taxis and group taxis, there are also *tempos*. Prices are a matter of negotiation. Normal taxis have a meter. However, often an extra fee is charged because of the changing prices for gasoline. Private automobiles and taxis can be rented through travel agencies and hotels; mostly with driver (per day in the Kathmandu Valley ca. 600 rupees; outside the valley ca. 1,200). At night you pay double or at least 50 percent on top of the basic price on the meter. The same is often true in bad weather! There is a night taxi service, Tel: 224374. The Yellow Cabs drive day and night, Tel: 414565.

Bicycle rickshas: These are used for private city sightseeing and shorter distances. They are almost exactly as expensive as taxis; the price should be negotiated before the trip.

Motorcycles and bicycles: Inquire at your hotel about the per hour, per day or per week prices. For a motorbike you will have to present your driving licence and often pay a deposit. By the way – if you mortally wound a sacred cow, you will have to spend 12 years in prison!

National Parks / Reservations

For Chitwan, Sagarmatha, Langtang, Shey Phoksundo and Rara National Parks, see the chapter "National Parks."

Royal Bardia National Park: in western Nepal in the outer Terai. Commercial flights from Kathmandu to Nepalganj, then further by car or bus. By bus to Motipur, then the remaining 8 km on foot. The park will be better accessible when the Mahendra Highway is finished. For tourist accomodations in the park there is a campsite on the banks of the Karnali River and a 24 bed rangers' house in Chitkaiye in the area of the park headquarters. Booking only through the West Nepal Adventure Company, a subsidiary of Tiger Tops, the office of which is in the Durbar Marg in Kathmandu. Otherwise one has to completely fend for

himself – this means bringing along camping equipment and food.

Suklapantha Wildlife Reserve: in the Terai, in the southwest of the country. Weekly flights to Mahendranagar airport, which directly adjoins the reservation. Except for Silent Safari Camp, which is only open during the season, there are no further tourist arrangements.

Koshi Tappu Wildlife Reserve: located in southeast Nepal in the Terai. Daily commercial flights to Simra, from there on further by bus to the headquarters in Adhabar. Here there is, however, no sort of board or overnight accomodation possibilities, so that you must undertake your sightseeing either from Hetauda or Birganj, arranged through the simple hotels.

Shivapuri Reservation: located in Kathmandu above Budhanilkantha. Can be reached by bus, taxi, bicycle or on foot, no overnight accommodations.

Khaptada National Park: in western Nepal in the central mountain country. One can fly into the following places from Kathmandu, Nepalganj or Dangarhi: a) Bajhang – from there a two day hike. b) Doti (Dipayal) – from there a three day hike. c) Bajura (Kolti) – from there a four day foot-march. d) Acham (Saphebagar) – from there a two day foot-march. No facilities for tourists. For sleeping and other needs you have to provide for yourself. More detailed information: King Mahendra Trust for Nature Conservation, Sakya Kunj, P.O. Box 3712, Kathmandu, Tel: 526571.

Travel Restrictions

Most of the restricted areas, above all those in the central Himalayas, have been opened to tourists since 1992. Those areas include Humla, Mugu, Dolpo, Mustang, Narphu and Rongshar. Visiting these areas is tied up with certain conditions (which do not cover the Annapurna and Everest regions). You must apply for a trekking permit at a local agency. The cost for the new destinations is markedly higher.

Furthermore, restrictions on the number of tourists and the size of the groups are being considered. As has been the case, expeditions and trekking groups must have an official Nepalese leader. This condition also applies to the outer Dolpo region and for the trekking routes of Kanchenjunga in the east (from Taplejung, which is accessible by airplane, to the base camp). Both regions have been open since 1989. The number of visitors here is limited in order to keep environmental damage at a minimum.

If your travel schedule includes some new routes, be prepared for a few surprises as the infrastructure is lagging behind somewhat. The immigration office and trekking agencies can provide you with the most recent information (you should inquire as conditions are continuously in a state of change). The newly accessed regions often have difficult road conditions. Equip yourself properly and do not overestimate your strength. Trekking agencies abroad and in Nepal tend to play down the difficulties of these treks. Be careful of altitude sickness!

Trekking permits

Trekking permits are issued by the Immigration Office in Kathmandu. At the Pokhara office the only permits issued are for the Annapurna and the Jumla regions. The permits can only be applied for in Nepal. You will need two photos of yourself. If you are planning two separate treks you will have to fill out two separate applications.

Trekking permits can be paid in Nepalese rupees except in the newly opened North Mustang (US$ 70 per day) and Manaslu regions (US$ 90 per week). The Kanchenjunga Dolpo region costs US$ 10 per week and US$ 20 per week for an extension of over four weeks. Other regions such as Langtang, Everest, Annapurna / Manang, Jumla, Gurkha, Dhad-

ing, Sindhupalchok, Simikot, etc. cost US$ 5 per week and US$ 10 per week for extensions over 4 weeks.

Beware! Trekking permits will not be extended beyond the validity of your visa. For the regions of Kanchenjunga, Mustang and Manaslu there are no individual trekker permits. And trekking permits are no longer considered substitutes for a visa.

Trekking permits for Mustang are only valid until Lomanthang (Lo Mantang).

Acquiring a trekking permit over a trekking agency usually saves time. Take along an adequate supply of passport photos. The permit must be carried during the trek and shown at checkpoints along the way.

Round Trips

The Kathmandu Valley and Pokhara are the traditional sightseeing areas for tourists. Almost all travel agencies organize sightseeing tours in the three royal cities of the Valley. In addition there are organized excursions to the surrounding villages, such as Dakshinkali, Budhanilkantha/Nagi Gompa-Shivapuri, Phulchowski, Kakani, and Kodari. The prices vary considerably. You can either join one of these group tours or hire a guide by yourself. Freelance guides can be ordered through hotels.

There are round trips offered between three and fourteen days in length; these vary in their degree of comfort. At best, rely on the following travel agencies:

Bhrikuti Himalayan Treks, Nagpokhari, Tel: 417459. President Travel & Tours, Durbar Marg, Tel: 220245/ 226744. GSS Travel & Tours, Bisal Nagar, Tel: 226639. Lama Travels, Nag Pokhari, Tel: 418657. Lukla Travels, Lazimpat, Tel: 415346. Marco Polo Travels, Kamal Pokhari, Tel: 414192/416432. Tibet Travel & Tours, Keshar Mahal, Tel: 410303/415126. Gorkha Travel, Durbar Marg, Tel: 224895. Himalayan Explorers, Jyatha, Tel: 226142. Gaida

Wildlife Camp, Durbar Marg, Tel: 220940/ 220186. Machan Wildlife Resort, Durbar Marg, Tel: 225001/227001. Temple Tiger, Thamel, Tel: 221585.

PRACTICAL TIPS

Accommodation

Nepal offers overnight accommodation for any budget and every taste. A list of hotels published by the Hotel Association of Nepal is made available by the Tourism Ministry. It is urgently recommended that you make prior reservations at your desired hotel during the tourist season from October to April. Because Nepal maintains no tourist offices in foreign countries, hotel reservations can only be arranged either through a travel agency which specializes in Nepal or directly with the hotel itself.

Besides the renowned large hotels in Kathmandu, there are many smaller hotels and lodges with the most exceptionally reasonable prices. Since it is frequently difficult to find means of tranportation in the time at hand, it is recommended to seek your lodging – if at all possible – in the city center. For those who want to stay in Kathmandu for an extended period, very reasonable flat rates are available at lodges.

Accomodation during a trek is organized by the responsible trekking organizers. Single travelers who have a trek in mind can also have their tour arranged through a trekking office. There are only a few hotels along many of the trekking routes. Houses of the local residents or the tent one has brought along serve for overnight stays.

Alcohol

The buying and selling of alcohol in Nepal requires no special permission. There are good domestic spirits, which are produced at three distilleries. Some spirits which have become especially famous are the red Khukri rum and vodka from distilleries in Kathmandu as well as the fruit brandies from Marpha and Tukche (on the Jomosom/Muktinath trek). The Nepalese are not familiar with wine, however, attempts have lately been made at producing fruit wines with similar methods. Foreign alcoholic beverages are comparatively expensive due to the high import duties on them.

Banks

The teller windows are open from 10 am to 2 pm Sunday through Friday. Only the exchange windows in the airports are open longer and on Saturdays. With few exceptions the banks stay closed on official holidays. Domestic and foreign banks have their representative offices all around the Durbar Marg. Money transfers can take – in our experience – a very long time; therefore you would be better off to take sufficient checks with you.

Bookshops

There is an enormous selection of English-language and other foreign literature in the bookstores of Kathmandu – books as well as magazines, etc. The leading book dealer and simultaneously the largest publishing house in Kathmandu is Ratna Book Distributors in Baghbazar (Tel: 220501/223026, in front of the French cultural house) with further sales locations distributed around the city. Ratna Books publishes a catalogue with an outstanding index of the literature of Nepal. Some further interesting booksellers include, for example: Educational Enterprises (Mahankal, diagonally opposite the Bir Hospital); Himalayan Book Sellers (at the Clock Tower), and Pilgrims Book House (Thamel, in front of the Tukche Peak Hotel).

Cinema

Primarily, Hindi films are presented in the numerous cinemas of Kathmandu. The majority of foreign cultural institutes or embassies also have film programs.

Customs

The international customs regulations apply here: Don't bring in or out any illegal drugs, weapons and radio equipment; cigarettes and alcohol in the usual amounts; articles for personal use, for example film and photography equipment in appropriate amounts. Sometimes value assessments are entered into passports upon entry; upon exiting these must be presented again.

Keep in mind that antiques which are more than 100 years old can not be taken out. If you are not sure of something in connection with this, have the Archaeology Department give you a certification: Ram Shah Path, Kathmandu, open Sunday–Thursday from 10 am to 4 pm, Friday 10 am to 3 pm.

Electricity

The electrical current carries 220 volts (alternating current). The variations are very large however, and frequently the current stops completely! The majority of sockets in Nepal are three-pronged.

Festivals / Calendar / Vacations

The dates of Nepalese festivals are set according to the Moon Calendar (the official calendar of Nepal is called Vikram-Sambat and originated in 57 B.C.) and are thus newly calculated by astrologers year for year.

Most of the travel agencies in Kathmandu have lists of the dates. Besides this, there are the Newar calendars: The Nepal-Sambat, which began ca. A.D. 790 and the Shakya Sambat (it originated A.D. 77/78). The official holidays, such as the King's Birthday (end of December), the Day of Democracy (beginning of February), and Constitution Day (end of December) are also set according to the Moon Calendar. On the other hand, international holidays are based on the western Gregorian Calendar. Famous festivals in the whole of Nepal are:

Dasain (festival in honor of the goddess Durga, beginning of October, starts on the day after the new moon, highpoint ninth and tenth days).

Lakshmi-Puja/Tihar (Festival of Lights New Year for the Nepal Era, end of October, new moon).

Bhai-Tika (brothers are honored by their sisters, end of October, second day after new moon).

Holi (several-day-long festival in worship of the god Krishna, paint fight; March, full moon).

For further festivals see Guidepost Kathmandu Valley.

Food

In the first few days you should avoid consuming the local food, which is cooked with a lot of oil and heavily spiced. Most of the restaurants in the Kathmandu Valley and Pokhara offer a variety of culinary delights. Besides Nepalese cuisine, you can find everything from Italian to Russian food. In some of the restaurants in the larger hotels you can eat in the evenings until midnight, in other places until around 10 or 11 pm.

Guides

There are numerous tourist guides in Kathmandu who have mastered English or another foreign language. You can get guides or organized tours through any travel agency, in Kathmandu sometimes also through hotels. Fees per day are set according to the guide's degree of knowledge and the goodwill of the travel agency and the guide. On average you should count on a price of between 500 to 1000 rupees for a tour through Kathmandu, for example. The guides must have completed an examination and have a license.

Hospitals

There are public and private hospitals, partly run by foreigners:

Kalimati Clinic: Tel: 71873. **Bhaktapur Hospital**: Tel: 610798. **Bir Hospital**

(Kanti Path): Tel: 226963. **CIWEC Clinic** (Baluwatar): Tel: 228531. **Kanti Hospital** (Maharajganj): Tel: 411550. **Maternity Hospital** (Thapathali). Tel: 211243. **Teaching Hospital** (Maharajganj): Tel: 412303. **Teku Hospital**: Tel: 211344. **Patan Hospital** (Lagankhel): Tel: 522266. **Nepal International Clinic** (Hitti Durbar): Tel: 412842. **Ambulance** (Bhimslusthan) Tel: 211959.

At the Red Cross on Exhibition Road (Tel: 228094) **AIDS tests** can be performed. There are already several cases of AIDS in Nepal. Each embassy has its own confidential doctor – please inquire.

Pharmacies

Medications can be purchased here without prescriptions. They are less expensive than in the West.

Photography

In most places in Nepal photography is allowed, except at military installations and certain holy places. If you want to take individual photographs of the inhabitants, please first ask them in a friendly way if this is possible. For religious reasons some Nepalese will refuse. Film is available everywhere in Kathmandu and Pokhara. Development is also possible and is good. However, you should always have slides developed at home.

Postal Service

The postal service works very unreliably. You would be better off not using mail boxes. Mail should be handed in directly at the post offices, and you should have the stamps cancelled. You can also send your mail from the large hotels. Letters can be sent to the main post offices of cities, where it will be stored until it is picked up: Name (underline family name), G.P.O. poste restante. Parcels and packets are handled in Kathmandu next to the General Post Office in the Foreign Post Office – it is, however, very time-consuming, and the customs formalities are nerve-wracking. G.P.O. business hours: 10 am to 4 pm Sundays through Fridays; 10 am to 3 pm Saturdays.

Press

Newspapers are published in English and the native languages. The *Rising Nepal*, *Kantipur* and the *Independent* are the only daily newspaper appearing in English. On the New Road in Kathmandu there is the so-called "newspaper tree" where the majority of newspapers are sold.

Radio and Television

Radio Nepal is the only Nepalese radio station. At 8 o'clock mornings and evenings news in English is broadcast; the evenings news is followed by one-half-hour English program. A television station existes, but the program can only be received in the Kathmandu Valley, Pokhara and a few villages in the Terai. English language news are broadcast at 9.40 pm. Satellite television is widespred. Programmes from India and Hongkong are popular (Star-TV).

Rescue Helicopter

If you become seriously ill during a trek, a rescue helicopter can be ordered from the next radio, telegraph or telephone station through your trekking agency or embassy. It is important that you have a surety voucher in Kathmandu which guarantees the assumption of the costs. The flight costs between US$ 600 and US$ 1,700 per hour, depending on the type of helicopter. A rescue flight to Everest or Annapurna takes about 2.5 hours. For further information: Himalayan Rescue Association, Thamel, Tel: 222906/418755.

Rules of Conduct

The codes of conduct of the Nepalese bears the impressions of various religious concepts and particularly the system of castes. Especially the rules which determine what is "pure" and "impure" are impenetrable and confusing for most of the foreigners.

Therefore, in general you should observe the usual international forms of politeness. Most Nepalese will overlook unfamiliarity with the usual rules of the country. Shaking hands for greetings and saying good-bye is not common. Instead, one puts the palms of ones' hands together and greets with the word "*namaste*," especially when addressing women. The Newar in the Kathmandu Valley greet each other with a slight shaking of the head, which in general in Nepal is also as a gesture of affirmation. Bodily contact such as embracing or kissing is still very uncommon between men and women in Nepal and often generates animosity toward foreigners.

If you should be invited into a Nepalese household, please pay heed to the fact that it is seen as impure to the household not to remove one's shoes before entering the dining room. Entering the kitchen is subject to strict taboo in the majority of Hindu households. It is considered the extremity of impoliteness to show someone the soles of your feet. This can very easily happen when you are eating on the floor, as is common to a degree.

As soon as you have eaten only a tiny morsel from a plate, it becomes impure, just as do the eating utensils you have used. Therefore observe this when passing food around, and drink out of a canteen. Don't sample something out of a cook-pot twice with the same spoon. In Hindu households it is uncommon for women to eat together with the men. This also applies to guests. To insist otherwise would be impolite. Don't be surprised when you are not immediately thanked if you bring a hospitable gift with you. Mostly these are immediately put aside and also not unpacked. In no case does this represent an insult.

Nepalese behave very loosely in temples and other religious establishments. Leather articles are not admissible in such places, therefore one usually takes off ones' shoes.

Shopping

With a lot of time and leisure, you can make a wonderful shopping trip in Nepal. Haggling is, however, a prerequisite! Finished handicrafts are on sale everywhere, for example, statues of deities made of brass and bronze, beautiful wood carvings, religious pictures called thangkas – painted following old traditions, and fine works of stonecutting (for example in the old quarter of Kathmandu, Bhaktapur, Patan Industrial Estate, Thimi, Thamel).

The jewelry of the Nepalese gold and silversmiths is especially beautiful (in Kathmandu and Patan). Hand-woven textiles like linen and cotton material as well as silk from Nepal, China and India; printed or painted in the most beautiful colors available (in the tourists centers in Thamel, Durbar Marg, Asan Tole, Indra Chowk Balaju in Kathmandu and the old quarter in Bhaktapur). Batiks, cloth handbags, clothing, wool blankets (particularly of the light, fleecy Pashmina fabrics of fine sheep and goats' wool) and hand-knitted sweaters can be bought in all sorts of variations.

Meanwhile in Thamel and Durbar Marg there now exists a variety of fashion boutiques with some noteworthy designer pieces – but these are also correspondingly expensive. Hand-woven Tibetan wool carpets (which are now been being produced in Nepalese weaveries too) are available in all sizes and colors (carpet centers are Bodnath and Patan/Jawalakel).

Calendars, art prints, gift wrapping paper, memo books and postcards from hand made tussore silk are popular mementos (everywhere, especially in Thamel). Music cassettes with classical pieces and Nepalese folk music have become sought-after souvenirs (in the New Road).

Telecommunication

You can call foreign countries or send a telegram in Kathmandu from the Central Telegraph Office, which is near the National Stadium. In most hotels you can also call foreign countries directly. Ask first about the price per minute – it changes from time to time. Nepal's international dialing prefix is 977-1 for Kathmandu, 977-61 for Pokhara and 977-5620 for Chitwan.

Time

Nepalese Standard Time is 5.45 hours ahead of Greenwich Mean Time (in central Europe, add 4.45 hours in the winter time and 3.45 hours in summer time.

Tipping

Luggage porters receive about 10 rupees per piece of luggage. Room service waiters receive 10 % of the bill, errand runners get 20 to 40 rupees and hotel pages about 20 rupees. Porters on trekking tours receive, besides the previously-agreed daily pay, an extra 5 to 10 percent of their total earnings.

Normally, waiters receive 10 percent. Granted, in hotel prices the tips are inclusive, however, it is usual to give somewhat more for good service. Luggage carriers, hotel pages, maids, waiters and errand runners then receive between 20 and 40 rupees. With group trips or private rides with chauffeur the driver usually receives an additional gratuity.

Tourist Information

The Department of Tourism maintains information offices at the following locations. Kathmandu: New Road in the area of the Durbar Square, Tel: 220818. Kathmandu Tribhuvan International Airport, Tel: 410537. Pokhara, Tel: 20028. Birgunj, Tel: 20083. Bhairawa, Tel: 304.

Janakpur, Tel: 20755. The offices are open daily from 9 am to 6 pm (in winter until 5 pm) except for Saturdays and holidays. On Fridays the offices are open until 4 pm.

The Ministry of Tourism is located behind the National Stadium.

To date there are no Nepalese tourist information offices in foreign countries.

Weights and Measurements

The metric system has been introduced in Nepal, however, in the country and the mountains calulations are made, as ever, in the traditional units of measurements. Silver and gold jewelry are sold by weight, expressed in *tolas*, which correspond to about 11.5 grams. The value of gems depends on their carat weight – a carat corresponds to 0.2 grams.

ADDRESSES

Embassies / Consulates

Australia: Bansbari, Tel: 411578. **Belgium**: Lazimpat, Tel: 414760. **Austria**: Kupondole, Tel: 410891. **China**: Baluwatar, Tel:411740. **Denmark**: Kantipath, Tel: 227044. **Finland**: Khichpokhari, Tel: 220939. **France**: Lazimpat, Tel: 412332. **Germany**: Gyaneshwar, Tel: 416527. **Great Britain**: Lainchaur, Tel: 411789/ 414588. **Holland**: Kumaripati, Tel: 522915/ 524597. **India**: Lainchaur, Tel: 410900/414913. **Israel**: Lazimpat, Tel: 411811/413419. **Italy**: Baluwatar, Tel: 412280/412743. **Pakistan**: Lazimpath, Tel: 410565. **Sweden**: Khichpokhari, Tel: 220939. **Switzerland**: Jawalakhel, Tel: 523468. **USA**: Pani Pokhari, Tel: 411179/412718.

Royal Nepalese Embassies

China: Beijing, No. 1 Sanlitu Yilujie, Tel: 521795; Tibet, Lhasa, Norbulingka Road, Tel: 22880. **France**: 75008 Paris, 7 rue de Washington, Tel: (33-1) 43592861 **Germany**: 53197 Bonn-Bad Godesberg, Im Haag 15, Tel: (49-228)

343097. **Great Britain**: London W8 4QU, 12A Kensington Palace Gardens, Tel: (44-71)2291594. **India**: New Delhi 110001, Barakhamba Road, Tel: 3329969; Calcutta 700027, 19 Woodlands, Sterndale Road, Tel: 452024. **Japan**: Tokyo, 14-9 Todoroki, 7-Chome, Setagaya-ku, Tel: (03)7055558. **Pakistan**: Islamabad, Attaturk Avenue, House No. 506, Tel: 823642. **Thailand**: Bangkok 10110, 189 Sukhumvit 7, Tel: 3917240. **USA**: Washington DC, 2131 Leroy Pl. NW, Tel: (1-202)6664550.

Airlines

Aeroflot Soviet Airlines – Kantipath, Tel: 226161. **Air Canada** – Durbar Marg, Tel: 222838. **Air France** – Durbar Marg, Tel: 223339. **Air India** – Kantipath, Tel: 212335/211730. **Air Lanka** – Kantipath, Tel: 222290. **Alitalia** – Durbar Marg, Tel: 220215. **British Airways** – Durbar Marg, Tel: 222266. **Cathay Pacific** – Kanti Path, Tel: 411725. **China Airlines** – Kamatadi, Tel: 412778. **Dragon Air** – Hong Kong, Durbar Marg, Tel: 227064/ 225166. **Druk Air**/Bhutan – Durbar Marg, Tel: 225166. **Indian Airlines** – Durbar Marg, Tel: 419649. **Japan Airlines** – Durbar Marg, Tel: 222838/ 224854. **KLM** – Durbar Marg, Tel: 224895. **Korean Air** – Kantipath, Tel: 212080. **Kuwait Airways** – Kantipath, Tel: 222884. **Lauda Air** – New Road, Tel: 227315. **Lufthansa** – Durbar Marg, Tel: 223052. **Pakistan International Airlines** – Durbar Marg, Tel: 223102. **Royal Nepal Airlines** – Kantipath, Tel: 220757. **Singapore Airlines** – Durbar Marg, Tel: 220759. **Swissair** – Durbar Marg, Tel: 222452. **Thai Airways** – Durbar Marg, Tel: 223565/ 224917. **TWA** – Kantipath, Tel: 411726.

EXPRESSIONS IN NEPALI

Hello / Goodbye . . . . *Namaste*
What is your name? . . . .
. . . . *Tapaaiko naam ke ho?*
My name is... . . . . *Mero naam... ho*
I live in . . . . . . *Mero ghar... ma ho*
Where is the...? . . . . *Io... kaha chha?*
How far away is...? . . . .
. . . . *Kati tadha chha/parchha?*
How do I get to...? . . . .
. . . . *Ma... makassari pugna sakchhu?*
How much does that cost? . . . .
. . . . . . *Esko kati parchha lagchha?*
That is expensive! . . *Io mahango chha*
Could I have the menu? . . . .
. . . . *Malai menu dinus*
I would like something to drink . . . .
. . . . *Malai piune kura dinus*
The bill please! . . . . . . *Bill dinus*
I am staying here for... days. . . . . .
. . . . *Ma iaha... din baschhu*
What is that? . . . . *Io ke ho?*
What is he doing? . . . .
. . . . *Whaha ke garnuhunchha?*
I don't feel well . . . .
. . . . *Malaai sancho chhaina*
What time is it? . . . *Ahile kati bajyo?*
I . . . . *ma*
you . . . . *tapaai/timi*
we . . . . *haamiharu*
okay . . . . *thik cha*
yes . . . . *ho*
no . . . . *hoina*
large . . . . *thulo*
small . . . . *saano*
today . . . . *aaja*
afternoon . . . . *diuso*
evening . . . . *saanjh/beluka*
night . . . . *raati*
week . . . . *hapta*
month . . . . *mahina*
year . . . . *Saal/barssa*
clean . . . . *saafa*
dirty . . . . *phohar*
hot . . . . *tato*
cold . . . . *chiso*
please . . . . *kripaya*
thank you . . . . *dhanyebaad*
less . . . . *thorai/alikati*
more . . . . *dherai*
come . . . . *aaune*
go . . . . *jaane*
price . . . . *mool/mullye*

shop . . . . *pasal/dokan*
medicine . . . . *aussadhi*
market . . . . *basar*
room . . . . *kotha*
vegetables . . . . *tarakari/sabji*
water . . . . *paani*
tea . . . . *chiya*
milk . . . . *dudh*
yoghurt . . . . *dahi*
rice . . . . *bhat/bhuja*
sugar . . . . *chini*
salt . . . . *nun*
butter . . . . *nauni*
food . . . . *khaana*
breakfast . . . . *nashtaa*

1 . . . . *ek*
2 . . . . *dui*
3 . . . . *tin*
4 . . . . *char*
5 . . . . *paanch*
6 . . . . *chha*
7 . . . . *saat*
8 . . . . *aath*
9 . . . . *nau*
10 . . . . *dos*
20 . . . . *bis*
25 . . . . *pachhis*
30 . . . . *tis*
35 . . . . *paitis*
40 . . . . *chaalis*
45 . . . . *paitaalis*
50 . . . . *pachhaas*
60 . . . . *saathi*
70 . . . . *sattari*
80 . . . . *assi*
90 . . . . *nabbe*
100 . . . . *saai/eksaai*
1,000 . . . . *hazaar*
10,000 . . . . *dos hazaar*

AUTHORS

Susanne von der Heide graduated in ethnology/art history and is employed at the Museum for East-Asian Art and the Rautenstrauch-Joest-Museum in Cologne, Germany. Her special relationship with Nepal developed after her first trip to Nepal in 1978. Since then her knowledge of Nepal has deepened through long years of residence there. She is active in the German section of the King Mahendra Trust for Nature Conservation in Nepal.

Hansjörg Brey studied ethnology, sociology and geography. Since 1978 he has traveled in Nepal regularly. His academic work as a geographer has given him an insight into the problems of Nepal. His special fields of interests are South Asia and South Eastern Europe.

Wolf Donner has studied political economy, sociology, and economic geography and was for twelve years an advisor for agricultural development in service to the United Nations (FAO). From 1966-1969 he worked in this function in Nepal. He is the author of numerous books and articles, among them *Nepal: Raum, Mensch und Wirtschaft.*

Toni Hagen, engineer and natural scientist, was employed in 1952 as a government geologist in Nepal and performed geological exploratory surveys under contract from the United Nations, for which he worked out plans for rural development from 1959-1960. He is the author of handbooks on developmental and catastrophic assistance; since 1989 he has advised for the King Mahendra Trust for Nature Conservation.

Jürgen Huber was for many years a trekking guide in Nepal.

Wolfgang Koch is a qualified chemist, however his greatest interest today is the study of the Chinese and Tibetan languages as well as ethnology. He has achieved international renown as a travel guide and mountain climber.

Axel Michaels studied indology, law, and philosophy and was the director of the Nepal Research Center in Kathmandu from 1981-1983. Today he is an academic counsellor at the University of Kiel, Germany. His research work in Nepal is concentrated primarily on the temple area of Pashupatinath.

Hemanta Raj Mishra, one of Asia's most pre-eminent zoologists, was born in Nepal. Today he is responsible for the leadership and conception of the King Mahendra Trust for Nature Conservation. In 1987 he was awarded the J. Paul Getty Prize for Natural Protection. Dr. Mishra has become internationally famous as the author of numerous books and films on wildlife research.

Joanna Pfaff-Czarnecka has been concerned with Nepal since 1979, where she collaborated in research projects as an ethnologist. Since 1989 she has worked as a scientific assistant at the University of Zurich. She is primarily known for her scientific publications on the Nepalese caste system.

Philip Pierce studied indology, linguistics and Greek at the University of Kiel, West Germany. He has lived in Nepal since 1984, where he works as a scientific assistant at the Nepal Research Center. He has collaborated as author in numerous publications about Nepal.

Ludwig von Savigny, internist and cardiologist, has visited Nepal regularly since 1980. In the years 1980/81 he worked at the Kanti Childrens' Hospital as well as the Bir Hospital. Later he resided predominantly in the North of the country, there developing an understanding of the natural healing methods and shamanism.

Ganesh Lal Shakya, born in Patan, has studied economic geography in Munich, Germany, since 1987. As a Newar he has devoted his attention above all to his own culture in Nepal. He is the owner of the Lukla Travels agency in Kathmandu, guides trekking groups and cultural tours.

Satis Shroff, a Nepalese journalist living in Germany, studied biology and geology in Nepal. At present he is studying medicine in Germany. He is owner of the Lukla Travels agency in Kathmandu in charge of German language trekking groups and study trips.

Gert-Matthias Wegner studied musical ethnology. Since 1982 he has researched the musical life of the Newar in the Kathmandu Valley. He is famous for his concerts and films, which provide insight to the cultural background of Newar musicians.

PHOTOGRAPHERS

Bondzio, Bodo   1, 2, 22, 37, 38, 42, 46, 52, 64, 70, 82, 98, 226, 229
Brey, Hansjörg   152
Chwaszcza, Joachim   10/11, 20, 28, 31, 34, 40, 51, 54l, 59, 80, 87, 95, 107, 112, 118, 119, 208, 221, 225, 233 229, 231
Frommelt, Ursula   130/131, 137
Grosse, Heinz   55, 91, 139
v. d. Heide, Susanne   26, 60/61, 123, 140, 184, 185, 188/189, 192, 194, 197, 204, 207, 211, 219, 230
Hinze, Peter   23, 32, 36, 62/63, 71, 74, 92, 102/103, 109, 223
Huber, Jürgen   174/175
Kaempf, Bernhard   27, 75, 94
Koch, Wolfgang   136, 232
Kubitzer, Tim   161, 166, 168
Maeritz, Kai   8, 14, 43, 79, 116, 117, 120, 121, 142/143, 151, 235
Müller, Ernst   108, 209
Müller, Kai Ulrich   72, 73, 212
Nelles, Günter   148, 162, 169
Poncar, Jaroslav   56
Proksch, Oliver   156, 165, 170, 172
Savigny, Ludwig v.   39, 47, 50, 54r, 97, 122, 128, 180, 182, 205, 231, cover
Schwarz, Berthold   124, 149, 183 l/r, 190, 198/199
Shakya, Bishwa   29, 45, 207, 213
Shroff, Satis   217
Spiess, Jürgen   204
Thapa, Ram Pratap   214, 222
Tomlinson, Ian   12/13, 25, 48, 57, 83, 89, 125, 126, 127, 154/155, 164
Vajracharya, Min   193
Wegner, Gert-Matthias   218
Wolf, Edda   163